SYSTEMS SOFTWARE
An Introduction to Language Processors and Operating Systems

FRANK MADDIX and GARETH MORGAN
Department of Computer Studies and Mathematics
Bristol Polytechnic

ELLIS HORWOOD
NEW YORK   LONDON   TORONTO   SYDNEY   TOKYO   SINGAPORE

First published in 1989
Reprinted 1992 by
ELLIS HORWOOD LIMITED
Market Cross House, Cooper Street,
Chichester, West Sussex, PO19 1EB, England

A division of
Simon & Schuster International Group
A Paramount Communications Company

© F. Maddix and G. Morgan/Ellis Horwood Limited, 1989

British Library Cataloguing in Publication Data

Maddix, Frank
Systems software: an introduction to language processors and operating systems. –
(Ellis Horwood series in computers and their applications).
1. Computer systems. Operating systems.
1. Title   II. Morgan, Gareth.   III. Series
005.4'3

Library of Congress data available

ISBN 0–13–877721–7
ISBN 0–13–877713–6 pbk

Typeset in Times by Ellis Horwood Limited
Reprinted and bound in Great Britain
by Hartnolls, Bodmin

Contents

Note on trademarks   9
Preface   11

INTRODUCTION

1 Why study systems software?
   1.1 What is systems software?   15
   1.2 Systems and applications software   16
   1.3 Types of systems software   17
   1.4 Why use systems software?   21
   1.5 The study of systems software   22

PART I — LANGUAGE PROCESSORS

2 Principles of programming languages
   2.1 Introduction   29
   2.2 Generations of programming languages   31
   2.3 Procedural and non-procedural languages   34
   2.4 Language elements   35
   2.5 Formal language definitions   39
   2.6 Desirable features of programming languages   42

3 Assembly language and assemblers
   3.1 Assembler principles   46
   3.2 Assembly language   47
   3.3 The GOAT machine   53
   3.4 Functions of an assembler   56
   3.5 Operation of an assembler   59
   3.6 Practical issues   64

4 Compilers: function and purpose
   4.1 The compilation process   66
   4.2 Translation of different constructs   68
   4.3 Outputs of a compiler   76

5 Compilers: structure and operation
   5.1 Compiler structure   78
   5.2 Lexical analysis   81
   5.3 Syntax analysis   83

5.4	Code generation	89
5.5	Additional issues of compiler design	95

6   Compilers: run-time environments
6.1	Introduction	100
6.2	Error and exception handling	101
6.3	Standard routines and file handling	103
6.4	Storage management	105

7   Linkers and loaders
7.1	Introduction	110
7.2	Modular programming and linkage editing	110
7.3	Translator output	114
7.4	Task of the linkage editor	115
7.5	Simple loaders	116
7.6	Relocating loaders	117
7.7	Multi-phase linking and dynamic loading	118

8   Interpreters and fourth-generation languages
8.1	Interpretive execution	120
8.2	Interpretive languages	121
8.3	Structure of interpreters	125
8.4	Comparison of compilation and interpretation	126
8.5	Fourth-generation languages and mixed compiler/interpreters	128

PART II — OPERATING SYSTEMS

9   Introduction to operating systems
9.1	Introduction	135
9.2	Operating systems — an overview	135
9.3	Conclusion	142

10   Files and directories
10.1	Introduction	143
10.2	Files	143
10.3	File access mechanisms	148
10.4	Directories	150
10.5	Conclusion	153

11   Input and output
11.1	Introduction	155
11.2	Hardware independence	155
11.3	User layer	155
11.4	Kernel level I/O: handlers and drivers	157
11.5	An example: time of day clock	158
11.6	Real drivers	160
11.7	Multitasking	161

12   Controlling the machine
12.1	Introduction	164

12.2 Multitasking 164
12.3 Memory management 176
12.4 An advanced microprocessor — the Intel 80386 181
12.5 Conclusion 183

13 Some real systems
13.1 Introduction 184
13.2 OS/2 184
13.3 VMS 188
13.4 Unix 189
13.5 Other systems 195
13.6 Conclusion 196

14 System services
14.1 Introduction 198
14.2 Types of system service 198
14.3 Calling system services 199
14.4 MS-DOS system services 199
14.5 VAX/VMS system services 200
14.6 Unix system services 202
14.7 Conclusion 203

15 System utilities
15.1 Introduction 204
15.2 The software development process 204
15.3 Software development tools 204
15.4 Project management 208
15.5 Project management software 208
15.6 Conclusion 211

CONCLUSION

16 Current and future developments
16.1 Introduction 215
16.2 Hardware 215
16.3 Software 218
16.4 Operating systems 222
16.5 Conclusion 225

Index 227

Note on trademarks

All names of real products mentioned in this book should be taken to be trademarks of the manufacturer of supplier concerned. In particular:

Unix is a trademark of AT&T Bell Laboratories.
MS-DOS and OS/2 are trademarks of Microsoft.
VMS is a trademark of Digital Equipment Corporation.
IBM and PC-DOS are trademarks of IBM Corporation.
Intel is a trademark of Intel Corporation.
Ada is a trademark of the United States Department of Defense.

The name 'GOAT' is a hypothetical creation for the purpose of this book, and any similarity to the names of any real products is purely coincidental.

Preface

An appreciation of the functions of compilers and operating systems is an essential part of most information technology and computer science courses, yet students beginning in this area are faced with a shortage of material at a suitable level. Particularly in the field of language processors, there is often nothing between the one chapter introductions in general computer studies books, and the advanced texts on compiler theory which are too technical for those who are new to the subject.

This book is primarily intended to accompany an introductory course in systems software, either at undergraduate level, or on post-graduate courses for graduates converting from other disciplines. It should also be suitable for professional examinations such as British Computer Society Part I, and as supplementary reading for those taking A-level computer studies. On elementary courses it will serve as a text in its own right; on more advanced courses it will provide an introduction from which students can tackle more detailed books such as those listed in the further reading at the ends of the chapters.

After an introductory chapter, Part I of the book deals with language processors: programming language principles, assemblers, compilers, and interpreters. Part II covers the field of operating systems, and a concluding chapter then discusses current and future implications for systems software. We believe students will find it convenient to have both the main areas of systems software in a single volume, but Parts I and II can be used independently for distinct courses. Part I has been prepared by Gareth Morgan and Part II by Frank Maddix, but there are extensive cross references between the chapters, particularly on topics such as linkers and software development environments, which could be treated under either of the main headings.

No background knowledge is assumed other than an introduction to computer concepts and machine architecture, and some experience of programming.

The emphasis is in looking at systems software very much from the user view, but covering just sufficient detail on internals to enable a general understanding of how a language processor or operating system might function. The authors believe that whilst it is important for all serious computer studies students to understand the principles of systems software, only a very few will ever be involved in its development, so the book is *not* intended as a manual on compiler or operating system design.

We have aimed to keep the book as broad in application as possible, so examples are taken from many different programming languages and a variety of real operating systems. For reasons of space, the examples are necessarily selective, and many important techniques used in certain systems are either omitted or mentioned only briefly; it is anticipated that a lecture or seminar programme would supplement the text with examples from the systems software actually used.

We would wish to acknowledge the support of many people in making this book possible, particularly our respective partners, Claire and Sharon, who have generously taken on other tasks to free us for this and assisted with checking parts of the text. We are also grateful to our students at Bristol Polytechnic who have impressed upon us the need for an introductory text in this area, and to the staff of Ellis Horwood Limited for their encouragement.

October 1988   Frank Maddix and Gareth Morgan

Introduction

1

Why study systems software?

1.1 WHAT IS SYSTEMS SOFTWARE?

When people start to use computers, they usually have a fairly clear idea of what is meant by the hardware, even though with a big multi-user system they may never get to see the machine room that contains the central processor. Very quickly, they gain an idea of what is meant by applications software in terms of instructing the computer to carry out tasks for their specific applications.

But systems software is often much more of a mystery; the user is frequently unaware of anything other than the application and the hardware. Indeed many application systems are nowadays deliberately designed in such a way that the end user has no contact with the operating system or any other aspect of systems software.

The simplest definition of systems software is that it is software which bridges the gap between application software on the one hand and hardware on the other.

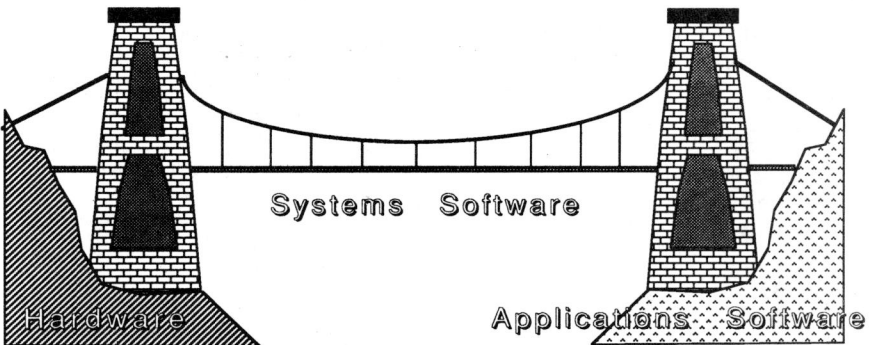

Fig. 1.1 — The bridge view of systems software.

The words **systems** and **software** are both significant. The fact that we are studying a particular kind of *software* is important: language processors and operating systems are still very much programs and they control the computer by sequences of instructions, in the same way as any other programs. They are quite distinct from the hardware — even though the hardware and systems software may have been designed for use together. But the term *systems* software stresses that these programs are related to the control and management of the computer system as a whole, rather than to a particular application.

For the user who is concerned only with the results of an application, the systems software is usually quite irrelevant. But for the programmer or systems designer, the systems software is vital, as it saves the application developer from having to be concerned with the details of hardware operation.

1.2   SYSTEMS AND APPLICATIONS SOFTWARE

In clarifying the role of systems software it is helpful to assess the differences between applications and systems software, which Table 1.1 sets out. Many

Table 1.1 — Systems versus application software

Applications software	Systems software
Carries out application	Controls system
Manages application data	Manages machine resources
Provides services to end user	Provides services to programmer or to application software
Usually written in a high-level language	Often written in assembler
Only runs for duration of a given application	May run at all times computer is on
May be a software package or a bespoke (one-off) development	Almost always a package — one-off developments of systems software would be prohibitive
Program is usually just a single step-by-step process	Commonly handles several processes at once

of these comparisons are generalisations and do not apply in all cases, but they help us see the distinctive nature of systems software, and hence the reasons for studying it as a subject in its own right.

These distinctions vary over the years — for example, with the emergence of programming languages such as C it is becoming much more common for systems software (or large parts of it) to be written in a high-level language. Also, there are plenty of examples of research projects where a compiler or operating system has been developed purely for one organisation. But such instances are quite rare: if you visit a large commercial computer user, you would not be surprised to find they had developed their own management accounting software, but it would be very surprising to find they had a compiler or operating system which had been developed on a one-off basis.

Furthermore, some of the comments in the right-hand column would not apply to all systems software — in fact from the point of view of the operating system, a compiler usually just appears to be another application program. But the basic issue of systems software bridging the hardware and the application remains applicable in all cases.

One issue which firmly applies to both systems and applications software is the *user*. For applications software, it is usually quite obvious who is the actual user. For systems software, the user is normally the developer of the application software.

It is sometimes assumed that, since the end user may have little or no contact with the systems software, issues of usability are of minor significance in relation to systems software. In fact, nothing could be further from the truth. An application developer is usually making very intensive use of both the operating system and language processors needed for a particular project, and the nature of the user interface can make enormous differences to the developer's productivity, and hence to the overall cost of the system. Moreover, a language processor with unfortunate limitations can lead to seriously increased risks of errors (bugs) in the final system.

The field of software engineering has shown how important the development environment is for the production of good quality software, and this has led to the integration of diagramming and documentation tools, language processors, and program-library systems into integrated project-support environments.

In addition, the interface presented by the operating system to the application software is very important: if this is messy or complex, it will make the development of applications considerably more difficult and more prone to error.

Therefore within this book we shall on many occasions be raising issues to do with the usability of the system software considered.

1.3   TYPES OF SYSTEMS SOFTWARE

We can conveniently divide systems software into three broad categories: language processors, operating systems, and utilities.

Language processors enable programs written in high-level languages to be executed on a machine which, as a piece of hardware, only operates in low-level machine instructions. The two main categories of language processors are translators and interpreters.

Operating systems control the detailed operation of the machine while application software is running. The operating system also has many functions in managing machine resources such as memory and disk space, controlling security, and starting the system initially.

Utilities carry out a wide range of other system-oriented tasks, such as formatting disks, initialising files, taking backup copies of data and so on.

In different ways, all these three categories provide a bridge between the applications software and the hardware, in line with our definition, and we shall now look at these a little more closely. Moreover, we shall see that the effect of this bridge is to give the application a simpler environment to work with than the raw hardware. Often this simpler environment is described as a **virtual machine** because it is like a real computer — a real machine — in being able to carry out instructions, but it does not physically exist in hardware terms. Only with the hardware and systems software together does the virtual machine arise.

1.3.1   Language processors

The most common example of a language processor is a compiler, translating a program written in a high-level programming language into the machine instructions which can actually run on the CPU (central processing unit).

In such cases, the compiler is not actually present while the program is running: its task is completed once the program is translated. But without the compiler, there would be an impossible gulf between a program written in a language such as Pascal or COBOL, and the actual instructions which the hardware is capable of executing. The compiler has thus provided a very real bridge between these two very different environments.

An alternative type of language processor is an interpreter, which generally takes each statement of a high-level language program and carries it out. The interpreter is itself a program consisting of machine instructions, and by carrying out the requests of the high-level program it is therefore executing that program on the machine, so providing the bridge that is needed between the high-level program and the low-level machine.

What the language processor has done is to create a virtual machine for which the application developer can design programs —, in other words it appears to the programmer that he or she is working with a machine that can understand a language like Pascal or COBOL. The systems software has created a simpler and more convenient environment than the real environment of the hardware.

Language processors thus make it possible to write programs in high-level languages without any detailed knowledge of machine code and machine architecture. They are described further in Part I of this book, where the distinctions between translators and interpreters will be explored more fully.

1.3.2   Operating systems

In most cases, the operating system is loaded as soon as the computer is switched on, and it remains in control of the system at all times. A great many hardware functions, especially inputs and outputs involving peripheral devices are first handled by requests from the application program to the operating system. The operating system itself then issues the appropriate hardware instructions to the devices concerned, so saving the application program from being concerned with the 'nitty gritty'.

For example, if a program wishes to read the next record from a disk file, it will usually just issue a call to the operating system to do this. The actual determination of which track and sectors on disk are needed, and the actual signals that have to be sent to the disk controller hardware to obtain these is left to the operating system. Moreover, the operating system may be able to arrange for another program to run, thus making good use of the CPU, while it is waiting for the disk to respond.

The operating system is thus offering the application program a simpler environment — a virtual machine — rather than all the complexities of the real machine. Indeed some operating systems actually divide the real machine up into many virtual machines, in order to support several applications at the same time. How similar these virtual machines are to the real machine depends on the design and purpose of the operating system.

We see the operating system acting very clearly as a bridge or interface between the application and the hardware — indeed this is often viewed in layers like those of an onion. The operating system acts as the layer that joins the application software to the hardware, as shown in Fig. 1.2; in particular it

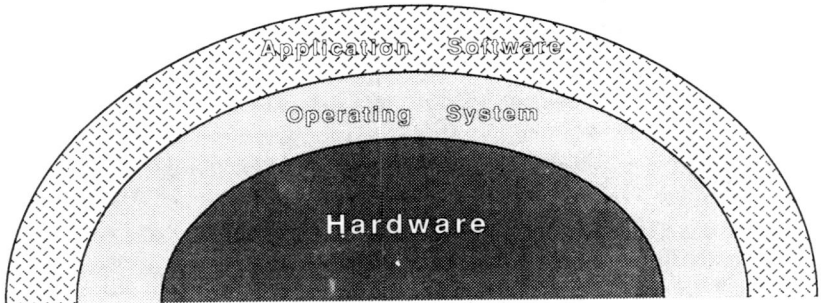

Fig. 1.2 — Application, operating system and hardware.

specifically prevents the application program from accessing certain hardware facilities other than through carefully controlled operating system functions. In Part II of this book, this issue will be described in greater detail; in particular it will be seen that the operating system itself has several layers within it.

The operating system is bridging the gap between the application and the hardware by interpreting application software requests (system calls) into the actual hardware instructions required.

1.3.3 Utilities
System utilities also assist in the task of providing a bridge between application requirements and actual machine effects. For example, it is

often possible to type in a simple command to copy a disk, and the utility will access the disk physically in such a way as to make the copy at maximum speed.

As items of system software, utilities are very often carrying out low-level tasks that would be meaningless to an application program. For example, in copying a disk, a flexible utility program will typically read all the tracks and sectors one by one and copy them directly to the new disk, with no regard to the actual files on disk or their structures.

In most cases, utilities are provided free with the operating system; their role is considered further in Chapter 15. In design, they tend to be quite simple (compared to, say, an operating system or compiler) but it is important to appreciate that without the ability to format a disk, for example, no software at all could operate on the hardware. Therefore, in terms of providing a bridge between the needs of the application and the reality of the hardware, utilities are very important items within the overall systems software heading.

1.3.4   Other kinds of systems software

A number of other items of software should perhaps be classed as systems software, in that they provide some kind of system function which is not specific to a particular application; some of these would be regarded as application untilities.

We shall briefly mention four items in this area. However, it is important to appreciate that, as program development environments become increasingly sophisticated, it is impossible to draw a totally clear-cut boundary between systems and applications software.

Editors are needed to allow programmers to key in and modify the source code of a program before it is read by a language processor; they are also used to create files of commands for use with operating systems and for many other purposes. Some interactive compilers and interpreters actually provide an editor as part of the language processor itself, as discussed in Chapters 5 and 8, but in most cases the editor is a distinct program. The distinction between an editor and a word-processing program is often quite subtle — indeed it is usually possible (provided certain options are specified) to prepare programs with a word-processing program.

Sort programs are used with many different applications to sort the records of a file into a specific order. Their importance has decreased slightly over the years with the move towards on-line systems and keyed files, but it still remains the case that many applications need data to be manipulated into a specific order before it can be processed, particularly for reporting. Particularly when there are too many records on a file to sort them all in memory, some very elaborate algorithms are required to make the process reasonably efficient.

Teleprocessing (TP) monitors are sometimes built as software separate to the operating system itself, particularly on certain large mainframes. As far as the operating system is concerned, the TP monitor may appear to be just one large application program, but it may in fact be controlling the passing of messages to and from many hundreds of on-line terminals, and invoking appropriate transaction processing programs to deal with these. The most well known example is IBM's CICS/VS. However, with most multi-user operating systems developed since the 1970s, the functions of the TP monitor are provided as part of the operating system itself.

A **database management system (DBMS)** provides all the software to control a database, ranging from initial definitions of the database structure to accessing the database when requests are made by application programs. By supporting the elaborate structure of a database, it allows the user or the application to be even further removed from the hardware detail of data storage than would otherwise be the case. In some cases this too is provided as part of the operating system, as an extension to its filing system. Either way, a DBMS is providing a further important bridge between the application and the hardware.

1.4   WHY USE SYSTEMS SOFTWARE?

From what has been said, it might be assumed that systems software is essential before one can create application programs. But in fact that is not the case. It is perfectly possible to write programs in machine language, so avoiding the need for a language processor. It is also possible to write application programs to carry out the direct low-level control of the hardware and peripherals, without using an operating system.

In certain cases, particularly as an educational exercise, people do follow this kind of approach. One of the greatest difficulties is how actually to get the program into memory in order that it can be run — without a language processor to read a source file and without an operating system to load the program from disk. It is possible to use a very simple piece of systems software that is purely a program loader, which overwrites itself as the user's program is loaded. Alternatively, a program can be 'blown' semi-permanently into PROM (programmable read-only memory) — but this usually involves another computer. Failing that, the program would have to be entered one binary digit at a time, using sets of switches. This was certainly the only way of loading in the first program on early computers.

Another reason for not using an operating system may be in an embedded system, where a computer processor is built into other equipment in order to control it — this can apply to anything from washing machines to cars, to missiles, or to scientific equipment. In such cases, the computer will only ever be used for this one application, and it is a waste to incorporate all the general facilities of an operating system, most of which will never be needed.

It is rare, however, for serious work to be done without a language processor. Even if the software must be written in individual machine instructions, it is much easier to write in assembly language and use an assembler (see Chapter 3) than to write raw binary machine code.

However, in most cases, the virtual machine offered by the systems software is so preferable to the complexities of the real machine, that the advantages of using systems software are overwhelming.

Programmers' productivity (in terms of the time taken to code and test a program) can be improved ten or more times by using good high-level languages, rather than by working in machine code. Moreover, the quality and reliability of the application is likely to be much better with all the facilities of a high-level language and the ability to concentrate on the user's needs, rather than on the machine.

Likewise, if all the detailed control of peripherals which is provided by the operating system had to be incorporated into every application, it would lead to vast amounts of effort being duplicated for every program that is developed. When it comes to more advanced operating system functions, such as allowing more than one process to share the machine, it becomes absurd to implement applications which try to do this themselves, without a central control program of some kind.

So, whilst it is important to appreciate that it is technically possible to do without systems software, the reasons for having systems software are enormous. Only in the most specialised environments would any consideration be given to doing without the crucial services that language processors and operating systems provide. Indeed, it is the developments in systems software from the 1950s onward which have led to some of the most important revolutions in information technology.

1.5 THE STUDY OF SYSTEMS SOFTWARE

Only a small proportion of those engaged in computer studies courses are ever likely to find themselves writing compilers or operating systems at any time in the future, and it is sometimes asked: what is the point, therefore, of studying systems software?

There are in fact many reasons why all computer practitioners need a strong appreciation of the principles involved in systems software and some of these are described below. The aim of this book is to look at systems software from these points of view, rather than as something to be studied as a highly technical discipline in its own right.

1.5.1 Reasons for studying systems software

(a) An understanding of systems software is one of the central areas that distinguishes a computer *professional* from someone who is simply a *user* or even an inexperienced *developer* of computer systems.

With a well-designed application, an end user generally needs no knowledge at all of language processors, and no knowledge of operating systems apart from how to start the required application program, and any associated housekeeping. However, many working full time in data processing may use language processors and operating systems on a daily basis, but with little understanding of what they actually do. Lack of knowledge in this area has led to systems which are very complex, expensive, inefficient or even impossible to implement in the particular systems software environment to be used.

An appreciation of what the systems software is doing is thus one of the most important skills needed by a professional computer practitioner. As such, this area rightly features in professional examinations for those seeking qualifications from the recognised computer societies in each country.

(b) The quality of the systems software has a big influence on the successful development of new computer-based systems. For example, some language processors handle more extensive versions of a programming language, allowing more rapid programming. Some operating systems allow sequential files to be read backwards (starting with the last record) which can make system designs possible that make less demands on the use of sorts. Some editors and utilities support much more convenient use and hence higher productivity than others.

The largest cost in developing applications software is usually the time of the programmers responsible. How quickly and accurately they can complete the task will often be a major determinant in the viability of the project. Apart from the calibre of the staff concerned, the systems software they use is often the largest factor in productivity. An awkward to use development environment, with an inconvenient programming language, can easily lead to a tenfold increase in development time compared to a good environment.

Anyone managing a project involving software development will therefore give considerable attention to choosing the best systems software available or — if there is no choice — to allowing for limitations which the systems software may impose. Many a project has been wrecked by (for example) a poor compiler which has made it impossible to complete the application on schedule.

(c) Because systems software is concerned with interacting with the hardware at a low level (indeed its whole function is to save the user from concern with this) the study of systems software is very useful for helping to consolidate one's knowledge of computers at that level.

For example, many people find the concept of interrupts quite difficult as purely a hardware issue, but when it is seen how an operating system processes interrupts, it becomes much clearer. Similarly, looking at the kind of code which is generated by a compiler in translation of a given high-level language statement helps many people relate a brief study of assembler language programming into the way in which the computer hardware processes instructions that make up real applications.

A true computer professional must understand (at least in principle) the concepts of a computer system right from the outside to the inside. This is not to encourage unnecessary dabbling in low-level technicalities, but simply to say that a sound appreciation of what the systems software is doing can greatly increase the chances of being able to solve problems that arise.

(d) Systems software raises some important design issues which are fundamental to many different aspects of computer systems, and some of which can arise in more complex applications software too.

For example, operating systems have to be able to control a number of different processes; they cannot just carry out a fixed number of steps in a given order. This leads to ideas of concurrency that affect many other applications, particularly in artificial intelligence. Language processors have to be able to break programs down into smaller and smaller units, which requires the widely used programming technique of recursion. Both operating systems and language processors can need some important data structures, such as trees and linked lists, which are of much wider importance.

Thus the study of systems software provides an interesting and useful way to explore these broader issues.

(e) Systems software usually has a much greater effect than applications software on machine performance — that is, how much information a system can process in a given time. Even though hardware is getting cheaper, and the days are long past when programmers had to worry about every wasted microsecond, sooner or later any system may reach the limits of the machine for which it is designed and expensive upgrades to new hardware may be required. Therefore, performance issues are one factor which computer professionals must always bear in mind.

It is not at all unusual in commercial systems for 80% of the machine instructions executed to be part of the operating system and only 20% are in the application programs; this is because of the dominance of input/output requests. An inefficient operating system will have a much more severe effect on overall performance than an inefficient application.

Moreover, with a multi-user on-line system, a small reduction in system throughput can lead to large increases in response times experienced at terminals, because queues can build up. A compiler which is generating inefficient object code can also severely reduce performance, particularly if the inefficient code is in a deeply nested program loop.

Therefore, even if for performance reasons alone, a computer professional needs a good appreciation of the principles underlying systems software.

For all these reasons, the study of systems software is a challenging and useful field, and the remainder of this book looks at the different aspects of language processors and operating systems in order to appreciate their function. Our emphasis throughout is on what they do, particularly from the user's point of view, with a brief discussion of how, but without exploring their operation at a level which would only interest those involved in compiler and operating system design.

FURTHER READING

Calingaert, P. *Assemblers, compilers and program translation* (Computer Science Press, 1979).

Gear, C. W. *Computer organization and programming* (McGraw-Hill, 4th edn, 1985).

Keller, L. S. *Operating systems — communicating with and controlling the computer* (Prentice Hall, 1988).

Lister, A. M. *Fundamentals of operating systems* (Macmillan, 3rd edn, 1984).

Part I
Language processors

2

Principles of programming languages

2.1 INTRODUCTION

The input to a language processor — whether interpreter or translator — is a source program, written in a programming language. So, before discussing the different types of language processors in any detail, we need to look at programming languages in general: how they are categorised, why they take the forms they do, and so on.

The intention of this chapter is not to act as an explanation of any particular programming language, but rather to look at the nature of language itself, in the context of programming languages specifically.

It is convenient to define a programming language as *a way of expressing a computer program in a human-readable form, that can also be processed by machine*. The essence of a programming language is thus as a means of human–computer interaction, for the specific purpose of describing a computer program. Of necessity, most programming languages have some characteristics that are relatively meaningless to a person who has no knowledge of computers, because of their need to describe a program, a task to be carried out by computer. But at the same time, most programming languages are designed to be fairly readable by people, and are thus usually rather different to the internal machine instructions that the CPU hardware actually executes.

It is sometimes suggested that in the ideal world, special programming languages would be unnecessary, and we would simply program computers in our natural language (English, French, Swahili, etc). Then, it is argued, there would be no need for people to spend time learning specialised languages in order to program computers. However, there are a number of snags with this argument.

Natural language systems, that is computer systems which can accept a degree of natural language input, are now beginning to be more common, largely as a result of developments in artificial intelligence. For special types of tasks, such as ad hoc enquiries on a database, a natural language system has much to offer the user. But natural language systems are very complex, and demand very large amounts of machine resources: they are hardly the simplest means of input to an ordinary compiler.

Natural languages suffer from a major problem of ambiguity. Often natural language systems have to ask supplementary questions — as another person would — before being certain what the user intends. This is very tedious and is not at all suitable for concise expression of an algorithm to be carried out by computer.

There are also a number of technical requirements in the field of information processing which mean that even if we were to use natural language, we would have to employ a large number of technical terms which are used in a different sense from everyday speech (fields and records, reading and writing, for example). Moreover, it is crucial to be able to refer later in the processing to some data which was used previously, so we need the ability to give names (identifiers) to items of data. If we were to start with a natural language and incorporate all these needs, we would end up with something similar to a programming language anyway.

Furthermore, natural languages are often very inconsistent. We may want the same task done twice, but may issue quite different instructions a second time. Or we may just say 'do that again' without being entirely clear what 'that' refers to.

A final problem is that natural languages lack conciseness: it takes much space to explain a simple task. By using keywords and symbols, programming languages allow us to express an operation in many fewer characters than it would take to describe the process in English. Thus, even allowing for the time taken to learn the language initially, programming languages make programming much quicker.

For all these reasons, therefore, natural languages would make a very poor form of input to a language processor, and specific programming languages have much to commend them.

Although we are looking in this chapter at programming languages before going on to consider their language processors, it is important to realise that a programming language and its translator or interpreter are not totally distinct. The design of a new programming language and the design of its language processor usually go hand in hand.

Many decisions about a language are affected by questions of how it is to be compiled — for example, compiler writers are usually keen to avoid language constructs which require a great deal of looking ahead before a phrase can be understood. In English it is quite permissible to put a condition at the end of a sentence as in 'Go and buy some food if you feel hungry' whereas almost all programming languages will insist that 'if' must come at the beginning of a sentence, so that the compiler knows immediately it is dealing with conditional processing.

The development of the language itself and its first compiler or interpreter thus go hand in hand, and are usually part of the same research project. There is little interest in a language until a language processor exists so that programs can be written in it. In the case of an assembly language, the design of the language goes hand in hand with the design of the hardware.

2.2 GENERATIONS OF PROGRAMMING LANGUAGES

Programming languages have become more sophisticated over the years, and a rough terminology has developed which categorises them into generations. It must be stressed that this is only a crude categorisation, and not all languages fit clearly into a specific generation, but the generations are still helpful in general discussion.

The early languages were very closely related to the machine hardware; later languages have been designed more for programming particular classes of problems and for higher productivity. There is some parallel between these categories and the generations sometimes used to categorise developments in hardware, but the parallels are limited and should not be taken as read.

The **first generation** of programming languages were machine languages: simply ways of writing down the binary machine code which the CPU accepts. These date from the 1940s when the first electronic computers were being developed. The crudest form of machine language is simply to write down the program in binary, or for greater readability, in octal or hexadecimal (base 8 or 16). A simple program is required to read in the hexadecimal characters and place the appropriate digits in the required storage locations, but such a program is hardly a language processor in any significant sense. The only significant use of first generation language nowadays is for low-level debugging.

The **second generation** are the assembly languages, which date from around 1950. These are discussed further in the next chapter. In assembly languages, the programmer still specifies each individual machine instruction, but does so in a much more readable way than in raw machine language. The key advantages are the provision of symbolic codes to indicate different machine instructions, and the ability to use programmer-defined names to refer to storage locations, rather than having to specify explicit addresses. More advanced assembly languages allow the use of **macros** whereby a whole group of instructions can be incorporated in the program by a one line statement. An assembly language is processed by a language processor known as an assembler, which translates the assembly source into binary machine code. (The term 'assembler' is also used as an abbreviation of 'assembly language'.)

Some people speak of machine language and assembler as though they were almost the same, but in fact assembly languages offer greatly improved programmer productivity over raw machine language, and well-written clearly commented assembly language programs can be quite maintainable. Although the use of assembler has been decreasing for many years, it is still widely used for many technical systems that require low-level machine control, and much systems software currently in use is written in assembler.

The first and second generation are known as low-level languages; the remainder are high-level languages.

The **third generation** languages account for the vast majority of popular programming languages in use: COBOL, FORTRAN, Pascal, C, and so on. These are often called problem-oriented languages, because they are oriented towards the problems or applications which the software is to process, in contrast to the first and second generation which are machine-oriented. The earliest was FORTRAN, for which the first compiler was released in 1957.

Because of the problem-oriented approach, there are an enormous variety of third-generation languages, many suited to different types of applications. Moreover, within the third generation it is possible to see a strong history of development, the later languages offering higher-level ways of describing the processing and much more advanced methods of program structuring.

FORTRAN has always been primarily a scientific language, with strong emphasis on floating-point arithmetic and extensive use of mathematical formulae. COBOL was conceived as a language for commercial data processing with an emphasis on structuring records into fields and extensive facilities for file processing. However, the early versions of both FORTRAN and COBOL were relatively crude in terms of program structuring, and this led to the definition of ALGOL as a highly structured language for expressing algorithmic processing, in particular, ALGOL-type block-structured languages make it possible to write programs without the use of GOTOs.

Over the years there have been a number of attempts to develop a 'universal' language that could be used for all kinds of applications, of which the key example is PL/I, largely an amalgamation of all the key facilities of FORTRAN, COBOL, and ALGOL, but such amalgamations are necessarily very rich and powerful, offering a vast range of facilities, which means the learning time is high, as is the risk of mistakes by the inexperienced programmer. A more recent example is Ada, which, although primarily developed for military purposes, is also a rich general purpose language, and has met similar criticisms.

The 1960s also saw the development of more specialised languages such as SNOBOL for text processing and Simula for simulation. There was also a need for easily learned languages to permit the rapid teaching of programming to new users, which led to BASIC, although more recently this has been widely used as a major programming language on microcomputers, due to its ease of implementation. It is particularly suited to interpretive (rather than compiled) execution. Another language that is normally interpreted is APL, which uses a very large character set to define numerous operators that are particularly powerful for array processing.

Another language developed mainly for teaching was Pascal, launched in 1970. It was based on the block-structured approach of ALGOL, but avoiding features of ALGOL which were difficult to compile or implement, thereby ensuring Pascal could be implemented efficiently on a wide range of computers. At the same time a number of important additions were made, including standardised input/output routines (which was ALGOL's biggest deficiency) and data-structuring facilities, including user-defined data types.

It too is now used much more widely than just for teaching, the portability of Pascal programs between different machines being an important advantage.

The 1970s also saw the emergence of C, a language developed very much for systems programming (that is for writing systems software) — it allows the programmer to have low level controls of registers and physical addresses in a way that is necessary for operating system development; its use is closely related to the Unix operating system. Modula 2 was a development of Pascal incorporating extensive software engineering facilities for modular structured design.

The fourth and fifth generations are much more recent, and there is much less agreement about the use of terminology. **Fourth-generation** languages (4GLs) are generally taken to refer to a wide range of products designed for very rapid system development, without all the detailed specification of every step of processing that occurs in third-generation languages. The most common products placed in this category are program generators, report generators, and relational database query languages, sometimes collectively called very high-level languages. The emphasis of these products is on very high application-development productivity, coupled usually with a need for little technical knowledge, meaning that some 4GL products are aimed mainly at end users rather than programmers. The first application and report generators with sufficient flexibility to be regarded as languages date from the mid-1960s.

In the fourth generation, the boundary between the language and the language processor often becomes completely blurred, as many products in this category do not have an actual source language in which a program can be written and then passed to the language processor; often the program is defined in an interactive session, involving processes such as **screen painting** where the developer simply types on to a VDU screen how the program output is to appear. From this, fields may be defined, files specified, and the process of transferring data between the screen and the file may then be generated by the product, without explicit programming. The high productivity is usually gained at the expense of some limitation of function, and applications involving complex data manipulation may remain more suitable to third-generation languages. The processing of fourth-generation languages is considered further in Chapter 8.

Fifth-generation programming languages are usually taken to be the languages popular for artificial intelligence and similar work. There is a movement in this area away from the traditional von Neumann hardware with its step-by-step instruction processing, towards machine architectures that incorporate much more parallel processing — although all popular languages in this category can be implemented on traditional machines. There are currently three main categories under the fifth-generation heading. The functional (or applicative) languages build on the third-generation notion of function calls, the most well-known example being LISP, which dates from 1960, but which has only achieved significant use much more recently. One of their key aspects is to eliminate the use of assignments in the same way as the later third-generation languages sought to eliminate

GOTOs. Logic programming languages such a Prolog centre on the specification of what is required in terms of logical statements, and leave the language processor to perform the deductions, based on evaluating large numbers of statements which can be true or false. The use of Prolog dates from the mid-1970s. Object-oriented programming relies on the notion of independent objects sending messages to each other: the main example is Smalltalk, which dates from 1972; it is considered further in section 16.3.3.1.

One of the important features of many fifth-generation languages is the lack of a strong distinction between program and data. The program can thus modify and extend itself in ways which could not have been predicted initially, which is central to many artificial intelligence applications. Languages processors for fifth-generation languages are discussed briefly in Chapter 8, and some longer-term implications are raised in Chapter 16.

2.3 PROCEDURAL AND NON-PROCEDURAL LANGUAGES

A further important distinction between programming languages depends on the notion of procedural and non-procedural languages.

A procedural language is one in which the processing to be performed by the computer is specified as a series of steps to be carried out one after the other, rather like a recipe. In other words, the programmer is defining a procedure that the computer is to carry out. Procedural languages in concept relate quite closely to the underlying von Neumann architecture of most computers as step-by-step instruction processors.

A procedural language can be high or low level, depending on whether each step represents some extensive processing or just a single machine instruction. Machine and assembly languages for conventional architectures are necessarily procedural, as are all the popular third-generation languages, and many fourth-generation languages.

Non-procedural languages rely much more on stating what is to be done, in terms of requirements, rather than how the processing is to take place. In a non-procedural language there is no suggestion that one statement will be performed chronologically after the one above it — often they will be evaluated in parallel. The non-procedural approach allows a much wider class of problems to be tackled, especially in artificial intelligence, because we do not have to know how a problem is solved in step-by-step terms before attempting to evaluate it by machine.

Languages categorised as belonging to the 'fifth generation' are necessarily non-procedural, but many fourth-generation languages also take a non-procedural approach. For example, in many report generators, the step-by-step reading of records is taken for granted: the user simply specifies the criteria on which records are selected and how the results should be tabulated. It is often suggested that removing the need to specify processing in procedural terms makes it much easier for end users without programming ability to use computers for their own problems. There are also some third-generation languages which take a non-procedural approach, the most common example being simulation languages such as Simula. In these, the programmer is using the computer to assist in simulating activities whose consequences over a period of time are uncertain. The programmer is thus working much more in terms of events which can arise in various orders, and the sequencing of time is left to the language processor.

2.4 LANGUAGE ELEMENTS

In discussions about programming languages and the operation of language processors, many terms are used to describe the different elements of the language that are not always familiar to those who have only used a language for writing programs. Most of these terms are used across a wide range of languages, and enable us to discuss the operation of language processors in general terms without being tied to any specific language. The definitions here relate to the context of third-generation procedural languages; some of these terms are used slightly differently in other contexts such as assembly languages (see Chapter 3).

The lowest level element of any language is the **character set** used for writing programs. Typically this is the same as the character set of the computer to be used (nowadays usually offering 256 characters in all) but many characters are often for use only in quoted strings and are illegal elsewhere. The early versions of COBOL and FORTRAN were designed for use with printers that could only use 48 different characters, so their character set is very small; in particular programs can be written without using greater or less than symbols, square brackets, per cent signs, and so on. At the other extreme, APL requires an enormous character set and can only be used with specially configured screens and printers.

The characters are used to build up the individual **symbols** or **tokens** of the language, such as identifiers, keywords, literals, and operators. In most languages these can be presented as free-format input to the language processor, but some languages, notably COBOL and FORTRAN assign special meanings to the use of different columns in the source records.

Identifiers are programmer-defined words. In most high-level languages they must begin with a letter but can be followed by letters or digits; there may be a maximum length. The most common use of identifiers is to define **variables**, that is, named items of data to which the programmer can assign values as execution proceeds. However, identifiers are also widely used as names for procedures, files, branch labels (where allowed), and for many other purposes. Languages such as Pascal also allow the programmer to give names to constants and to data types.

Many languages allow a group of variables to be referred to by a single name known as an **array**, and a **subscript** (which can itself be a variable) indicates which of the array **elements** is required. Typically a notation is used such as A[I] where A is the name of the array, and I is the subscript; the value of I indicates which element of A is required. Arrays may have one or more **dimensions**, e.g. B[I,J,K] is an element of a three-dimensional array.

Keywords are usually imperatives such as READ, DO, PERFORM that help to identify the different actions to be carried out by the program. In many languages, keywords are **reserved words**, that is they cannot be used as identifiers, though this can make for mistakes if a programmer did not realise a certain word was reserved, so some languages such as PL/I avoid this restriction and recognise keywords by the context.

Literals define values immediately by their appearance. Numeric literals define values such as 3, −7.456, or 1.247E−17, whilst character literals usually appear in quotes, such as 'Hello'. Symbols such as TRUE and FALSE may be used for logical literals.

A **constant** is a value that does not change during the execution of a program. A constant is often expressed simply by use of a literal, although some languages allow constants to be defined once and referred to by an identifier, which makes for ease of maintenance if the program subsequently has to be modified. Literals may also be used to indicate initial values of variables, as in the COBOL VALUE clause. It is thus important to appreciate that literals and constants are not necessarily the same.

Operators usually indicate processing to be performed: typically a '+' sign indicates that two values are to be added (an arithmetic operator) while a '>' sign may indicate that two values are to be compared (a relational operator). Most operators are diadic, that is they operate on two values, but monadic operators, such as a '−' used to indicate negation, are also frequently used. Triadic and more complex operators are possible in principle, but readability tends to suffer, and operations involving three or more operands are usually handled more easily as built in functions. Operators are not necessarily single characters, but may be denoted by reserved words such as 'AND' or 'MOD'.

Most languages support a number of different **data types** such as integer, real (floating-point), character, and logical (often called Boolean). It may be possible to combine several items of data of different types into a record structure, which can then become a **user-defined type**. Specialised languages may support further special types: for example FORTRAN permits the use of complex numbers, which have real and imaginary components, whilst languages that place emphasis on text processing facilities may offer both fixed and variable length character strings. Languages that support list processing allow **pointers** as a data type.

Variables and constants can be combined by means of operators to produce **expressions**. Usually parentheses are allowed to indicate the structure of an expression, similar to ordinary mathematical use. $(A+3)*B$ would be an arithmetic expression, that is its value is an arithmetic quantity (assuming A and B are arithmetic variables). It indicates to the language processor that at run time the value to be used at this point must be determined by adding A to 3 and multiplying by B. On the other hand, $A>B$ or X AND Y would be logical expressions: they generate a result which is either true or false.

Most languages nowadays allow expressions to be used almost anywhere a value is required, but there may be restrictions on the type: typically the keyword IF can only be followed by a logical expression, whilst the initial and final values in a FOR loop may be restricted to arithmetic expressions.

Variables acquire values most frequently by **assignments**, often denoted by the symbol '=' or ':='. Thus $A := B+3$ indicates that the expression $B+3$ is to be evaluated and the result assigned to the variable A. All subsequent references to A will yield this result until A is assigned another value.

Assignments are one kind of **statement**, but most languages allow many different statement types; usually a program consists of a sequence of statements.

Statements can be classified as **declarative** or **executable**. Declarative (or non-executable) statements provide information for the language processor, such as indicating the type of a variable or the dimensions of an array, but such statements do not indicate any actual processing to be carried out. Many languages insist that variables must be declared textually prior to their use in an executable statement; in others, standard assumptions are made about undeclared variables, their type possibly being ascertained from the initial letter of the name.

Executable statements indicate processing which the programmer is instructing the computer to perform. There are three main categories: data manipulation statements (e.g. assignments); input/output statements; and control statements (loops, IF statements, etc.), which serve to control the sequence of program execution.

The notion of parentheses not only applies within expressions: many languages allow statement parentheses, typically by keywords such as BEGIN and END, to group a number of statements, and allow a control statement to treat them as one.

Languages normally allow the programmer to define **subroutines** or **procedures** which are sections of code that can be **called** from elsewhere in the program. When a procedure is called, instructions in the procedure are executed until the procedure **returns** whereupon processing continues in the calling routine, starting with the statement immediately after the procedure call. In some languages a keyword such as CALL or PERFORM is used to invoke a procedure; in others a procedure call statement may consist simply of the name of the procedure.

Many languages also allow procedures which can be invoked from within an expression to return a value — for example to calculate a square root or to provide the next input character — such procedures are usually called **functions**. Thus a function call is not a statement in its own right, but simply a portion of another statement such as an assignment. Collectively, procedures and functions are called **sub-programs**, though the precise usage of these terms varies slightly between languages.

Sub-programs may be **internal**, **external**, or **built-in**. Internal procedures are submitted to the language processor as part of the same source code as the routine which calls them, whereas external procedures may have been separately compiled at a different time. Built-in functions or procedures are provided as part of the language and do not have to be written by the programmer. Scientific languages usually provide a large range of built-in mathematical functions to calculate logarithms, trigonometric functions, etc. Other languages may offer built-in functions to supply sub-portions of a character string or to allow the program to obtain the system date. A number of languages implement all input and output by means of calls to built-in procedures.

In the majority of cases, communication of data between the calling routine and a sub-program is assisted by some means of **parameter passing**. When a procedure is called, a number of **arguments** may be listed, which are variables or expressions representing data to be passed to the procedure, or variables to receive data which the procedure may return. These are frequently listed in parentheses after the procedure name. The procedure itself defines a number of **parameters** which are variables that correspond with the arguments of the calling routine, and enable the procedure to work with the values that the arguments represent. This has the advantage that a procedure may be called on different occasions with different arguments.

The terms *arguments* and *parameters* will be used in this sense in this book, but unfortunately they are also used in many different ways in the context of different languages. Some languages, for example, speak about arguments and dummy arguments, or about actual parameters and formal parameters.

Although parameter-passing mechanisms are quite widespread, they are not universal, particularly with internal procedures. The traditional versions of COBOL (using PERFORM) and BASIC (using GOSUB) offer no means of parameter passing for internal procedures. Many languages do not support functions, or possibly offer them only as one-line definitions rather than as a sequence of statements involving loops and conditional processing.

A further distinction between languages, which is of considerable importance in the design of the language processor, lies in the parameter-passing *mechanism*. There are four commonly used mechanisms of associating arguments and parameters, and programmers who have only encountered one mechanism frequently make the mistake of assuming other languages work in exactly the same way. In certain cases, programs can give quite different results according to the parameter passing mechanism used.

The simplest mechanism is passing by **value** where the value of the argument is copied into the parameter. Subsequent modifications to the parameter have no effect on the argument. The most popular mechanism is probably passing by **reference** where simply the address of the argument is passed, and all references to the parameter refer to and modify the actual storage location of the argument. Passing by **value result** is like passing by value, except that the final contents of the parameter are copied back to the argument when the procedure returns, so enabling the argument to be updated. Unlike call by reference, there is no access to the actual storage location of the argument while the procedure is executing, so the effect can be different where, for example, the same variable appears more than once in the list of arguments. The most complex mechanism, mainly used in ALGOL 60, is calling by **name** where the effect is defined to be as though the name of the argument were textually substituted everywhere the parameter occurs. Where the argument is an expression, this means it is re-evaluated every time the parameter is referred to.

Where passing by value is used, another mechanism is normally offered as well, otherwise the procedure cannot return values to the calling routine. The range of mechanisms used is one difficulty encountered in attempting to call sub-programs written in a different language.

The other method of communicating with sub-programs is to use **global data**, that is variables which can be accessed by both the calling routine and the sub-program. In many languages all data is global between a program and its internal procedures. Most block-structured languages, on the other hand, allow procedures to declare their own **local** variables which cannot be accessed by the calling routine; however, any variable declared in the calling routine is usually global and can be accessed by the procedure, unless the procedure has declared a local variable with the same name. This gives rise to the notion of the **scope** of a variable, that is, the parts of the program in which a particular variable can be accessed, and when there are several levels of internal procedures, the scope rules of a language may become quite complex. Where there are global and local variables of the same name, the language processor has to follow the scope rules carefully to ensure that the correct variable is accessed for given statement.

Some languages also allow global data between a program and its external sub-programs, usually by explicit declaration such as through the FORTRAN COMMON statement or the PL/I EXTERNAL attribute. The main program and sub-program (or two sub-programs) are thus enabled to refer directly to the same area of storage, without use of parameter-passing mechanisms.

2.5   FORMAL LANGUAGE DEFINITIONS

It is clear that a programming language, although much simpler than a natural language, is still quite complex, and the rules about how the language elements may be combined to give a valid program may be difficult to explain.

To overcome this, various attempts have been devised to allow a formal definition of the syntax of a language, showing all the possibilities that can lead to a valid program. Such definitions can then be used both by programmers and by those responsible for the language processor. The complete syntactic definition is known as the **grammar** of the language. Some more elaborate methods have also been devised which attempt to define not just the syntax of the language (how it is written) but also the semantics (the meaning) of the different elements, but these will not be persued here.

By far the most well known method of formal language definition is **Backus–Naur Form** (BNF), named after those who devised it: its first major use was in the definition of ALGOL. It allows block-structured languages, in particular, to be defined very concisely. BNF is a **meta-language**, that is a language for defining languages. The fact that BNF is written according to strict rules is very useful to designers of language processors, a point which will be investigated further in Chapter 5.

The BNF definition of a language consists of a substantial number of definitions, starting with the definition of low-level elements and building up to the definition of a program (or vice versa — the order of the definitions does not matter greatly).

The language elements are separated into *terminals* and *non-terminals*. Terminal symbols are symbols that can appear in the program as it is actually written — they are characters in the language's character set. Non-terminal symbols define language elements that build into other elements to form a program. Thus, for example, most BNF language specifications contain the definition:

<digit> ::= 0|1|2|3|4|5|6|7|8|9

The use of angle brackets indicates that <digit> is a non-terminal; whereas the symbols on the right — the actual printed figures — are terminals. The '::=' is read as 'is defined as'. The vertical bar is read as 'or'. Thus the language element known as a digit can consist of any one of the figures 0 to 9; there are no other possibilities. It is easy to see from this that 3 is a valid digit but X or 99 cannot conform to the definition of a digit.

From the definition of digit, larger language elements can be defined, for example:

<unsigned integer> ::= <digit>|<unsigned integer><digit>

This definition is recursive: it shows that an unsigned integer can consist of just a single digit, or it can be anything that is a valid unsigned integer followed by another digit. In practice this means that any sequence of digits satisfies the definition of an unsigned integer.

Assuming that the non-terminal <letter> has been defined in a similar way to <digit> above, an identifier can typically be defined by:

<identifier> ::=
    <letter>|<identifier><letter>|<identifier><digit>

showing that an identifier can be a single letter, or anything that is a valid identifier followed by a letter or followed by a digit. This allows identifiers such as A, B1, CAB, but not 1A or A$$.

Assuming <constant> has been suitably defined, building on the definition of <unsigned integer> we can proceed to define expressions:

<factor> ::= <identifier>|<constant>|(<expression>)

<term> ::= <factor>|<term>*<factor>|<term>/<factor>

<expression> ::= < term>|<expression>+<term>|
            <expression>−<term>

This shows the syntactic structure of expressions very clearly as a sequence of terms built up from left to right, each of which can consist of factors multiplied or divided (showing syntactically that multiplication and division have priority over addition and subtraction). It also shows that if you take something which is a valid expression — no matter how complex — and put parentheses round it, you have what is treated as a single factor (the parentheses in the definition of <factor> are terminals, whereas <expression> is a non-terminal).

From this it is relatively simple to define an <assignment statement>, and once other statements are defined, we have the general definition of <statement>. A sequence of statements can then constitute a <block> and by the addition of declarations, we reach the definition of a program such as:

<program> ::= <program statement><declarations><block>

Any legal program must satisfy this definition and by following these definitions down to the lowest levels we can in theory generate all possible valid programs. Conversely, given something which purports to be a program in the language, a language processor may be able to determine whether it could have been arrived at by following these BNF rules, and hence whether it is in fact a legal program. This discussion has avoided most of the issues that differ from one programming language to another, but the actual BNF definition will, of course, be specific to each language.

This style of definition can be written in many ways. It is common to see an arrow used instead of '::=' and sometimes the alternatives are written by offering several definitions of the same non-terminal instead of the 'or' symbol, for example:

<unsigned integer> → <digit>

<unsigned integer> → <unsigned integer><digit>

or for brevity, the definition may dispense with the use of long names in angle brackets and denote non-terminals by lowercase (or Greek) letters, such as:

u → d

u → ud

When this is done, the definitions are more often called *productions* (that is they show how the language is produced). There is a great deal of theory in this area, much of it due originally to the philosopher Chomsky, who identified different classes of grammars. Most programming languages conform mainly to his definition of *context-free grammars*, and BNF is designed for the definition of these. In more complex context-sensitive grammars (including most natural languages) it is not possible to define everything with a single non-terminal on the left of all productions.

An alternative, more readable approach was used in the definition of Pascal, which is to express the definitions in terms of syntax diagrams that are interpreted intuitively as railway tracks. Any path along the tracks (moving in the direction of the arrows) generates a valid possibility, with branches in the tracks being used to allow alternatives, and loops in the tracks allowing multiple iterations. Using this approach, an identifier could be defined by Fig. 2.1.

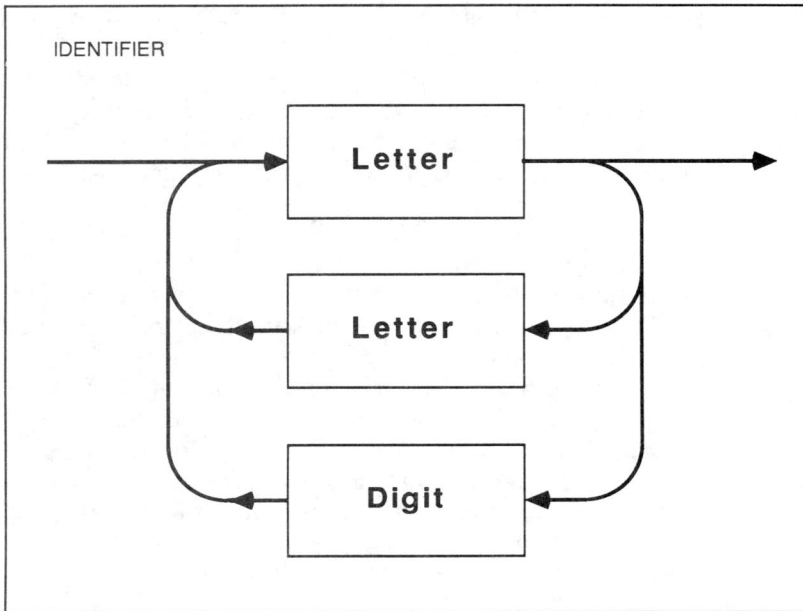

Fig. 2.1 — Syntax diagram definition of an identifier.

The disadvantage of this diagrammatic approach is the relative difficulty of processing the definitions by machine.

It must be stressed that the grammar only tells us a certain amount about the language, and there may be further rules which can only easily be expressed in terms of narrative clarifications — for example if numbers cannot exceed a certain length, or if identifiers must be declared before they are used. In particular, the grammar of the language tells us nothing of the semantics of the language elements used. Nevertheless, the ability to define language syntax in formal ways such as BNF is of immense help in understanding how languages are handled by a language processor.

2.6   DESIRABLE FEATURES OF PROGRAMMING LANGUAGES

From the issues examined so far, it becomes clear that there are many different aspects which one would like to see reflected in a programming language. No one language can satisfy all that we would wish, which is partly why there are so many languages available. One can possibly summarise the main desirable features as follows.

2.6.1 Ease of use

A programming language should be easy to use — though languages are used in different ways by different people. An ideal language would be easy to use in terms of writing programs, in readability, in the ability to maintain and modify existing programs, and for debugging. In particular, a language should allow high productivity in all these tasks.

Even these issues, however, are open to debate. Some languages are easier to use for particular applications than others. Some languages are easy to use for the beginner but contain frustrating limitations for the more experienced programmer. Some languages are quick to write but hard to read (a criticism often levelled at APL).

2.6.2 Power

A powerful language imposes few constraints on the programmer and thus acts as a highly flexible tool for program development. Generally speaking a powerful language will also lead to higher productivity, as it will be possible to accomplish more processing with less writing.

On the other hand, the danger of very powerful languages is that they are more open to programmer mistakes than simple languages. This is particularly a problem in maintainability if people amending a program do not realise the full implications of statements they are changing.

2.6.3 Portability

A highly portable language enables programs written in that language to be transferred from one machine to another with little or no modification. A number of languages (notably Pascal) have been designed specifically with portability in mind.

However, for the programmer developing an application which will only ever run on one type of machine, the portability can be restrictive. For example, portable languages have to avoid building in features which are dependent on particular operating systems, because such features may not be available on other machines. A program which specifically requires use of such features may therefore have to be developed in another language. Or the compiler writer may build in extensions to the language for use on specific machines, which removes the portability if any of those extensions are used.

2.6.4 Reliability

Some languages are much better than others for developing highly reliable software. In the worst case a program may be unreliable because of bugs in the language processor, rather than in the source code of the program itself. Even if this is ruled out, some languages do lead to frequent programmer mistakes — perhaps because of two similar constructs which are easily confused — and if these are not easily detected by a compiler they may have a serious effect on software reliability.

More subtle issues to do with reliability apply to the ability of the program to handle exceptional conditions. Many languages automatically terminate the program if an error is encountered during file input/output, for example. The impact of this on the end user can be quite serious. A language more oriented towards software reliability would allow the program to detect such a condition and take suitable action.

A final issue of reliability relates to verifiability. In general, it is much easier to check a program and to be certain of the logic flow if the use of GOTOs and labels is avoided, which is assisted much more in some languages than others. If formal program proving is required, it may be necessary to restrict the language further; functional programming languages are particularly valuable in this context.

2.6.5 Efficiency

It is no use having a superb language to use if programs written in it are too slow to be of use.

Where a compiler is used, both the efficiency of compilation and the efficiency of execution need to be considered. Some languages are extremely slow to compile, because of their complexity, even though programs written in the language may execute efficiently. In some cases the fault is with the compiler design, but in other cases it may be the language design which causes the difficulty.

Equally there are languages which can be compiled very quickly but which lead to inefficient execution, perhaps because of facilities that involve large run-time overheads of storage management (see Chapter 6).

Where the execution is interpretive, issues of efficiency become even more important, because of the overheads of interpretive execution, as discussed in Chapter 8. Some languages, such as BASIC, are particularly designed for interpretation, and can be interpreted fairly efficiently. With other languages, interpretation may be possible, but the syntax may be such that it can only be accomplished with very substantial overheads.

2.6.6 Summary

Overall, there is no such thing as a good language, but there are programming languages which are strong in particular areas. In a given situation, the choice of language for a project will be highly dependent on the language processors available, and it is impossible to separate consideration of the quality of the language from questions about the quality of the language processors. It is frequently the case that a certain programming language largely spurned in a given installation becomes very advantageous when a new compiler is available.

It is thus clear that the issues raised in this chapter regarding the nature of programming languages are incomplete in themselves. In order to answer many of the problems, we need to look at the language processors these programming languages use, which is the purpose of the next six chapters.

FURTHER READING

Ghezzi, C. and Jazayeri, M. *Programming language concepts* (John Wiley, 2nd edn, 1987).

Eisenbach, S. (ed.) *Functional programming* (Ellis Horwood, 1987).

MacLennan, B. J. *Principles of programming languages* (Holt, Rinehart & Winston, 2nd edn, 1987).

Higman, B. *A comparative study of programming languages* (MacDonald, 1967).

Malone, J. R. *Comparative languages* (Chartwell-Bratt, 1987).

Meek, B. *FORTRAN, PL/I and the Algols* (Macmillan, 1978).

Nicholls, J. E. *The structure and design of programming languages* (Addison-Wesley, 1975).

Pratt, T. W. *Programming languages — design and implementation* (Prentice-Hall, 2nd edn, 1984).

Tennent, R. D. Principles of programming languages (Prentice-Hall, 1981).

3

Assembly language and assemblers

3.1 ASSEMBLER PRINCIPLES

The function of an assembler is to translate assembly language programs into the internal machine formats required for execution. Assemblers are essentially simpler than compilers, because the selection of individual machine instructions is done by the programmer rather than by the translator. It is thus convenient to look at the processing of assembly language before proceeding in later chapters to consider language processors for high-level languages.

It is sometimes supposed that assemblers are very simple, even trivial, language processors, on the grounds that the assembly language programmer has specified all the machine instructions, and that therefore the assembler has no more than a minor reformatting task to perform.

On closer examination, however, it is seen that with most assembly languages, the assembler has to do a great deal more than this. Features such as symbolic addressing and the use of macros (described below) demand extensive processing; indeed it is not unusual for a sophisticated assembler to be a larger program than a simple compiler. In particular, facilities such as macros are common in assembly languages but are only supported by a few high-level languages, so it is not surprising that an assembler can be a fairly elaborate kind of language processor.

Much of the processing carried out by an assembler is, however, equally applicable to other kinds of language processors, but it is much easier to understand how symbols are handled, for example, if we do not have to worry about the complications of compiler code generation at the same time.

For all language translators, both assemblers and compilers, the input language which the translator accepts is referred to as the **source code** and the machine code translation which the translator produces, is **object code**.

An assembler is, by definition, a translator, producing binary machine code from the assembly language source. Although it is possible to construct interpreters for assembly languages, they have little practical use for most assembler applications, as much of the reason for writing in assembler is to achieve the maximum performance in program execution. The overheads of an interpreter would, in most cases, totally destroy the benefits of programming in assembler. However, there are exceptions, particularly where it is desired to run assembler programs written for one machine on a completely different machine. In such cases, an **emulator** is frequently used, that is, a program running on one machine which interpretively executes the instructions of a program written for another machine.

Before considering assemblers in any detail, we need to look more closely at assembly languages in their own right. We shall then proceed to outline a hypothetical machine which will be used to illustrate this and the remaining chapters of Part I.

3.2   ASSEMBLY LANGUAGE

It is convenient to define assembly language as *a means of programming where every machine instruction is specified by the programmer, but with various aids in the language to make it more convenient than raw machine code.*

Because such languages are tied to a particular set of machine instructions, assembler languages necessarily differ from one machine to another (unless the machines have the same architecture). There may be similarities — for example many assembly languages on different machines use the directive ORG to allow the programmer to indicate a starting address for the program — but the actual instructions of the assembly language must correspond to the machine for which the program is written.

It can also arise in certain cases that there is more than one assembly language available for one machine; this is mainly when the original assembler provided by the computer manufacturer is felt to be relatively weak, and others are developed independently. For popular architectures such as the Intel 8086 and related families of processors, there are a number of competing assemblers offered by different software houses, and programs written for one cannot always be assembled using another, as there may be differences, for example, in the programmer directives allowed, or in the maximum length of symbols, even though the machine instructions are the same. It can also be that different assemblers generate output for different linkage editors. If more than one operating system is available for the machine there will also usually have to be different assemblers that run under the different operating systems, otherwise one would have to load a different operating system purely to assemble a program!

Second-generation languages thus lack the standardisation that can apply to machine-independent higher-level languages, and any discussion of assembly language can only be representative; individual assemblers are bound to have certain unique features. This also means that the use of terminology varies slightly, and not all assembly languages use the term 'literals', for example, in precisely the way it is used here. Other features, such as the specification of different addressing modes, will be included as part of the assembly language only where the machine architecture so requires.

Most assembly languages are written in a standard format, with one machine instruction per line. Typically each line is divided into four fields:

| *label* | *operation* | *operands* | *comments* |

for example:

| NEXT | LDA | TOTAL | Allow for final value |

Sometimes the fields must begin in certain columns, but more commonly they are simply separated by a convenient character such as a space. Some assemblers insist that the comments must be preceded by a character such as an asterisk or semicolon, which means that there can be spaces within the operand field without confusion as to where the comments begin.

The label field is optional, and is used only where the programmer wishes to give a name to the storage location at which that instruction is assembled. The comments are similarly optional, but for readability it is regarded as good practice to comment the majority of instructions when writing an assembler program, the comment serving to relate the machine operation to the problem task. The operation field is usually compulsory except on lines consisting solely of comments, and, depending on the machine architecture, each instruction will have one or more operands, which are frequently symbols defined by their appearance in other lines in the label field.

The features most commonly provided in an assembly language can be summarised as follows.

3.2.1   Mnemonic operation codes
Probably the strongest distinction between assembly language and raw machine code is that the machine operation codes (**op-codes**) are denoted mnemonically by short alphabetic codes rather than by the numeric codes understandable by the CPU. Thus the instruction to load the accumulator may be denoted LDA rather than hexadecimal 01.

This makes for much greater readability as it is very quick to see what operation is performed on each line of the program. Although the allocation of mnemonic codes to instructions is in principle a matter in the design of the assembly language, it is usual for hardware designers to specify a mnemonic for each op-code as part of the CPU specification.

3.2.2   Symbolic addressing
The ability to refer to addresses by means of symbols (identifiers chosen by the programmer) is probably the most powerful aspect of assembly languages, and approximates towards the ability in high-level languages to name variables at will.

The principle of symbolic addressing is that the programmer does not have to specify absolute addresses when writing instructions; instead a symbol is inserted in the label field of any instruction whose address is required elsewhere. The symbol can then be used wherever the address of that location is required. For example, at some point in the program which contained the line above, we may find the instruction:

| JUM | NEXT | Continue loop |

from which the assembler generates a machine instruction whose address field contains the address of the location of the LDA instruction above.

The freedom which symbolic addressing gives to the programmer is immense. It saves the programmer from concern with the number of locations occupied by each instruction in order to know where in memory each instruction will lie. It makes programs much more modifiable, because if instructions are inserted or deleted it is not necessary to alter branch addresses: the use of a symbol to refer to the address takes care of this. Symbolic addressing also allows the whole program to be relocated in memory, as it does not matter which part of memory the program actually occupies, so long as all references to symbolic addresses are correctly assembled relative to some particular starting address.

3.2.3 Pseudo-instructions

In addition to the machine operations, assemblers allow a variety of **pseudo-instructions** or **directives** which are simply included in the program as information for the assembler. Lines containing pseudo-instructions do not assemble into machine instructions, but are analogous to declarative statements in a high-level language.

Pseudo-instructions are commonly used to define the origin or initial address of the program (from which all symbolic addresses are calculated); to reserve storage for data areas, that is locations which will not be used to hold machine instructions; to indicate page breaks in the program listing, to equate a symbol to a particular value, and so on. ORG, EQU, DS, DC, DEFW, DEFS, BSS, MACRO, END are all pseudo-instructions used in a variety of assembly languages. For data areas, different pseudo-instructions are normally used for initialised and non-initialised areas. With initialised data, the assembler must ensure that the required value is found in a given location at the time the program is loaded.

3.2.4 Values

The assembler programmer needs to be able to refer to explicit values as well as to symbolic addresses. The need for this is most obvious with initialised data areas.

For example, if a given location is to hold the value 27 one typically needs a line such as:

    CONVRATE   DEFW   27   Conversion rate

where DEFW is a pseudo-instruction defining a location for constant (initialised) data.

The assembly language could insist that all values were indicated in (say) hexadecimal, but it is much more convenient to allow a choice of data types and number bases. Numeric values are assumed to be decimal unless otherwise specified; hexadecimal values may be distinguished by devices such as 1CH, X'1C', or &H1C. Similar approaches are used if binary or octal values are permitted. Character data is usually surrounded by quotation marks, possibly preceded by a character C, thus in IBM 360/370 assembler, C'HELLO' indicates a character value five bytes long.

As far as the assembler is concerned, however, different data types are simply used to give the programmer a choice of how a value is defined. There are none of the restrictions of high level languages that only allow certain types in certain contexts. One can perfectly well use 'B' as an address: if the machine operates using the ASCII character set this would be taken as a reference to absolute address 66. The fact that this is rather meaningless is a matter for the programmer, not for the assembler.

3.2.5   Expressions

It is frequently necessary to refer not just to a given symbolic address, but to a location which is a given offset away. For example if the symbol REC denotes the first location of an area of storage containing a data record, REC+4 can be used to refer to a location offset four bytes into the record (assuming one byte per location). REC−1 refers to the byte immediately before the start of the record.

Most assembly languages allow **expressions** such as these, as they avoid the need to assign a symbol to every possible location to be referenced. It is vital to appreciate, though, that these expressions are determined at assembly time, and a single resultant address is obtained. (They are unlike expressions in high-level languages which usually indicate calculations to be performed during program execution.) Thus the instruction:

$$LDA \qquad TOTAL+8$$

is *not* a request to load the value of TOTAL into the accumulator and add 8 to it: on most machines that could not be done in a single machine instruction. Rather the programmer is indicating that the number held in a location that is eight locations after TOTAL is to be loaded into the accumulator. If after determination of symbolic addresses, TOTAL is found to correspond to the hexadecimal address 20C0, then TOTAL+8 is the address 20C8. If the operation code for LDA is hexadecimal 01, the above instruction will assemble to the hexadecimal:

    0120C8

which is a single machine instruction.

Assemblers vary in the complexity of expressions they will allow. Addition and subtraction are normally supported; it is particularly useful to be able to subtract symbols to give an offset. For example if RECEND denotes the first location following the record, then RECEND−REC yields, at assembly time, the length of the record, which may perhaps be the value by which a register is to be incremented. Multiplication and division are more complex: if REC is in principle an address that could be relocated anywhere in the machine, REC+4 has some meaning, but REC*2 (where the * denotes multiplication) is rather meaningless.

To cope with more elaborate expressions, most assemblers distinguish between relocatable and non-relocatable symbols, with multiplication and division of relocatable symbols being disallowed. Any symbol defined by being placed in the label field of an instruction is relocatable, as its value would change if the start address of the program were altered. But symbols defined in other ways may be non-relocatable, for example using the pseudo-instruction EQU one might define:

```
        CR          EQU         13                      Char code for
                                                        carriage return
or
        RECLEN      EQU         RECEND-REC   Length of record
```

where CR and RECLEN will have absolute (non-relocatable) values.

Expressions referring to the current location are often allowed, the current location frequently being denoted '*'. Thus

```
            JUM         *-4
```

assembles to an instruction which jumps back four locations (though the use of such techniques is questionable in terms of program maintainability). Such a facility can be offered by the assembler irrespective of whether the *machine architecture* allows addressing relative to the current location.

3.2.6 Literals
On many machines, calculations involving constants require that the constant is held in a suitable storage location, separate from the instruction. For example, to multiply the contents of the accumulator by 100, something on these lines is usually required:

```
            MUL         HUNDRED     Convert to pence
            :
            :
            :
HUNDRED DEFW         100
```

This is inconvenient as the programmer has to write the MUL instruction and also assign a location for the constant somewhere within the data area; it also means an additional symbol is used, and furthermore, the programmer does not usually mind where the value is held (so long as it is not in the middle of the instructions). To get around this, some assemblers support **literals** in a similar way to high-level languages; the literal is used where needed and the assembler allocates a convenient location. The character '=' may be used to denote a literal; thus the above code could be written simply:

```
            MUL         =100        Convert to pence
```

which is taken as a request to the assembler to place the value 100 in a convenient location, and insert the address of that location into the instruction, thus achieving the same effect as when the symbol HUNDRED is manually defined.

This is, of course, quite different to the instruction

$$\text{MUL} \qquad 100$$

which is simply a request to multiply the accumulator by the contents of *address* 100.

3.2.7 Macros and conditional assembly

Certain sequences of instructions — for example to perform input or output operations — may occur frequently in assembler programs. In such cases, it is helpful if the programmer can have a shorthand to avoid writing them out in full each time. **Macros** provide one such approach.

The notion of a macro is, in fact, a totally general concept that could apply to any kind of text; it is not restricted to programming languages, but in this context we discuss macros in relation to assembly languages.

To define a macro, certain pseudo-instructions are used, such as MACRO at the start and MEND at the end. Symbolic parameters may be defined, in this case beginning with the character &, indicating information which is to be substituted when the macro is invoked.

Suppose that a certain program requires frequent use of a three-instruction sequence to increment the contents of a location by a given value. This could be defined as a macro thus:

```
MACRO
INCR          &LOC,&VAL
LDA           &LOC
ADD           =&VAL
STO           &LOC
MEND
```

These instructions can then be invoked simply by using the macro name INCR as a pseudo-instruction, with operands that will be substituted for the symbolic parameters. Thus

```
INCR          TOTAL,4
```

causes the assembler to generate and then assemble the instructions:

```
LDA           TOTAL
ADD           =4
STO           TOTAL
```

thereby saving the programmer a good deal of writing.

It is important to appreciate that macros are quite different to subroutines, even though the effect may be similar. A subroutine involves a branch being taken at *run time* to a portion of code away from the mainline code. This necessarily involves some run time overhead, particularly if there are parameters to pass. By contrast a macro is expanded at *assembly time* and the required instructions are inserted into the code at the point required, though this does require more memory if large macros are frequently invoked.

Assemblers that support macros are often called macro assemblers. The macro facilities usually allow macros to be held in a library, so that they can be invoked in different programs, or to be defined at the start of a particular program. Many macro assemblers incorporate quite elaborate **conditional assembly** facilities, whereby the macro can generate quite different code, dependent upon the symbolic parameters. It is thus possible to define very complex routines to meet a wide variety of situations, which can be incorporated by a programmer of only limited experience, simply by invoking the macro with suitable operands.

3.3   THE GOAT MACHINE

In order to discuss the use of assembler in this chapter, and to consider issues of compiler code generation in later chapters, it is convenient to use a hypothetical machine for illustration. The use of a hypothetical machine has the advantage in that we can design it to include only those features necessary for illustrating a point and can avoid irrelevant complications of real machines. The illustrations in the previous section were based on this, by implication. Readers who have experience of assembler programming on real machines will be able to detect certain similarities whilst also appreciating ways in which other machines may differ from the one used. This hypothetical machine is similar to many used by other authors; its architecture is deliberately somewhat crude compared to current machines.

The GOAT (Grand Old Architecture Trainer) is a byte-oriented machine (that is each location holds one eight-bit byte) with just 64K locations. Thus an address can be specified in 16 bits, and instructions contain the full address of the data location referenced. The ASCII character code is used. All instructions are three bytes (24 bits) long, and consist of an eight-bit op-code followed by a data address.

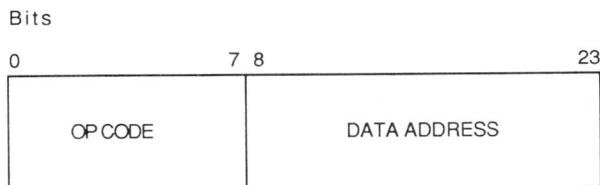

Bits

0	7 8	23
OP CODE	DATA ADDRESS	

Fig. 3.1 — GOAT instruction format.

There is only one general purpose register: a 16-bit accumulator (AC), and all arithmetic operations are performed between memory and AC, with the result being placed in the AC. Unless otherwise specified, instructions operate on a 16-bit (two-byte) operand, located in the address specified and in the following location; such operands must commence on an even-numbered byte. (Thus an instruction to load from 2000H will fetch the contents of 2000H and 2001H.)

There is also a 16-bit index register (IX) which can be used for address modification. Only two addressing modes are supported: direct and indexed. With direct addressing, the effective address is the data address specified in the instruction. With indexed addressing, the effective address is obtained by adding the contents of the index register to the instruction data address. Indexed addressing is indicated by the first bit of the op-code being set to 1 (that is, by adding 80H to the normal op-code). Where indexed addressing is used in an instruction that alters the contents of IX, the effective address is calculated before the instruction is executed.

Instructions are fetched into the instruction register (IR) where they are decoded and a program counter register (PC) maintains the address of the next instruction to be executed: it is thus incremented by 3 as each instruction (other than a jump) is executed; a successful jump places the effective address into the PC.

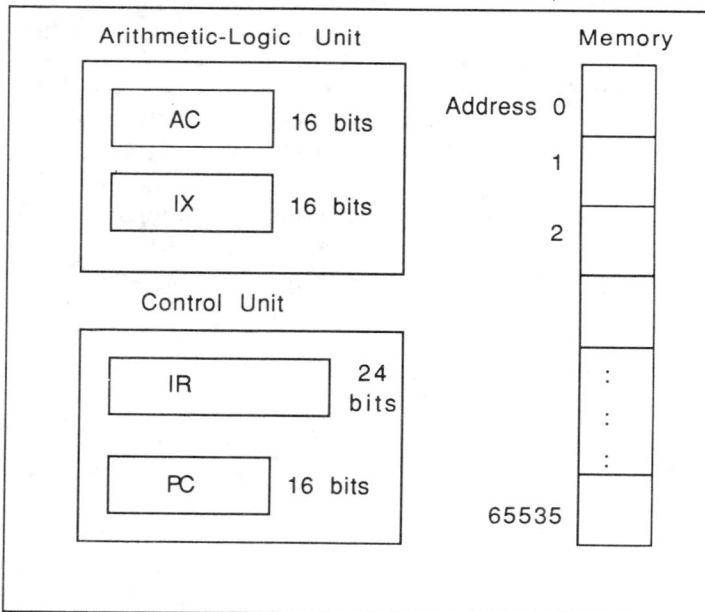

Fig. 3.2 — GOAT machine structure.

The following instructions are provided.

OP-CODE	MNEMONIC	DESCRIPTION
01H	LDA	Loads 16-bit integer into AC from contents of effective address.
02H	STO	Stores 16 bits from AC into effective address.
03H	ADD	Adds 16-bit integer at effective address into AC; result is placed in AC.
04H	SUB	Subtracts 16-bit integer at effective address from AC; result is placed in AC.
05H	MUL	Multiplies AC by 16-bit integer at effective address; any overflow is ignored.
06H	DIV	Divides AC by 16-bit integer at effective address; any remainder is ignored.
07H	SLA	Shifts AC left by the number of bits indicated by the value of the effective address.
08H	SRA	Shifts AC right by the number of bits indicated by the value of the effective address.
09H	LDI	Loads AC with *value* of effective address (i.e. the effective address is taken as an immediate operand).
0AH	LDC	Loads one character at the contents of the effective address into low-order bits of AC; high-order bits of AC are set to zero.
0BH	STC	Stores one character from the low-order byte of AC into the location specified by the effective address.
11H	LDX	Loads IX with 16-bit integer at effective address.
12H	STX	Stores IX contents (16 bits) at effective address.
19H	LXI	Loads IX with the *value* of the effective address (i.e. the effective address is taken as an immediate operand).
1AH	LXA	Loads IX from AC (data address has no effect).
21H	JUM	Jumps to address specified by the effective address.
22H	JP	Jumps to address specified by the effective address only if contents of AC are positive.
23H	JZ	Jumps to address specified by the effective address only if contents of AC are zero.

OP-CODE	MNEMONIC	DESCRIPTION
24H	JN	Jumps to address specified by the effective address only if contents of AC are negative.
25H	CAL	Subroutine call: jumps to location specified by effective address and places address of the next instruction in IX.
31H	INP	Inputs one byte from the peripheral device whose number is indicated by the effective address; this byte is placed in the low order bits of AC and the high order bits are cleared. (CPU waits until a byte is ready.)
32H	OUT	Outputs the low order byte of AC to the peripheral device whose number is the effective address. (If the device is not ready, the CPU waits until the instruction can be completed.) (The operator's keyboard/VDU is device number 1, the standard printer is device number 2.)

In GOAT Assembly Language, indexed addressing is indicated by a '*' after the op-code. Pseudo-instructions used include ORG to indicate an address at which to start assembling a program, DEFW to define a two-byte integer storage cell, DEFC to define character constants (length determined by the operand) and END to denote the end of the program. Comments can occupy a full line if they commence with an asterisk.

It will be noted from the descriptions that the instruction

LDI*   0

can be used to load IX into AC, and

JUM*   0

can be conveniently used to return from a subroutine, as it causes a branch to the address in the index register. The index register can be incremented by constant values using LXI*, thus

LXI*   2

adds 2 to the contents of the index register.

Additional instructions would be needed to support a worthwhile operating system, but the above architecture is sufficient to consider the implications for language processors.

3.4 FUNCTIONS OF AN ASSEMBLER

It is convenient to define the assembler itself as *a piece of software that translates assembly language source code into machine code.*

The nature of assembly language makes it clear that there is indeed a translation process involved, particularly to handle symbolic addressing, macros, literals, and so on; the assembler is doing a good deal more than a simple reformatting exercise.

The tasks that an assembler has to perform can be grouped under a number of headings (though the tasks are not necessarily carried out in this order).

3.4.1   Op-code translation

The mnemonic op-codes used in the assembly language must be replaced by the numeric op-codes used by the machine architecture to identify different instructions.

On a machine like the GOAT, this is a very simple process involving just a look-up table; the only complication is to add a 1 bit in the first place if the op code is followed by an asterisk to indicate indexed addressing.

However, before translating a mnemonic op-code, the assembler must be sure that it is indeed an instruction op-code rather than a pseudo-instruction or macro invocation. Some assembly languages complicate this by allowing the programmer to redefine instruction mnemonics or by allowing macros which have the same name as an instruction. In these cases there will be a number of tables: instruction mnemomics, pseudo-instructions, redefined mnemonics, program macros, and library macros, which will be searched in a carefully defined order.

With more complex machine architectures, including most microprocessors, the number of bits in the machine op-code can vary, so the process of assembling each instruction may be more complex. Also a number of assembly languages allow one mnemonic to cover several different hardware instructions for example, in Z80 assembler the mnemonic LD is used for all instructions that involve loading data from one place to another, and only by inspecting the operands field of the source instruction can the assembler determine the actual machine op-code required.

3.4.2   Allocation of addresses

As the assembler scans the lines of the source code it must determine the actual address into which each instruction or piece of data is to be assembled. In order to do this, the assembler maintains an internal working variable known as the **location counter**.

At the top of the program, the location counter is set to a suitable initial value, and as each instruction or data area is assembled, the location counter is incremented by the size of that item. When the symbol '*' is used by the programmer to refer to the current location, the assembler can simply replace it by the current value of the location counter.

The value in the location counter may be an absolute address, or an address relative to the start of the program if the output of the assembler is to be processed by a relocating linker or loader. The implications of relocatable object code are considered in Chapter 7, and for the remainder of this chapter we shall assume, for simplicity, that the assembler is dealing with absolute addresses.

A pseudo-instruction such as ORG typically appears at the start of the program to define the initial value for the location counter.

3.4.3 Resolution of symbolic addresses

Where symbols are used in instruction operands to refer to addresses, the assembler must replace these with the actual numeric address to which each symbol refers. This is usually done by making two passes through the program and building a symbol table, as described below.

3.4.4 Conversion of constants to binary

All values that are defined explicitly, whether by decimal digits, hexadecimal characters, or text fields, must be converted to their internal binary representation, before they can form part of the machine code program.

3.4.5 Evaluation of expressions

Where constant values and symbols are combined in expressions, the expressions must be evaluated by the assembler to yield a single binary value that can be inserted in the object code where required.

3.4.6 Allocation of storage for literals

If the assembly language supports literals on the basis described above, literals must, once their value is known, be allocated to a suitable storage location, and the address of that location is then inserted in all instructions which refer to the literal.

3.4.7 Building instruction address fields

Once the value of symbols and constants are known, any expressions used in operand fields of the instructions can then be evaluated. Once the actual data address is determined, this is inserted into the machine instruction, following the op-code.

On the GOAT this is a relatively simple process, but on machines with more elaborate addressing modes there may be several different formats in which the instruction address may have to be presented.

3.4.8 Macro expansions

Where macros are invoked, the expanded body of the macro must be inserted into the program at that point, including any substitution of symbolic parameters as required. Where the macro uses conditional assembly features, the appropriate conditions must be determined, and the macro text to substitute is selected accordingly.

Where a macro is invoked, the macro expansion task must actually be carried out ahead of all the tasks listed above, as the expanded code will normally require op-code translation, symbolic address resolution, and so on, as though the code had been written out in full by the programmer.

3.4.9 Miscellaneous tasks

In addition to those tasks directly concerned with producing the object code translated from the assembly source, assemblers must also issue suitable error messages, for example to indicate undefined symbols, invalid instruction mnemonics, or syntactically incorrect expressions. Many assemblers also produce source code listings, often showing the assembled object code in octal or hexadecimal for assistance in debugging.

Once the assembly is complete, the object code must be output in a suitable form — under most operating systems it will be written to a disk file from which it can be loaded when the program is to run, or processed by a linkage editor. It is not usually necessary for the assembler to be able to hold the object code of the entire assembled program in memory, but it will be written out in stages, as the assembler completes its final pass through the program.

3.5 OPERATION OF AN ASSEMBLER

In order to complete the tasks required, most language translators (both assemblers and compilers) will normally make several **passes** through the source program, that is several scans through the program from beginning to end. Information, usually in the form of tables, is collected on each pass which can then be used in the final pass to build the object code.

The first pass always reads the source code itself; subsequent passes may re-read the source, or may use some intermediate form of code, but at each stage more information is gathered. The approaches are illustrated in Fig. 3.3.

The main reason why assemblers need more than one pass is because of the so-called *forward reference problem*. When an instruction uses a symbol that is not defined until later in the program, as in the example below, the assembler cannot know the address represented by the symbol ALLOK when it encounters the JP instruction on the first pass.

```
            JP          ALLOCK
            :
            :
ALLOK       LDA          TOTAL
```

Most assemblers therefore use a two-pass approach. On the first pass, the assembler scans the instructions, incrementing the location counter, and building a symbol table with names of all the identifiers and the addresses (values) they represent. A literal table is also built if the program uses literals. On the second pass, using the symbol table, the full object code is generated.

If macros are used, some assemblers make a preliminary pass for macro expansion purposes, giving three passes in all, but it is frequently possible to handle macro expansion as part of the normal first pass, and thereby still keep the assembly process to two passes in total.

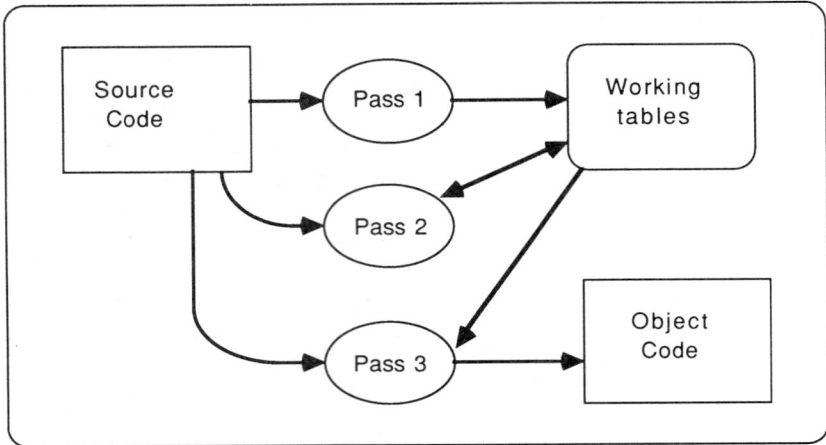

(a)

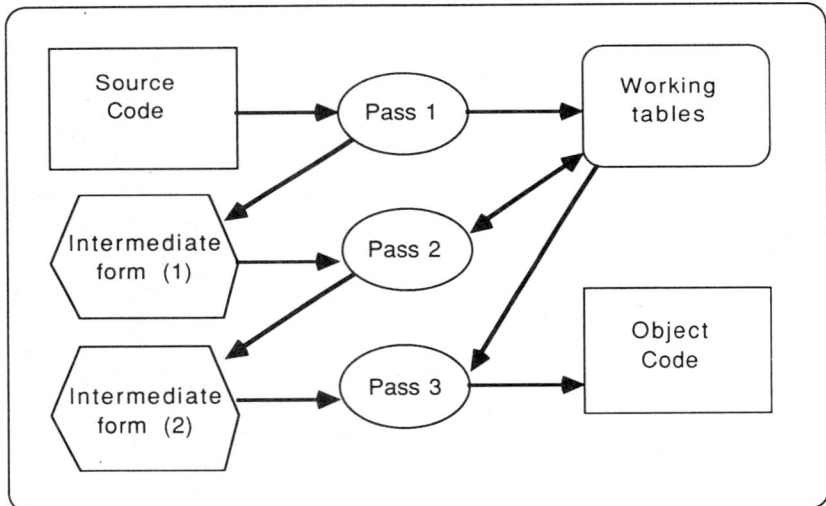

(b)

Fig. 3.3 — Possible approaches to multi-pass translators: (a) source code is re-read
on each pass; (b) intermediate code generated by each pass.

A one-pass assembler is a possibility, but only with considerable restrictions. It is possible if the assembly language disallows forward references,
but this is a very severe restriction which destroys much of the value of
symbolic addressing in the first place. A one-pass approach is also possible if
the entire object program can be held in main memory together with the
assembler itself, so that addresses can be inserted anywhere in the program
as they become known, but of necessity this means an upper limit on

program size which is smaller than the total program memory available. Alternatively, it is possible for the assembler to scan forward through the source whenever a forward reference is encountered, until the required symbol is found, and then to go back and continue assembling from the point reached. Although this does involve reading much of the source more than once, it may be less than doing two complete passes if there are not too many forward references and if they are mostly defined only a few lines ahead of where the symbol is used.

The normal two-pass approach works as in the following example. (The program fragment is not intended to achieve any meaningful execution, but it is a syntactically correct module in GOAT assembly language.)

```
* EXAMPLE PROGRAM IN GOAT ASSEMBLY LANGUAGE
* SUBROUTINE TO OUTPUT A–Z ON PRINTER
            ORG      2000H        Program address
            LDI      'A'          Initial char
NEXT        OUT      2            Output
            STO      CHARVAL      Save
            SUB      ='Z'         Are we at Z?
            JZ       EXIT         If so, return to caller
            LDA      CHARVAL      Char to increment
            ADD      =1           Next char
            JUM      NEXT         Continue
EXIT        JUM*     0            Return to caller
CHARVAL     DEFW     0            Value of current char
            END
```

On pass one, the assembler passes over the two comment lines, and finds the pseudo-instruction ORG before any lines of code. The location counter is thus set to an initial value of 2000 (all addresses in this description are in hexadecimal).

The next instruction, LDI, would thus be assembled starting at location 2000, but as there are no symbols on this line, no action is required on the first pass other than to increment the location counter by the number of locations (three) which the LDI instruction will require.

The value of the location counter is thus 2003 as the next instruction (OUT) is inspected. On this line the symbol NEXT is defined by being in the label field, so the assembler can insert this as the first entry in the symbol table.

Name of symbol	Value
NEXT	2003

No other symbols or literals appear on this line, so the location counter is incremented to 2006 and inspection of the STO instruction takes place. This uses a symbol CHARVAL which is not yet defined, so it is added to the symbol table with its value not yet known.

Name of symbol	Value (location)
NEXT	2003
CHARVAL	?

The location counter is incremented to 2009 for the SUB instruction. This line uses no symbols but has a literal — the character value 'Z'. The assembler will thus have to allocate to suitable storage location for the value 'Z' and insert the address of it in this instruction, on the second pass. The literal table thus begins to be built.

Literal	Location
'Z'	?

After the next three lines, the location counter has reached 2015, and the symbol EXIT and the literal 1 have been added to the tables. There has also been another reference to CHARVAL, but as this was already in the symbol table and as its value is still unknown, this has no further effect. The tables are then as follows.

Name of symbol	Value (location)
NEXT	2003
CHARVAL	?
EXIT	?

Literal	Location
'Z'	?
1	?

The JUM instruction then requires the value of NEXT, which is known as it is a backward reference, but it will not be used until the second pass.

The location counter has thus reached 2018 when the following JUM* instruction is examined, and on this line the symbol EXIT is defined. The value 2018 can thus be inserted in the symbol table against EXIT, and the location counter is incremented to 201B.

The next line is a pseudo-instruction DEFW, requesting that two bytes of storage be allocated to hold data, with the initial value zero. The location counter stands at 201B, but the assembler has to be aware of the rules of the machine architecture which require that 16-bit operands must be aligned on even numbered locations. Location 201B will thus be unused, and the location counter is incremented to 201C. Since the symbol CHARVAL is defined here, we can insert 201C in the symbol table. The location counter is now incremented by just two bytes, this being the size of the DEFW data.

At the end of the first pass, the tables look like this.

Location counter: 201E

Name of symbol	Value (location)
NEXT	2003
CHARVAL	201C
EXIT	2018

Literal	Location
'Z'	?
1	?

All symbols now have values, so there are no undefined symbols to report. Locations can now be assigned to the literals, and for convenience the assembler can place them at the end of the program. Both literals are 16-bit operands, so the first can be located at 201E and the second at 2020. Before the second pass the literal table is thus complete.

Literal	Location
'Z'	201E
1	2020

The location counter is now set back to the initial value (2000) for the second pass, when instructions are actually assembled.

The initial LDI instruction can be assembled without any reference to tables. The character 'A' is treated purely as a value according to its ASCII code and placed in the instruction address field, and the op-code table shows that the numeric code for LDI is 09. The assembled machine code of this line (in hexadecimal) is thus:

    09 00 41

Similarly, the OUT 2 instruction is simply assembled as:

    32 00 02

— the use of a symbol in the label field is of no interest in the second pass.

The following STO instruction requires the value of CHARVAL in its address field, and this is now readily obtained from the symbol table (201C), giving assembled code:

    02 20 1C

On the next line, the SUB instruction uses the literal 'Z', whose address, 201E, is now obtained from the literal table. The instruction thus becomes:

    04 20 1E

Notice the difference between this last instruction, which used a *literal* with the value 'Z', and the initial LDI instruction which actually placed the value 'A' in its address field.

The process continues, up to the JUM* instruction (where the op-code is adjusted to allow for indexed addressing). A slack byte is then inserted as described, and finally the value zero is placed in the two-byte initialised data word. The overall machine code output by the assembler is thus as follows (spaces are shown after each byte purely for readability — the actual output will simply be a stream of binary data).

    09 00 41   32 00 02   02 20 1C   04 20 1E   23 20 18
    01 20 1C   02 20 20   21 20 03   A1 00 00   00 00 00

3.6 PRACTICAL ISSUES

The symbol table is clearly at the heart of the assembly process, and the assembler will only operate efficiently if access to the symbol table is itself efficient.

For small programs with little more than fifty different symbols, there is little problem: the table can just be searched sequentially. However, for larger programs involving hundreds or even thousands of symbols, a more efficient approach is required, otherwise the time taken to assemble a program can become handicapped by searching of the table every time a symbol is defined or referenced.

There are many ways of improving symbol table access, and these apply equally to all types of language processors, not just assemblers; readers should consult the list of further reading for detailed descriptions.

The apparently simplest approach is to keep the symbol table ordered alphabetically by the names of the symbols; a binary search can then be used which is vastly more efficient than a linear search. However, to keep the table in order during the first pass, entries must be moved up when new symbols are encountered. Alternatively the assembler could manage with sequential searching during the first pass, and then sort the table prior to the second pass.

Hashing is a frequently used technique, whereby the table is allocated initially to a fixed number of locations, and a simple mathematical calculation on the characters of the name of a symbol is used to determine where to insert it. When the same symbol is encountered again, the function yields the same result enabling the symbol to be quickly located. Problems arise when a location is already used by a previous symbol; in such cases another location must be found or symbols must be chained by pointers into an overflow area.

For the assembly of very large programs it may be necessary to keep at least part of the symbol table on secondary storage, and access techniques must then be more elaborate still if the assembler performance is still to be reasonable.

In addition to other outputs, many assemblers provide a cross-reference listing of every symbol and the line numbers at which it is used. This can be achieved by a third pass purely to gather this information and sort it before printing, but it is more efficient to collect the information as the symbol table is built, recording not just the value of the symbol but also all the source line numbers where it is used. Of course some symbols may be referenced many more times than others, which means either that the symbol table entries will have to vary in size, or that pointers will be used to maintain a chain of references elsewhere in memory.

FURTHER READING

Barron, D. W. *Assemblers and loaders* (MacDonald/Elsvier, 2nd edn, 1972).

Calingaert, P. *Assemblers, compilers and program translation* (Computer Science Press, 1979).

Gear, C. W. *Computer organization and programming* (McGraw-Hill, 2nd edn., 1985).

4
Compilers: function and purpose

4.1 THE COMPILATION PROCESS

Having explored the operation of an assembler (a low-level language translator) we are ready to look at the process carried out by a high-level language translator, normally called a **compiler**.

This chapter looks primarily at *what* a compiler has to do; Chapter 5 considers *how* a compiler carries out its translation functions, and Chapter 6 discusses the operation of compiled programs as they run, and the support which they require from the compiler.

A compiler can conveniently be defined as *a program that will accept input in the form of a program written in a high-level language and translate it into the machine code necessary for execution on a given computer.* The terms **source code** and **object code** describe the input and output, as for an assembler.

Once the source code has been translated by the compiler, neither the source nor the compiler is required in order for the program to run — the only requirement may be a portion of the compiler which acts as a run-time environment (see Chapter 6).

It is crucial to note that the compiler is a *program* which carries out the translation; occasionally those new to the computer field assume that a compiler is a piece of hardware. Even if a compiler or interpreter is recorded permanently in read-only memory (ROM) it still remains a program, even though it does not have to be loaded from disk before it can run. Compilers in ROM are, however, fairly rare: usually the compiler is loaded only when a program needs to be translated.

The vast majority of compilers generate binary object code — usually to a disk file — in a form for processing directly by a linkage editor or loader. However, in a few cases, compilers have been produced which generate assembly language output, which must then be processed by an assembler.

4.1.1 Source languages and target machines

Normally a compiler is designed to take input in a given high-level language and generate object code for a given target machine architecture, for example 'A Pascal Compiler for 8086 Processors' or 'A FORTRAN Compiler for IBM 370'. It is thus clear that the potential number of compilers that may be required is quite large: if (say) there are fifty popular programming languages and forty popular machine architectures, it needs two thousand different compilers to be able to use every language on every machine. Fortunately, however, compiler writers do not have to start from scratch every time a new compiler is needed, as will be considered in the next chapter.

In most cases, the compiler itself runs on the same machine as the target machine; that is, the FORTRAN Compiler for IBM 370 is itself almost certainly a program that runs on IBM 370 machines. However, this is not necessarily the case; it is perfectly possibly to have a **cross-compiler** which runs on one machine and generates object code for another. Cross-compilers are particularly important in the early stages of development of new machines, so that programs can be written, edited and compiled on existing machines. Cross-compilers are also widely used in developing code for embedded systems where the target machine may be too limited (particularly in its peripherals) to run editors and compilers. (It is possible similarly to have a cross-assembler.)

4.1.2   Source language processing

One reason why compilers are relatively complex programs is that they must be able correctly to translate *any* program whatsoever written in the given high-level language. Some compilers impose upper limits to the maximum size of program they can handle or the maximum number of different identifiers in a program (say) — which is in itself inconvenient — but anything more serious than this would be quite unacceptable.

By way of example, many people have wanted to write Pascal compilers which can handle everything in Pascal apart from labels and the GOTO statement. They reason that the GOTO statement discourages structured programming and that they never use it, so why include provision for it in a new compiler. The answer is that the GOTO statement is part of the Pascal definition, and, unless the compiler can handle such statements, it cannot call itself a Pascal compiler; rather it compiles only a subset of Pascal and is thus very much less useful as it cannot handle the full standard language.

Most languages have extremely complex ways of expressing actions, which though hard to understand are nevertheless still legal in the language, and the compiler must be able to handle these; for example it is very poor if the compiler issues an error message and gives up simply because more than fifteen operators have been used in one expression. There may also be very similar constructs which take considerable care for the compiler to distinguish in order to avoid ambiguity, for example in FORTRAN IV

$$DO\ 3\ J = 1,8$$

is a DO loop, requiring iteration on the variable J, but the statement

$$DO\ 3\ J = 1.8$$

is an assignment statement, storing the floating point value 1.8 in the variable DO3J (spaces are not significant).

It is also a requirement that a compiler must be able to detect if the input is *not* a valid program in the language concerned, in which case an error message must be issued (see 4.3 below).

4.2   TRANSLATION OF DIFFERENT CONSTRUCTS

The main elements which make up a programming language: identifiers, keywords, statements, operators, procedures, and so on, were outlined in section 2.4. In this section, we look at what we need a compiler to do with some of these, that is, what object code we need the compiler to generate. Thus we will examine some statements and other elements in a high-level language and consider what these must become when translated to machine code; in the next chapter we consider how that translation can be automated.

The source examples are illustrative of common constructs in high-level languages, but are not intended as syntactically correct examples in any particular language. The object code examples are in GOAT Assembly Language (outlined in section 3.3), but this is only used for readability; the actual compiler output would be in raw binary machine code, as in the illustration of assembler output in section 3.5. The comments against the assembly code are likewise purely to assist the reader of this book and form no part of the actual compiler output.

4.2.1   Literals and constants
Literals such as 3, −7.98, 'Hello' or 1.24E−27 must be recognised and converted to their binary internal form. This is not always as easy at it seems, as the compiler must determine the characters at which the literal begins and ends. An important clue is that literals cannot, in most languages, begin with a letter; they either begin with a digit, a quotation mark, a decimal point, or something similar. However, where scientific quantities are expressed using 'E' notation to denote a power of ten, the conversion routine may be very elaborate to produce the correct floating point format required internally.

In most cases, literals must be assigned their own storage location, as with literals in assembler, and the address of this location will be inserted into all instructions which use the constant concerned.

4.2.2   Variables
All identifiers, including variables, will be placed in a symbol table as they are encountered. In a language where all variables must be declared before use, the symbol table entry is based mainly on the declaration.

However, a compiler symbol table is a good deal more complex than one for an assembler: the table must record not just the location of a variable, but also its data type, its dimensions if it is an array, and so on. Unlike an assembler, though, the compiler is usually free to allocate storage for variables as it wishes (in practice this is usually just allocated in the order of encountering a variable) as the programmer cannot normally specify particular locations.

The allocation of storage may, however, be much more complex in a high-level language, particularly a block-structured language. Variables may be allocated storage dynamically on a stack, as the program is running (see Chapter 6); indeed this is essential if the language allows recursion.

There may also be more than one variable of a given name, in programs in block-structured languages, as there may be a global variable A, say, and also a local variable A defined in a particular procedure. These must be treated quite differently by the compiler, which must follow the scope rules very carefully to ensure that all code accesses the correct variable at run time. Therefore in addition to keeping the name of each variable in the symbol table it is also necessary to indicate the procedure in which it was defined.

4.2.3 Statements

The compiler must have the ability to separate the distinct requests from the programmer; in most languages these are called statements. In most cases this is quite straightforward, as statements may be separated by characters such as a semicolon, or a new line.

However, there are often more complex cases. Most languages allow an IF statement to contain a statement within it. With multi-level IFs this can be quite complex, for example

```
if X = 2
then if K = 3
        then print X
        else print Y
else print K;
```

contains three PRINT statements and two IF clauses without a semicolon between them. In COBOL statements can run on one after the other, and are only followed by a full stop at the end of a sentence, which may comprise many statements. Block-structured languages which allow statements to be built into larger statements using BEGIN and END are even more elaborate.

So whilst the notion of statements is very important for compilers, compilation is much more than just reading statements one by one and translating them into object code. The actual identification of statements is only possible by appreciating the syntax of the language.

4.2.4 Assignments

The simplest form of assignment statement involves just a movement of data from one location to another. For example, if A is an integer variable the statement

A := 5

will translate to:

```
LDA          =5
STO          A
```

(bearing in mind that the machine code will contain the address of the literal 5, and the address of the variable A).

Some machines have special instructions to accomplish a move, but where, like the GOAT, this is not available, a load and store approach is needed. For character string data, this can be quite complex, e.g. if T is a fixed length eight-byte character variable, the statement

T := 'HELLO'

will have to be translated to:

```
LDA          ='HE'         First two chars
STO          T
LDA          ='LL'         Second two chars
STO          T+2
LDC          ='O'          Fifth char alone
STC          T+4
LDA          ='  '         Spaces to pad result
STC          T+5           Space in char 6 of T
STO          T+6           Spaces in chars
                           7 & 8 of T
```

Many assignments are more than a move, and require evaluation of an expression before the result can be stored. The classic

C := A+B

translates very simply to

```
LDA          A
ADD          B
STO          C
```

provided A, B and C are all integers (otherwise some complex data conversion routines may be needed). However,

X := (A+B) * (C−27)

is more subtle, and needs temporary storage on a machine like the GOAT which has only one working register. It translates to

```
LDA          A
ADD          B
STO          TEMP
LDA          C
SUB          =27
MUL          TEMP
STO          X
```

where TEMP is a temporary variable which the compiler must allocate; it is not defined by the programmer. More complex expressions may need indefinitely many temporary variables, which can be a problem for the compiler.

4.2.5 Conditionals
The translation of IF statements (and other kinds of conditionals such as WHILE loops) requires code to test the condition and branch around the statements that are *not* to be executed. The elegance of structured programming in the high-level language is translated into machine code that is very dependent on jump instructions, but provided the compiler does this reliably, the program is much more robust than one which uses extensive branching in its own right.

If the machine architecture does not incorporate compare instructions, a relational test (greater than, less than, equal to, etc.) involves subtracting the two values and inspecting the result.

Thus the code:

$$\text{if } A > B \text{ then } X := 1$$
$$\text{else } Y := 2$$

is translated to:

	LDA	A	Value to test
	SUB	B	Compare: AC contains $A-B$
	JN	LABEL1	If neg, $A < B$ so do ELSE
	JZ	LABEL1	If zero, $A = B$ so do ELSE
	LDA	=1	} THEN
	STO	X	} clause
	JUM	LABEL2	Jump over ELSE processing
LABEL1	LDA	=2	} ELSE
	STO	Y	} clause
LABEL2	...		Next statement

The labels have to be defined by the compiler, and may have to be inserted in an internal symbol table for processing in the same way as by an assembler. If there are many IFs in a program, the labels must of course be unique, and where there are nested IFs, the branches must go to the correct labels, with outer IFs branching round inner IFs.

A test involving character strings may require a loop, as they will have to be compared character by character.

4.2.6 Loops
FOR and DO loops are amongst the more popular features of high-level languages, as they save the programmer a great deal of work compared with coding the processing in assembler. A compiler thus has to generate a good deal of code in dealing with such statements; and this code will be split between the beginning and end of the loop. If the loop is a large one, and particularly if loops are nested, the compiler must maintain records —

typically on a stack — to indicate where code must be inserted at the end of a loop.

There are quite a number of ways in which loops can be coded; the simplest way is to keep all processing at the beginning and just have a single jump instruction at the end. For example, the Pascal loop

```
for I := 1 to 10 do
    begin
        :
        :
    end;
```

can be translated to:

	LDA	=1	Initial value
	STO	I	Store in index variable
	JUM	LABEL2	Omit increment on first time
LABEL1	LDA	I	
	ADD	=1	Increment
	STO	I	Save
	SUB	=10	Test against final value
	JP	LABEL3	If positive end of loop reached
LABEL2	:		}
	:		} Translation of body of loop
	:		}
	JUM	LABEL1	Loop round for next time
LABEL3	...		Next statement after loop

Different code is needed for a loop where the index variable is decremented, or where the initial or final values are variables, which may require a test even on the first time round.

For efficiency, particularly as index variables are often used as array subscripts (see below) it is often desirable to use an index register to hold the index variable, rather than loading and storing it every time round. However, this requires care when I is used within the loop, as its value will be in the register rather than in the storage location. Also if there are several nested loops and only one index register it should be used for the innermost loop, which the compiler must recognise.

4.2.7 Arrays

Arrays are another high-level language feature which saves the programmer a great deal of coding. When an array is declared it will be allocated a number of storage locations. For example, the Pascal array declared

var SALES: array [1..12] of integer

will occupy 24 bytes (twelve elements, each of which is a two byte integer). In the assembler code, we will use the symbol SALES to indicate the address of the start of the array. Thus SALES[1] is at location SALES, SALES[2] is at location SALES+2, SALES[3] is at SALES+4, and so on.

References to array elements with constant subscripts can be resolved at compile time, and the actual address can be inserted into the machine instruction, so, at run time, the processing time is the same when scalar (unsubscripted) variables are used. Thus

SALES[4] := 751

translates simply to

LDA	=751
STO	SALES+6

However, a reference to SALES[I] where I can only be determined at run time, means that code must be inserted by the compiler to determine the required address. Usually index registers are used for offsets due to subscripting. If the array starts at a subscript of 1 this must be deducted in calculating the offset, and allowance must be made for each element occupying two bytes; thus the actual address of SALES[I] is SALES+(I−1)*2.

Furthermore, it is highly desirable for the compiler to check that I is in fact between 1 and 12, and give a run-time error if not; otherwise storage areas totally outside the array will be inadvertently modified, causing very obscure program bugs.

Therefore, the apparently simple statement

SALES[I] := 0

may well generate the following code. (ERROR is the address of a run-time error handing routine, as discussed in Chapter 6.)

LDA	I	Load
SUB	=12	Upper subscript limit
JP	ERROR	Error if I > 12
LDA	I	Reload
SUB	=1	Lower subscript limit
JN	ERROR	Error if I < 1
MUL	=2	AC contains (I−1)*2
LXA	0	Put into IX
LDA	=0	Value to assign
STO*	SALES	Stored in reqd locn SALES[I]

With an array of two or more dimensions, the subscript calculation involves at least twice as many instructions. It is often the case with programs that use extensive array processing that more machine instructions relate to subscript calculations than to the actual data manipulation the program is performing.

4.2.8 Input/output

Input and output statements differ considerably from one language to another; even within a given language there are often significant variations between the implementations of that language on different machines due to different external constraints. In languages such as COBOL, which place emphasis on indexed file processing and database access facilities, a large number of special statements may exist; in other cases such as Pascal, input and output is handled simply by means of some special procedure calls.

The object code which a compiler must generate in translating input/output statements is thus equally varied, but it is often in this area that the most difficulties and exceptional cases arise. By definition, input/output statements require interaction with peripheral devices, which are outside the immediate realm of a program executing on the CPU.

Peripheral devices are usually controlled by the operating system, so the compilation of input/output statements almost always has to generate operating system calls (see Chapter 11). These will naturally vary between implementations, and the input/output code is necessarily operating-system specific. It is thus not sufficient to specify a compiler in that it translates a given source language into object code for a given machine; one must specify the operating system under which that object code will execute.

However, not every input/output statement necessarily generates a system call. For example languages like Pascal and BASIC allow a number of statements to output data to appear on one print line, but (at least on larger operating systems) the system call will not arise until the whole line has been built. The compiled object code must thus operate so as to build the print line and call the operating system to print it when it is complete.

Input/output statements also require data conversion: the simple BASIC statement

> PRINT N

(where N is an integer) requires that the internal binary form of N be converted to decimal, and each decimal digit output as a separate character, with leading zeros replaced by blanks, and a minus sign inserted if the value is negative. Only when these final characters to be output are available is it possible to call the operating system to transfer the data to a peripheral device. Graphical and other forms of output may require much further processing.

In general, therefore, the code required for input/output operations is too complex to insert in the object program at every point where an input/output statement is encountered. The usual solution is to compile a subroutine call to a standard routine in the run-time environment which handles all the detailed processing as well as the system calls required — this is considered further in Chapter 6.

4.2.9   Functions and procedures

Procedure calls are relatively simple for the compiler: most machines have a suitable instruction which will branch and save a return address; at the end of the procedure a suitable instruction returns control. On the GOAT this is handled by CAL at the point of call and a JUM* to effect the return. The name of the procedure is kept in the compiler symbol table and will be given a value which is the address at which the procedure begins. Where a function is invoked, the simplest approach is for the value (or the address of the value) to be left in a suitable register.

Usually there will be certain standard code incorporated at the head of every procedure, for example to save the contents of registers so they can be restored prior to return. Similarly if storage is allocated dynamically, the entry to the procedure will need to advance the stack pointer to allocate storage for the procedure's variables, and on return the stack will go back to its value at the point of entry.

The main complexities arise with parameter passing. It is simplest to illustrate the approach for call by reference (see section 2.4) but other techniques would mostly start similarly, then taking copies of the value if required. In the example below, the addresses of the parameters are placed immediately after the CAL instruction†.

The procedure call

    CALC (X,Y,Z)

is compiled as

CAL	CALC	Procedure call
DEFW	X	Addr of first parm
DEFW	Y	Addr of second parm
...		Next stmt (proc returns here)

The procedure can then be compiled as shown.

```
procedure CALC (I,J)
begin
    J := I * 2−7
end
```

* Procedure entry code			
CALC	EQU	*	Procedure call comes here
	STO	SAVEAC	Save AC
	STX	SAVEIX	Save addr of locn after CAL
	LDA*	0	Load addr of 1st parm
	STO	IADDR	Save as addr of I
	LDA*	2	Load addr of 2nd parm
	STO	JADDR	Save as addr of J

† This convention requires the CAL instruction to be aligned on an odd-numbered location so that the following addresses are correctly aligned without slack bytes. If necessary a no-operation instruction (such as LXI* 0) is inserted before the CAL to ensure this.

* Body of procedure — note indirect access to parameters

```
            LDX       IADDR       Addr of I
            LDA*      0           Load I
            MUL       =2
            SUB       =7
            LDX       JADDR       Addr of J
            STO*      0           Store result in J
* Procedure return code
            LDA       SAVEAC      Restore contents of
                                  AC
            LDX       SAVEIX      Restore contents of
                                  IX
            JUM*      4           Jump to 4 bytes after
                                  CAL
```

(SAVEAC, SAVEIX, IADDR, and JADDR are all temporary storage locations allocated by the compiler.) This code allows the procedure to be called from more than one place and with different arguments.

Every access to parameters in the subroutine has to refer back to the actual data in the calling routine; this is achieved using indexed addressing, but it requires extra instructions. The parameters I and J will appear in the symbol table with an indication that they are parameters; special action can then be taken in compiling any statement which refers to them.

There are in fact many possible linkage conventions as regards the use of registers and parameter addresses on procedure calls; placing the arguments on a stack is a common approach. Often the linkage technique is standardised throughout all programming languages on a given operating system. This makes it possible for procedure calls to invoke separately compiled external routines, which, subject to certain constraints, may even be written in another language.

4.3   OUTPUTS OF A COMPILER

The primary output of the compiler is the binary object code, much the same as from an assembler, as illustrated in section 2.5. As with an assembler, it will normally be written to a disk file, and will usually be relocatable code for processing by a linkage editor, as considered in Chapter 7.

However, other outputs are also very important, particularly the error messages. The function of a compiler in checking the syntactic correctness of the source program is almost as important as its translation function. Programmers rely heavily on compilers spotting errors such as undeclared variables, mismatched parentheses, or missing END statements, and these checks serve to help make high-level language programs more reliable.

Therefore, if any syntactic errors are found in the source program, these must be reported to the programmer in a clear and helpful manner. As we will see in the next chapter, it is not too difficult to produce a compiler that will issue the single message 'Invalid program'; it is much harder to make it pinpoint all the errors and give meaningful messages. In particular, a misspelled keyword can completely confuse the compiler as to the type of statement, and lead to large numbers of very unhelpful messages.

The messages themselves may have to strike a balance between being as informative as possible without wasting too much space (particularly if the same message appears many times). Some compilers offer a choice of long or short messages, long messages being preferred for a programmer of more limited experience. Large messages may also make the compiler itself too large, and may have to be held in a disk file, which can slow compilation.

There can thus be a trade off between the efficiency of a compiler and the quality of the error reporting: different compilers are best suited to different functions.

Most compilers also offer source listings, usually with the statements numbered for cross-reference to error messages; this is particularly helpful for run-time errors. In some cases the listing may be formatted, for example by indenting it in accordance with certain conventions. In addition to the source listing itself the compiler may give a list of all variables with their attributes, and possibly a cross-reference showing the statements in which each variable is used. Such aids are very helpful for program maintenance.

The object code may also be augmented by the inclusion of run-time debugging information, which will enable run-time errors to report not just the address at which the error occurred, but the number of the source statement, and possibly even the name of the variable concerned. Such debugging information will increase the size of the final object program, so it is best if it is included only as an option. Once the program is believed to be working, it can be recompiled without this.

Some compilers also offer the facility of an object code listing of the compiled program, in assembly language (or something close to it). This is mainly for complex debugging but such listings are extremely useful for getting to understand what a compiler is doing.

FURTHER READING

Berry, R. E. *Programming language translation* (Ellis Horwood, 1982).
Farmer, M. *Compiler physiology for beginners* (Chartwell-Bratt, 1985).

5

Compilers: structure and operation

5.1 COMPILER STRUCTURE

In the last chapter we saw what is needed for a compiler to carry out its task, and showed why that task is in many cases quite a complex one. In this chapter, we aim to take the covers off a compiler and see how its component parts accomplish the translation process. In this section some terminology is defined and the following sections deal with the three main compilation stages.

Compiler design is an enormous field, and the material in this chapter merely gives an overview with a few illustrations of possible techniques; many other approaches are possible.

5.1.1 Passes

The notion of a **pass** is used in relation to compilers in the same way as for assemblers (see section 3.5). Although some languages can be compiled in only one or two passes, it is quite common for a compiler to make up to about ten passes through the program, sometimes many more in a complex language like PL/I or Ada. However, these passes are normally based on successively refined intermediate code (Fig. 3.3b) rather than on frequent re-reading of the source. When compiling large programs, the intermediate code from each pass, and possibly the symbol tables, will be written to a disk file to be read on the next pass.

5.1.2 Stages

The gradual refining of the source into successively more machine-oriented intermediate code and finally into machine code, is usually grouped into three main **stages** of compilation: **lexical analysis** which is concerned with textual issues is the language input; **syntax analysis** where the compiler determines the syntactical structure and meaning of the program; and **code generation** where the final machine code is generated. These stages form the basis of most discussion about compiler operation, and they are each described in the sections that follow.

The three stages do *not* however have to be three distinct passes. In a simple compiler it is quite common for lexical and syntax analysis to be accomplished on a single pass; conversely a complex compiler may require several passes to complete the syntax analysis and several more for code generation.

Although these stages form a convenient basis for discussion, they are not absolute distinctions: some aspects of source code examination will be treated as lexical analysis by one writer and as syntax analysis by another. Other writers prefer to regard the determination of program meaning as a separate stage, semantic analysis, which follows the syntax analysis rather than being a part of it.

The intermediate code generated by the lexical analyser for processing by the syntax analyser is often referred to as the **S-language** (syntax-language), and the intermediate form passed from the syntax analyser to code generator may be known as the **C-language** (code-language) as shown in Fig. 5.1.

5.1.3 Compiler construction

The actual structure of the compiler itself, as a program, may differ again. A simple compiler may be just a single program (albeit with many subroutines), but larger compilers will be written as a number of separate programs which are loaded one after the other; each carrying out perhaps one or two passes. Where this approach is used, the separate programs are often called **phases** (as with many other large programs).

The multi-phase approach is less important nowadays with more memory being available, particularly in a virtual-memory operating system, but particularly for mainframe compilers it is still widely used. Writing the compiler in separate phases makes it easier to divide the development between different programming teams, and while the compiler is running it leaves more memory for tables and working data. There may also be certain complex types of statements which are processed in a specific phase, and if a program contains no statements of that type, it may be possible to omit a phase.

The total size of a compiler can vary enormously. A straightforward Pascal compiler with no elaborate debugging facilities may possibly be written in as little as ten thousand lines of code; but an advanced compiler with numerous programmer aids compiling a rich language into highly efficient object code to run on a complex machine architecture may well approach half a million lines of code.

To look at it another way, with good tools to avoid writing everything from scratch, it is possible to write a simple compiler as a student project with a team of three or four as a part-time exercise in six months or less. But to write a major production compiler for use with a mainframe operating system may require twenty or more person-years of effort.

Increasingly nowadays, the workload is reduced by compilers being written in high-level languages and then compiled using an existing compiler, rather than the compiler being written in assembler. However, to do this effectively, the language in which the compiler is written must have very good facilities for character scanning (at the lexical analysis stage); for building pointer-based structures and recursion (at the syntax analysis stage)

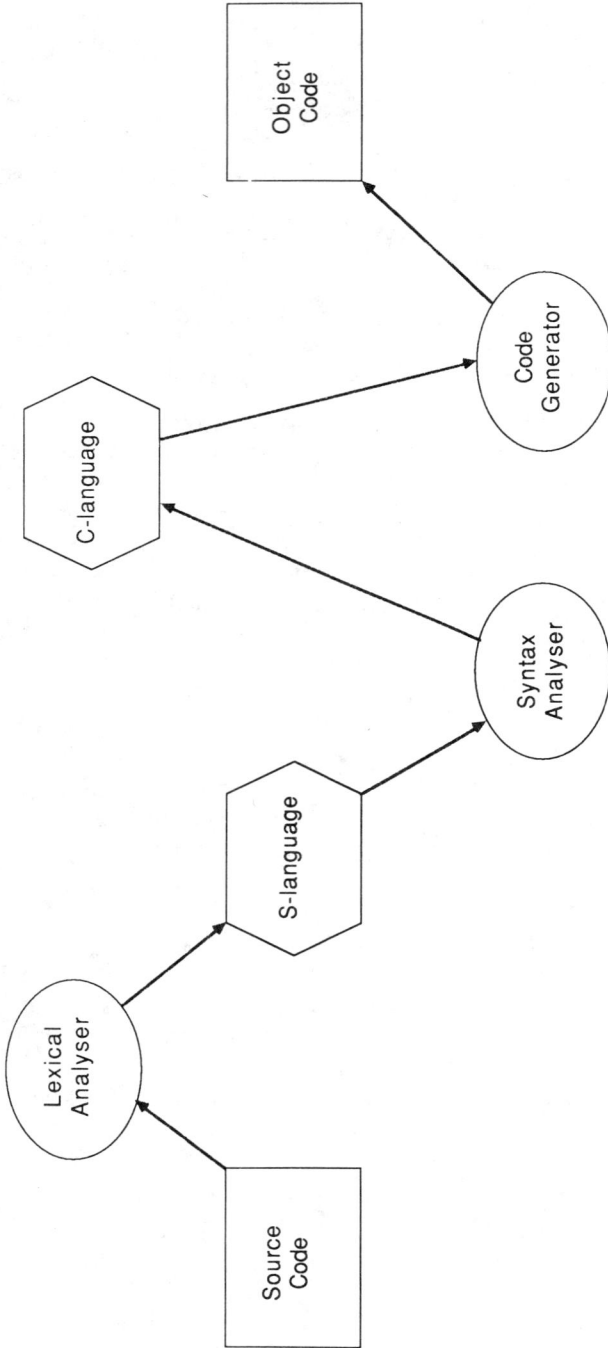

Fig. 5.1 — Stages of compilation.

and for bit manipulation (at the code generation stage). There can also be complications with the run-time environment of the language in which the compiler is written. Apart from languages such as C which are specifically designed for systems programming, few languages are strong in all these areas.

A further complication lies in the fact that many designers of new languages wish to write the compiler in the language that it is to compile! With no previous compiler this seems impossible, but by developing additional tools one can get round the problem.

The structure of the compiler is relatively unimportant for understanding compilation principles, but it may be important in implementation terms or in considerations of compiler performance.

5.1.4   Parsing

The term **parsing**, like many other terms used in compilation and programming language design, is taken from the field of linguistics. A compiler will parse a portion of a program in order to determine its structure: parsing at the character level takes place in lexical analysis, and parsing at the level of symbols takes place in syntax analysis.

Some techniques require that the compiler will make many attempts to determine the structure of a given sentence; it may try to parse it several ways. However, all such attempts would normally be accomplished on the same pass: despite the similarity of sound, a parse and a pass mean quite different actions. Parsing is concerned with determining syntactic structure; a pass is simply the process of reading through a program.

5.2   LEXICAL ANALYSIS

The input to a compiler is simply a stream of characters; the task of the lexical analysis stage is to give that stream a degree of structure which can then be analysed by the syntax analyser.

Typically lexical analysis is concerned with breaking down the source code into a sequence of **symbols**, which forms the S-language. The term 'symbol' is used here in a much broader sense than in the assembler context: to a compiler, a symbol may be an identifier, a literal, an operator, a keyword, or an item of punctuation, the idea being to break the source down to this level ready for syntax analysis.

The lexical analyser thus handles the actual reading of the source code. It is also responsible for identifying and then ignoring comments, unnecessary blank spaces, ends of lines (unless they are significant) and all such aspects which are important to the programmer, in terms of readability, but unimportant to the compiler.

Having reduced the source to those characters which are significant, it will scan them to determine where symbols begin and end; indeed some writers simply refer to the lexical analyser as the scanner. The extensive character scanning may frequently mean that lexical analysis, despite its relative simplicity, consumes over half of compiler execution time.

The first type of symbol to identify is character string literals, as these may contain absolutely any other characters within them. Having eliminated character literals, one can be absolutely confident in most languages that a '+' sign is to be parsed as an addition operator, for example, but while character strings remain it could just be part of some text the program wishes to output. Fortunately character strings are usually quite easy to identify as they are delimited by quote characters at each end, though it can be much harder if the compiler is to give helpful error messages when the programmer has forgotten to close a quote. Character literals will be stored away in a suitable area of memory, and the syntax analyser will just receive an indication that the next symbol is a character string.

Most operators are also quite easy to identify due to the special characters used. In most cases, the lexical analyser will simply treat parentheses as operators, along with actual arithmetic and logical operators; it is in syntax analysis that parentheses will be used to determine structure. Some operators may consist of several characters, such as '<=', '>=', ':=', '**', and so on; the lexical analyser must spot these and transmit them as single symbols to the syntax analyser.

After character literals are eliminated, most other literals can be spotted because they begin with digits, though finding the end of a numeric literal can require care. Numeric literals will be converted to binary and placed in a literal table, in a similar manner to an assembler. The information passed to the syntax analyser indicates a numeric literal (possibly with an indication of its data type — real or integer) and a pointer to the literal table entry.

Language elements beginning with letters will either be keywords or identifiers. If all the keywords are reserved words, the lexical analyser can just look up all input words in a keyword table: if found, the appropriate keyword is signalled to the syntax analyser by means of a simple code number. If the word is not found in the keyword table it is taken to be an identifier and is placed in a symbol table; at this stage only the name of the identifiers will be in the table but as compilation proceeds further information about each identifier will be added. (This approach does, however, have the disadvantage that a misspelled keyword is taken to be an identifier, which will mean unhelpful error messages later on when the statement is found to be syntactically incorrect.)

Where statement boundaries are readily identified by new lines or semicolons, these will also be identified by the lexical analyser. Similarly, if special characters are used to indicate that a statement is continued on a new line, the lexical analyser will build the lines together as it extracts the symbols; that way the syntax analyser is unaffected by the form of the input.

The S-language consists of a sequence of symbols, but these will probably be passed to the syntax analyser as a series of codes. For example, the Pascal statement

    for COUNT := 1 to 10 do

might take the following form in the S-language. Two pieces of data are provided about each symbol: the type of symbol and a number giving further information.

Symbol type	Details	Meaning
RW	23	Reserved word no 23: FOR
ID	12	Identifier, now stored in position 12 in the symbol table: COUNT
OP	5	Operator no 9: :=
NL	3	Numeric literal, now stored at position 3 in the literal table: 1
RW	8	Reserved word no 8: TO
NL	4	Numeric literal. now stored at position 4 in the literal table: 10
RW	24	Reserved word no 24: DO

With information presented in this form, together with symbol and literal tables, it is very easy for the syntax analyser to parse the program structure, as the symbols are clearly presented one at a time rather than just as a stream of characters.

The lexical analyser does not always complete an entire pass of the program before syntax analysis begins. It is quite common for a compiler to be structured with the lexical analyser as a subroutine of the syntax analyser: the syntax analyser calls the lexical analyser every time it is ready to receive another symbol.

5.3 SYNTAX ANALYSIS

The syntax analyser takes the S-language, examines the statements in symbolic terms, determines their syntactic structure, and from this it generates a C-language that can be processed by the code generator.

5.3.1 Approaches to syntax analysis

Whilst the principles of lexical analysis are fairly similar across all languages, syntax analysis can vary considerably according to the syntactic structure of the language. Block-structured languages whose syntax can be defined in straightforward terms using a formal language definition such as BNF (see section 2.5) can be handled using fairly standard approaches. Languages such as FORTRAN and COBOL which have little formal syntactic structure tend to require quite different approaches to syntax analysis for each statement type, and much of the syntax analysis may be done by informal methods.

Where a formal language definition exists, the syntax analyser will seek to build a tree structure showing how a particular portion of the program source fits into that structure. The structure that results is called a parse tree. It is possible to build a parse tree of the whole program, but for reasons of memory this is unlikely to be done in one go; typically parse trees are built for each statement, or for just a portion of a statement such as an arithmetic expression. Moreover, the tree will not usually go right down to the individual characters of the source (even though this is quite possible in principle) but only to the level of individual lexical symbols. Every level in the tree is obtained by applying one of the productions in the language definition.

For example, the statement

for COUNT := 1 to 10 do

(received by the syntax analyser in the S-language above) might be parsed as:

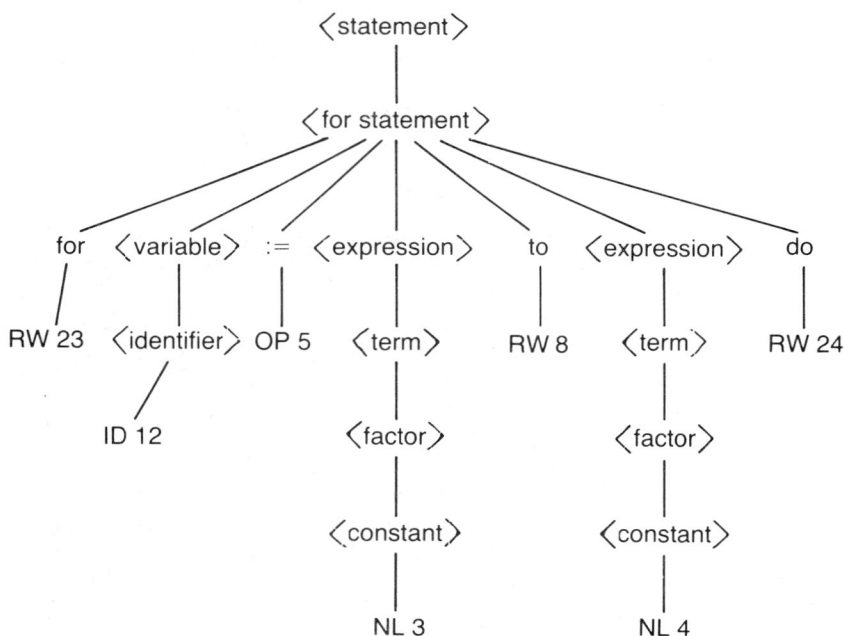

It is seen that each branch of the tree ends where a terminal symbol is reached, that is one which directly corresponds to an input symbol. Strictly speaking, symbols like 'RW 23' are not terminals, as they can be broken into their individual characters 'f', 'o', 'r', but if this has been done by the lexical analyser, the lowest level needed in syntax analysis is the lexical symbol.

Internally, the syntax analyser will represent all this using code numbers to indicate each language element, rather than with the full BNF type expressions above. The tree structure may be maintained using pointers, though not all methods of syntax analysis actually require the tree to be built in memory; in many cases the tree is merely a concept on which the parsing algorithm is based.

5.3.2 Methods of syntax analysis

There are many different methods of syntax analysis, but a detailed description is beyond the scope of this book; readers are referred to the further reading listed at the end of this chapter. Broadly, however, the methods can be categorised under the headings of **top-down** and **bottom-up** techniques.

Bottom-up techniques look at the input, symbol by symbol, and attempt to build the parse tree from the bottom by correctly grouping symbols into the larger language elements which form the next level up on the tree. Techniques based on operator-precedence grammars or on parsers which scan from left to right looking one symbol ahead — known as LR(1) — are widely used bottom-up methods.

Top-down methods start from the initial <program> or <statement> symbol at the top of the tree, and attempt to apply the productions of the language in various combinations, building the tree downwards until a bottom level result is found which corresponds to the string of input symbols. Common top-down techniques include recursive descent parsers, and parsers which take symbols from the left and productions from the left looking one symbol ahead — known as LL(1).

Typically the overall process of syntax analysis can be viewed in two stages:

(a) the input (S-language) is built into a parse tree
(b) the parse tree is converted into a suitable form (C-language) to pass to the code generator;

the first of these sometimes being described as analysis and the second as synthesis. The C-language will consist of a series of operations which the code generator can convert to individual machine instructions.

The precise action taken in the second stage is dependent on the statement type. Once a declarative statement is parsed, it will not generate any C-code at all, but the syntax analyser will insert appropriate information in the symbol table (for example) to indicate that a particular identifier is a variable of a certain type. The code generator will then be able to generate the correct instructions for any arithmetic operations which use that variable.

5.3.3 Output

As regards executable statements, the actual form of the C-language varies considerably between compilers, but many forms are based in some way on **reverse Polish notation**. Strictly speaking, this should be referred to as reverse Lukasiewiczian notation, after the Polish logician who devised it, but due to the difficulty of his name, the term 'Polish notation' is more common. The 'reverse' indicates that operators are placed after the operands concerned; in forward Polish they come beforehand.

The advantage of this notation is that arithmetic expressions can be represented in a way that can simply be read from left to right, without the need for parentheses. The approach can in principle be extended to all operations in a programming language, not just expressions.

The expression

$$a * (b-c)+d$$

is represented in reverse Polish as

$$a\, b\, c - * d +$$

where the rule for evaluating reverse Polish is based on a push-down stack. Every time an *operand* is found it is placed on the top of the stack. When an *operator* is read, the top two elements are removed from the stack, the operator applied to them, and the result placed on the stack. When the entire expression has been evaluated, there is only one item on the stack, which is the result of computing the expression.

Suppose the values are thus: a=2, b=4, c=1, d=5, so $a * (b-c)+d$ should give a result of 11. Evaluating the reserve Polish we proceed as follows. a, b, and c are each in turn placed on the stack which then looks like:

1	(c)
4	(b)
2	(a)

The next symbol is '−', so the top two items (c and b) are removed from the stack, subtracted, and the result put back, giving a stack:

3	(b−c)
2	(a)

The next symbol in the reverse Polish form (reading from left to right) is '*' so the top two elements are removed from the stack, multiplied, and replaced, giving a stack of just

6	(a * (b−c))

On encountering d, it is placed on the stack:

5	(d)
6	(a * (b−c))

so the effect of the final '+' operator is to remove these and add them, giving a final result:

11	(a * (b−c)+d).

With an interpreter (see Chapter 8) the evaluation of reverse Polish is extremely simple: the interpreter just has to follow the stack process described; but reverse Polish also offers a convenient basis from which to generate code to bring about later execution, as explained below.

5.3.4 Example
To give an illustration of syntax analysis, we shall look at the task of building a parse tree and converting it into reverse Polish, using the elements of

recursive descent parsing. This is one of the most widely used methods of syntax analysis largely because of its simplicity; in particular it can be based directly on a BNF or similar definition of the language. However, this is merely an approximation for illustrative purposes; readers seeking a full explanation of recursive descent parsing should consult the further reading.

We will illustrate the parsing of a reasonably large arithmetic expression. Expressions, because of their indefinite complexity and use of parentheses to indicate structure, are very useful for illustrating the flexibility needed in a compiler. Consider the expression:

$$(a+b*(c-d)) / (e-f)$$

To build the parse tree, we use a recursive routine which works as follows. (Readers unfamiliar with recursive programming and the building of tree structures using pointers are referred to programming textbooks that explain these issues.)

Its main principle is based on scanning the expression and counting the levels of the brackets: every time a left bracket is encountered, the bracket level increases by 1; every time a right bracket is found, the level decreases by 1. The figures below the expression indicate the bracket level at each point.

```
( a + b * ( c - d ) ) / ( e - f )
0 0 1 1 1 1 1 2 2 2 2 2 1 0 1 1 1 1 1 0 0
```

Procedure Parse (Currentexpr, Treeposn)

(1) If the expression consists of only a single symbol (no operators) that symbol is placed on the parse tree at the current position, and the procedure returns.
(2) If there are *matching* brackets at the outside of the expression (far left and far right) these are removed. (The outer brackets match if everything between them is level 1 or higher.)
(3) The outermost operator is found, that is the one at level 0 (not within any brackets). This is the central operator of the expression at this stage. This operator is placed on the tree.
(4) Parse is then called recursively with the expression to the left of the central operator, to add on to the left branch of the tree at the current point.
(5) Parse is called again with the expression to the right of the central operator, to add on to the right branch of the tree at the current point.
(6) If at any stage the brackets do not match, or if there is nothing on one side of an operator, a syntax error is recognised and compilation of the expression is terminated.

Thus, taking the expression above, the first invokation of Parse is at the root of the tree, dealing with the whole expression. There are no matching brackets to strip, and the central operator is the '/'. This is placed on the tree, and Parse is called to deal with the two sides.

```
      /
     / \
    /   \
```

On the left side, Parse is called to deal with (a+b*(c−d)). The outer brackets of this match and are stripped giving a+b*(c−d). There are now two level 0 operators: '+ ' and '*'. Additional rules are now needed to deal with operator priority: the '+' is less binding than '*', so '+' is taken as the central operator and added to the tree.

Calling Parse recursively on the left side involves just the symbol a, so this is added to the tree and Parse returns to the previous level.

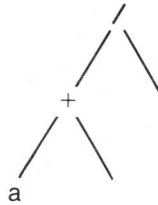

```
       /
      / \
     /   \
    +
   / \
  /   \
 a
```

Parse now deals with the expression to the right of the '+', and finds '*' is the outer level operator of b * (c−d), which is placed on the tree. To the left of this is just b.

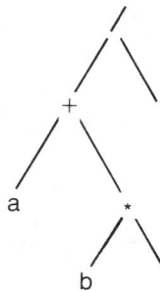

```
        /
       / \
      /   \
     +
    / \
   /   \
  a     *
       / \
      /   \
     b
```

On the right of the '*', the brackets are removed from (c−d), the '−' is added to the tree, with the individual symbols c and d on either side. Finally, Parse returns back to the top level to deal with the expression to the right of the '/' giving the final parse tree.

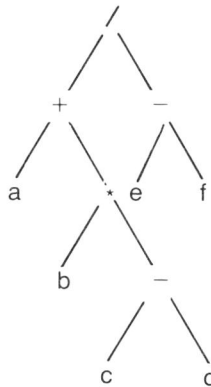

The expression now fully parsed is converted to reverse Polish by a further recursive routine that just gathers up the tree in the following way:

Procedure Gatherup (Treeposn):

(1) If current node is lowest level, output the symbol and return.
(2) Gatherup everything to the left of the current node.
(3) Gatherup everything to the right of the current node.
(4) Output the symbol at the current node.

Thus a simple tree:

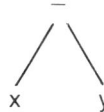

generates as output: x, then y, then −, producing the reverse Polish:

    x y −

Applying Gatherup to the full example parse tree gives

    a b c d − * + e f − /

which is the correct reverse Polish form of the expression.

The C-language will not actually be in this algebraic form, but will use codes similar to those used in the S-language. For example, operands will be recorded by way of references to entries in the symbol or literal table, and operators will just be codes.

5.4   CODE GENERATION

The code generator portion of the compiler takes the C-language, together with the symbol tables and literal tables, and uses these to generate machine code for the appropriate architecture.

The lexical and syntax analysis stages of compilation are fairly machine independent; Pascal syntax analysis is much the same whatever the target machine. By contrast the code generator is necessarily machine specific. Generating code for IBM 370 machines is very different to generating code for Z80 processors. This makes it much more difficult to automate the code generation stage and use standard algorithms that can be incorporated into many compilers; code generators nearly always have to be written individually.

In most cases it is not very difficult to produce a code generator which simply does its job: that is, it generates machine code which will correctly carry out the functions of the source program. It is a much harder task to produce a code generator that will generate machine code virtually as efficient as if the program had been written in assembler in the first place. The efficiency of the object code is most important in major production compilers, particularly when compiling programs which may have deeply nested loops, rather than in environments where programs are only used once or twice and then discarded.

5.4.1 Code generation tasks
The code generator has two main tasks: it has to allocate storage for all static data — constants, initialised data, working data — and for all variables other than those which will be allocated dynamically during program execution. This is done mainly from the symbol and literal tables. The code generator also has to generate the machine instructions corresponding to the C-language.

The second task is the generation of machine instructions. This falls into two main categories: the use of skeletons and the generation of individual instruction sequences.

5.4.2 Skeletons
Most compilers use standard groups of instructions, often called a **skeleton** which can simply be incorporated into the object program wherever a particular operation is encountered. Code skeletons are used for many tasks, such as subscript calculations or type conversions, and for many statements such as FOR loops, input/output, and so on, which require virtually the same instructions wherever they are used.

Many of the instruction sequences given in section 4.2 would in fact form the basis of code skeletons which a code generator could incorporate, substituting addresses of variables as required. For example, the general skeleton for the statement

    for <integer variable> := <lower limit> to <upper limit> do

could be:

                LDA   <lower limit>
                STO   <integer variable>
                JUM   <label2>

```
<label1>LDA    <integer variable>
        ADD    =1
        STO    <integer variable>
        SUB    <upper limit>
        JP     <label3>
<label2> :
         :     [Body of loop]
         :
        JUM    <label1>
<label3>...
```

(compare this with the specific case in section 4.2.6). The compiler would not, of course, hold the code in this assembler-like form but simply in binary machine code, with special codes to indicate where addresses have to be inserted (as indicated by the <---> symbols above). The process of incorporating skeletons and substituting specific addresses is very similar to the process of expanding macros and substituting symbolic parameters by an assembler.

The skeletons will be held simply in the data areas of the code generator, from where they can be copied into the object code being output. Where the skeletons take up too much space for this, the larger and less frequently used may well be obtained from a disk file. It is important to appreciate that the code generator is itself a program, but the data it is manipulating also consists of machine instructions. The code generator could, if desired, be written in a high-level language, but it must of necessity be dealing with machine code instructions as its data.

A compiler may well have several hundred different skeletons that can be used in different circumstances, as there are many different combinations of ways a statement can be used. For example, it is not sufficient to have one skeleton for FOR loops. Different skeletons are needed for loops where the index is incremented and for those where it is decremented. Different code is also needed for different data types of index variable. If an increment or decrement other than 1 is used, the code may have to be different again. Constant upper and lower limits are simpler than variable upper and lower limits, as with variable limits run-time checking is needed to determine whether to go round the loop at all. If the upper or lower limits are expressions rather than simple constants or variables, code must be generated to evaluate these before the skeleton can be used. A particularly awkward case arises in languages where the increment can be a variable and may be either positive or negative at run time: in such cases the skeleton code must allow for testing for passing the final limit in either direction. If the compiler uses index registers for certain FOR loops, rather than keeping the index variable in memory, different code is needed again. The example above was only the skeleton for: FOR loop, incrementing, integer index variable, no explicit increment (taken as 1), constant lower limit, constant upper limit, index variable in memory.

5.4.3 Generation of individual instructions

Many parts of a program are not, however, amenable to the use of skeletons, because the instructions needed are different in every case. The most common case of this is in evaluating expressions. There are infinitely many expressions that can be constructed by combining variables, operators, and parentheses in different ways, so skeletons could at best be used for a few common cases. Any compiler must, therefore, be able to generate the sequence of individual machine instructions needed to compute an expression.

The C-language received by the code generator will typically contain the expression in a form similar to reverse Polish, and individual instructions are generated from this.

Evaluation of reverse Polish, as described in section 5.3.3, is based on a stack principle, and for machines which incorporate stacks as part of the architecture, with push and pop instructions, machine code (albeit of a very crude sort) can be generated very easily. The rule is just based on the rules of reverse Polish itself: when an operand is encountered, push it on to the stack; when an operator is encountered, pop the top two items, apply the operator, and pop the result back.

The code for the sample expression:

$$a*(b-c)+d$$

which is represented in reverse Polish in the C-code as

$$a\,b\,c-*\,d+$$

becomes (on a hypothetical stack-based machine):

```
PUSH   a
PUSH   b
PUSH   c
POP    TEMP2          } Evaluation
POP    TEMP1          } of
SUB    TEMP1,TEMP2    } operator
PUSH   TEMP1          } −
POP    TEMP2,               } Evaluation
POP    TEMP1                } of
MUL    TEMP1,TEMP2          } operator
PUSH   TEMP1,               } *
PUSH   d
POP    TEMP2          } Evaluation
POP    TEMP1          } of
ADD    TEMP1,TEMP2    } operator
PUSH   TEMP1          } +
```

However, this code is quite long and involves a great deal of data movement to and from the stack. This example also assumes that a single instruction can subtract TEMP2 from TEMP1 and leave the result in TEMP1: on many machines this would need two or more instructions. If there is no hardware stack, one could be implemented by the program, using an index register, but each push or pop would then involve at least two instructions: one to load or store the data, and one to increment or decrement the stack pointer.

An assembler programmer wishing to evaluate the above expression on the GOAT would just code:

```
LDA   B      AC contains b
SUB   C      AC contains b−c
MUL   A      AC contains a * (b−c)
ADD   D      AC contains a * (b−c)+d
```

thereby completing the entire evaluation in just four machine instructions. It is thus clear that whilst the naive stack-based approach can be used in very crude compilers, a more sophisticated approach is needed in any code generator whose result has to be reasonably efficient object code.

A better approach is for the code generator *itself* to follow the reverse Polish on the stack, and generate code accordingly, rather than generate code which will execute with a stack at run time. The stack is now a *compile-time* rather than a run-time concept.

The rule for the code generator is now: on finding a symbol, push it on to the stack (do not generate any code); on finding an operator, remove the top two items from the stack, generate code to apply the operator to them; then pop the symbol 'AC' on to the stack to indicate that the current result would be in the accumulator.

Processing

$$a\ b\ c-\ ^*\ d+$$

proceeds as follows. (The code generator's working stack is shown left to right: top at the left.)

```
Symbol:    a   Code generated: —                   Stack: a
Symbol:    b   Code generated: —                   Stack: b a
Symbol:    c   Code generated: —                   Stack: c b a
Operator:  −   c and b removed from stack; code generated to subtract
               them; result is in AC.
               Code generated:  LDA    B
                                SUB    C         Stack: AC a
Operator:  *   AC and a removed from stack; code generated to multi-
               ply them; result is in AC. (When one of the operands is
               already in AC it does not have to be loaded first.)
               Code generated: MUL    A          Stack: AC
Symbol:    d   Code generated: —                  Stack: d AC
Operator:  +   d and AC removed from stack; code generated to add
               them; result is in AC.
               Code generated: ADD    D          Stack: AC
```

The code generated consists of the same four instructions that an assembler programmer would have coded, so by this approach there has been no loss of efficiency at all by writing in a high-level language. However, this expression is particularly simple, and avoids certain problems. If we consider the expression looked at for syntax analysis:

$$(a+b*(c-d))/(e-f)$$

which in reverse Polish became:

$$a\,b\,c\,d-*+e\,f-/$$

we have to proceed as follows.

Symbols:	a, b, c, d				Stack: d c b a
Operator:	−	Code generated:	LDA	C	
			SUB	D	Stack: AC b a
Operator:	*	Code generated:	MUL	B	Stack: AC a
Operator:	+	Code generated:	ADD	A	Stack: AC
Symbols:	e, f				Stack: f e AC

Operator: −   f and e are removed from the stack, but since the value in AC is still required, this must be saved in a temporary location and the reference to AC in the stack is amended accordingly.

Code generated:	STO	TEMP1	
	LDA	E	
	SUB	F	Stack: AC TEMP1

Operator: /   AC and TEMP1 are removed from the stack. Division and subtraction are non-commutative operators: x/y is not the same as y/x. In this case we need TEMP1/AC, not the converse. AC must first therefore be stored.

Code generated:	STO	TEMP2	Stack: TEMP2 TEMP1
	LDA	TEMP1	
	DIV	TEMP2	Stack: AC

The code to compute the expression has thus been generated with ten machine instructions using two temporary storage locations. This is quite acceptable, and many compilers would do no better than this, although an assembler programmer would probably have calculated (e−f) at the start rather than at the end, which would then need only eight instructions and one temporary location.

One of the major difficulties with temporary storage is that it is almost impossible to predict how many such locations are needed: they are only determined as code generation is underway. If the temporary locations are in static storage it thus becomes impossible to associate addresses with every symbol at the start of code generation. In some compilers this may necessitate an extra pass.

It must also be remembered that not all machines have hardware multiplication and division. In such cases a code skeleton (likely to be at least twenty instructions with an internal loop) must be inserted whenever a multiply or divide is required. Even when hardware multiply and divide are supported, the register usage is rarely as simple as on the GOAT, and additional loading and storing may be required.

5.5   ADDITIONAL ISSUES OF COMPILER DESIGN

Our description above has concentrated on a fairly traditional type of batch compiler working on a traditional machine architecture. Many modern compilers use techniques that go considerably beyond this model, and some of these are introduced briefly in this section; readers should consult the 'Further reading' for details.

5.5.1   Interactive and incremental compilers

Many modern compilers, particularly on microcomputers, incorporate an editor as part of the compiler, rather than requiring the programmer to use a separate editor to prepare the source code. Such **interactive compilers** can offer significant increases in programmer productivity simply through not having to switch between different software for editing and compilation, but usually they go considerably further.

Interactive compilers can often perform lexical and syntax analysis on each line of code as soon as it is entered, so that syntax errors can be highlighted (and thus corrected) immediately. Since the editor is language sensitive it can also provide automatic indentation, allow abbreviated entry of keywords, and support **folding** whereby individual blocks of code or procedures can be opened up for editing when needed, but are otherwise left with only the heading showing. Special debugging run-time facilities are also frequently provided, for use while a program is under test, permitting interruption of the program at specific statements, execution one statement at a time, display of variables, and similar features.

An **incremental compiler** not only performs lexical and syntax analysis as each statement is entered, but generates machine code as well. The program is thus developed incrementally: every time a statement is added or modified, the object code is adjusted accordingly. This has the advantage that one-line changes do not require the delay of complete recompilation. When the program is to be run there is only a very short 'binding' delay when jump addresses between different statements are inserted, and then execution begins immediately.

5.5.2   Optimising compilers

We have seen that it is possible for code generators to vary considerably in the efficiency of the object code they generate. For many applications, particularly in process control or on-line systems with multiple users, efficiency is very important, and programs would have to be written in assembler if the compiler-produced object code was substantially less efficient.

Optimising compilers aim to produce highly efficient object code by considering several statements together, rather than just performing a simple statement-by-statement translation. In some cases they can produce programs which may have as little as a 10% overhead on an equivalent hand-coded assembler program.

The optimisation may be done with a view to saving memory or time in execution (usually a combination of both). There are many different techniques of optimisation: some can be done by means of a further pass or passes after the main code generation stage; others may have to be built into the compiler as early as syntax analysis. Naturally optimisation increases compilation time, but the gains at execution time may well justify this.

5.5.2.1 Local optimisation

Local optimisation techniques save unnecessary instructions by considering the code for each statement in conjunction with those close to it.

Consider the statements:

(1)   X := Y+Z;
(2)   C := 2 * X;
(3)   X := 0

which a simple (non-optimising) compiler would translate as:

```
LDA     Y     }
ADD     Z     }  (1)
STO     X     }
LDA     =2    }
MUL     X     }  (2)
STO     C     }
LDA     =0    }  (3)
STO     X     }
```

An optimising compiler would spot that the value of X was left in the accumulator after statement (1) and thus by reversing the multiplication, statement (2) can be reduced to just two instructions:

```
MUL  =2
STO  C
```

A good compiler will also realise that a binary left shift by 1 bit achieves the same effect as a multiply by 2 but is likely to be many times faster on most machines, and will thus replace MUL =2 by SLA 1. (Similarly for other multiplication or division by powers of 2.) Also LDI 0 is almost certainly a faster way of zeroising the accumulator (and uses less memory) than LDA =0 which accesses a further storage location.

A rather more subtle optimiser might further realise that since X is reinitialised in statement (3), there is no need to save it at all, given that it is left in the accumulator for statement (2); thus the STO in statement (1) is now completely redundant.

The sequence of instructions is now reduced to:

```
          LDA        Y
          ADD        Z
          SLA        1
          STO        C
          LDI        0
          STO        X
```

— eight instructions have been reduced to six; slow instructions have been replaced by faster ones; and several bytes of memory have been saved. In itself this is a small saving but repeated many times throughout a program, and particularly with code in frequently executed loops, the savings can be substantial. In this case alone, at least a 30% saving in execution speed has been made for the instruction sequence concerned.

Subscript calculations also benefit from local optimisation. If arrays A and B have the same dimensions, then code such as:

$$A[I, J] := X;$$
$$B[I, J] := Y$$

only requires the subscript calculation on I and J to be carried out once. Since the subscript calculation may require twenty instructions, a very substantial saving is made by avoiding the repetition.

5.5.2.2   Global optimisation

Global optimisation techniques involve looking much more than just a few statements ahead and behind, and take account of the logical structure of the program.

One of the most common kinds of global optimisation lies in moving unnecessary code outside loops, so that processing which does not change each time round the loop is performed only once rather than many times. The number of instructions in the program is not usually reduced, but the number of instructions executed may drop dramatically.

In the code:

$$\text{for } J := 1 \text{ to } 1000 \text{ do}$$
$$A[I, J] := X * I + J$$

a good optimising compiler will appreciate that the calculation of $X * I$ yields the same result each time round the loop; it is only the addition of J that will vary. By breaking up the expression evaluation code and moving the calculation of $X * I$ so that it is done before the loop, 999 unnecessary multiplications are saved at run time. It may even be able to economise in the subscript calculation for A[I,J]: the part of the calculation on I could be done before the loop, so that only the offset for J is added within the loop. If J is then kept in the index register, rather than saved to memory each time round the loop, at least 1000 load and 1000 store instructions will also be saved at run time.

With large loops, an optimising compiler may well move code across many hundreds of statements in order to achieve a more efficient result.

One consequence of optimisation is that it is no longer possible to identify specific object code instructions with specific source statements — this can make the production of meaningful run-time error messages more difficult.

5.5.2.3 Machine-specific optimisation

Most of the optimisation techniques above would apply in general terms on almost any machine, but other techniques involve making the best possible use of particular machine architectures.

Having only a single accumulator, register allocation on the GOAT is not a problem. But most modern machines have a number of general purpose registers where operands of computations can be held, and making the best possible use of these is quite an advanced science. The techniques considered above in sections 5.4.3 and 5.5.2.1 to reduce unnecessary loading and storing become very much more elaborate when a number of different values can be kept in registers. (In some cases, though, because of the obvious difficulty, an optimising compiler can actually do better at register allocation than a human programmer.)

Some machines have elaborate instructions which will perform very extensive processing in a single machine instruction, which would otherwise have to be coded out quite a number of instructions — for example one important early machine had a three-way branch instruction. Such instructions are useful to assembler programmers in certain cases, and no doubt situations arise in high-level language programs where they could usefully form part of the object code. But only with very elaborate analysis is it possible for an optimising compiler to spot these cases: many compilers generate code which only ever uses at most two-thirds of the available instruction set.

The benefits of such instructions are thus denied to the high-level language programmer unless special statements are included in the source language to make use of them, and if the latter course is followed the language becomes rather machine specific. One solution to this is the emergence of reduced instruction set computers (RISC machines — see Chapter 16) which have a much smaller range of instructions, but these can be executed very rapidly. By keeping the range of instructions very simple, the code generated by a compiler can be as good as that written by an assembler programmer — but the program is developed vastly more quickly through writing in a high-level language.

5.5.3 Compiler-compilers

Much of the work in compiler writing is common to many different compilers and from the early years of compiler development, work has gone into developing tools to simplify the process. Particularly where a formal language definition is available, large parts of the lexical and syntax analysis stages can be driven automatically from the definitions: it is not necessary for new lexical and syntax analysers to be written afresh for every new language. A wide range of tools to assist in compiler development are collectively known as **compiler-compilers**.

The theoretical idea of an ultimate compiler-compiler is that it is a piece of software which given a language definition will translate that into a compiler, in the same sense that a compiler given a source program translates that into machine code. In practice no such tool exists, but several steps have been made in that direction, which greatly reduce the task of writing new compilers.

The simplest tools classed as compiler-compilers are just special systems programming languages particularly suited to writing compilers, for example by incorporating convenient facilities for symbol table access and for building data structures such as trees and stacks.

More elaborate compiler-compilers may automate the parsing, using the language definition, though most impose certain simplifying limits on the source language, so some parts of the parsing routines will still have to be hand-coded.

The code generation stage is the hardest to automate because it is so dependent on the target machine. Some economy can occasionally be made if several compilers (of different languages) on the same machine use the same C-language, as they can then in principle all use the same code generator. To be fully effective the C-language has to become a highly flexible form of **intermediate code**, sufficient to cover all the operations that may be required in all the languages, which is rarely possible. However, code generators which work from a defined intermediate code have been produced for some machines, and can be regarded as compiler-compilers in the broadest sense.

FURTHER READING

Aho, A. V., Sethi, R. & Ullman, J. D. *Compilers — principles, techniques and tools* (Addison-Wesley, 1985).

Brown, P. J. *Writing interactive compilers and interpreters* (John Wiley, 1979).

Davie, A. J. T. & Morrison, R. *Recursive descent compiling* (Ellis Horwood, 1981).

Foster, J. M. *Automatic syntactic analysis* (MacDonald/Elsevier, 1970).

Hopgood, F. R. A. *Compiling techniques* (MacDonald/Elsevier, 1969).

Hunter R. *Compilers — their design and construction using Pascal* (John Wiley, 1985).

Terry, P. D. *Programming language translation — a practical approach* (Addison-Wesley, 1986).

Tremblay J.-P. & Sorenson, P. G. *The theory and practice of compiler writing* (McGraw-Hill, 1985).

6

Compilers: run-time environments

6.1 INTRODUCTION

As well as the machine code translation for each statement, the object module of any high-level language program has to include a good deal of standard routines that will present in the object of *all* programs translated by that compiler: to cover initialisation, run-time error handing, and so on. This standard code is called the **run-time environment** (RTE).

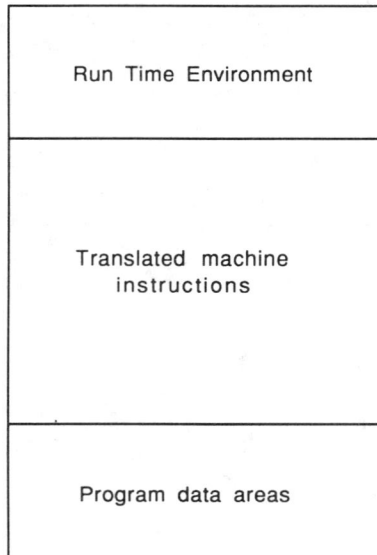

```
┌─────────────────────────────────┐
│                                 │
│       Run Time Environment       │
│                                 │
├─────────────────────────────────┤
│                                 │
│                                 │
│       Translated machine         │
│         instructions             │
│                                 │
│                                 │
├─────────────────────────────────┤
│                                 │
│       Program data areas         │
│                                 │
└─────────────────────────────────┘
```

Fig. 6.1 — Object module format.

In most cases the run-time environment is not produced as part of the code output by the code generator stage of the compiler, but is incorporated at the linking or loading stage, as discussed in Chapter 7. This means that the run-time environment can just be written as an ordinary program which is link-edited with object code output by the compiler, or the compiled object code may contain a few instructions at the start which loads the run-time environment when the program starts.

Writing the run-time environment is often quite a large task; it may be as much as a third of the total compiler development.

The essence of the run-time environment is that it provides facilities needed whilst the program is running in order that it can execute correctly. Typically it will include: file control routines, such as opening or closing a file; standard subroutines such as square root or input/output data conversions; error handling; and storage management routines. The remainder of this chapter explores these functions in more detail.

The nature of the language greatly affects what has to go in the run-time environment and this can greatly affect program size and efficiency. Many languages have a standard run-time environment always included, so for a small program, the run-time environment may be much larger than translation of the statements — which can be a very inconvenient overhead. More elaborate compilers will only include those parts of run-time environment actually required by a particular program; for example if a program does no file handling or no square roots those routines are excluded.

The quality of run-time environment is an important focus for considering run-time performance. If the run-time environment does lots of initialisation even for the smallest program, it may be that no program executes in less than half a second even if only one line. Many compilers, even though they may produce excellent highly-optimised object code, let themselves down by poor run-time environments that take up much program execution time and negate many of the benefits of the optimised code.

In other cases, serious limitations arise because of the error handling mechanisms used. If the programmer wishes to take certain action in response to certain file errors, for example, but the run-time environment simply issues a standard message that is rather meaningless to the end user, any other benefits of that high level language can be lost.

Also, if a firm is producing software to sell to others, it is necessary for the end users to have the run-time environment in order to operate the software on their own machines. Since the run-time environment is the copyright of the compiler supplier this can only be done with the supplier's consent, which is not always available or only at a high price. In this way too, the run-time environment can limit the use of an otherwise very attractive compiler.

Deficiencies in the run-time environment is one of the main reasons which drives people to write in assembler.

6.2   ERROR AND EXCEPTION HANDLING

A good compiler will ensure that programs do not just 'crash' while running with no indication of what is wrong, but will produce a suitable message. The run-time environment must handle all of this.

Types of errors that must be handled include:

(a) overflow in a calculation
(b) division by zero
(b) subscript out of range
(c) input/output error (typically a hardware problem — disk not in drive, printer out of paper, etc.)
(d) out of storage (though the run-time environment must leave enough to issue the message!)
(e) undefined variable (possibly)
(f) invalid argument to a built-in function (such as asking for a substring outside the string itself).

Some of these, particularly overflows and hardware errors, may well be checked by the hardware, and will cause interrupts if they occur. The interrupt will be detected by the operating system, as discussed in Chapter 11, but most operating systems allow application programs to define a special routine to be invoked if interrupts of this kind arise. At program initialisation, the run-time environment can define a special address to receive control on overflow (say), so when an overflow occurs this routine is automatically invoked and can arrange to issue a suitable message.

Most other errors, and all errors on machines that do not generate interrupts for events of this kind, must be checked by the compiler including checking code in the object program at each possible point of occurrence, with a conditional branch to a run-time environment. This was illustrated in respect of subscript checking in section 4.2.7.

When errors arise, the run-time environment must at the very least produce a clear meaningful decent message. Just displaying 'Overflow' is very unhelpful. It can usually give the address of the instruction where the error occurred, e.g. 'Overflow at 2F63C' but this is still very unfriendly. For it to be any use at all, the programmer must have a source listing which gives the hexadecimal address of the machine code of each statement (which can be quite difficult as it requires the code generator to refer back to the source). It is more helpful if the message can actually give a line number for the error — but this requires line numbers to be held in the object program.

Ideally, to assist debugging, the message would actually give the name of a variable if a problem occurs — e.g. 'Undefined value in TOTAL at line 276' — but this requires the names of all variables and their addresses (virtually the whole symbol table) to be included in the object program.

Therefore there needs to be a balance between ease of debugging on the one hand and the object program size on the other. Many compilers have options, so that the program can initially be compiled with full debugging options, and then recompiled to produce more compact object code once the program is tested. It is important, though, that even without the debugging options, there must be sufficient information produced (even if not in a very friendly form) to enable programmers to track down problems that may occur in live use.

For the development of major applications that will be operated by non-computer specialists, the run-time environment must also allow programmers to define program routines to handle errors themselves if desired. The software designer may not want the program to terminate with a message like 'Disk I/O Error', but may want to produce a more meaningful message, allow the user to take action and then re-try the task requested. Some languages include such **exception handling** statements to allow programmers to define action when errors arise (for example PL/I provides a wide range of ON-units, such as ON OVERFLOW and many implementations of BASIC provide ON ERROR statements). Usually the programmer wishes to handle some errors, but wishes the run-time environment to take standard action in other cases. When an error arises which the program is to handle, the run-time environment must invoke the program's own error routine. (Care has to be taken to avoid looping if the error recurs within the error routine itself.)

The run-time environment may also have further helps for program debugging, such as maintaining a statement execution count, procedure linkage history, flow history, or even one statement at a time interactive execution with the ability to stop and display variables.

6.3 STANDARD ROUTINES AND FILE HANDLING

It is not usually desirable for the code generator to make too much use of code skeletons that require more than twenty or thirty machine instructions, as the object code can get very large if a certain operation occurs many times. Therefore for more complex instances of standard processing, the code generator just compiles a subroutine call into the run-time environment, where a suitable routine is held.

The balance between using a code skeleton or a run-time environment routine is the same balance as an assembler programmer deciding whether to implement a frequently used operation by means of a macro or a subroutine.

Typical uses of standard run-time environment routines would be as follows.

6.3.1 File handling
Most file handling operations: open, close, read, write, are relatively complex and often require several hundred machine instructions including interaction with the operating system. (As considered in section 2.4.8, this approach also makes the compiler less operating system dependent — all the operating system specific parts are in the run-time environment rather than built into the code generator.)

6.3.2 Input/output data conversions
Any input/output operations involving numeric data require a conversion to be carried out between the individual characters used to write down a number in decimal, and the internal binary representation used in compu-

tations. For example, READ(N) takes characters and converts them to binary. On output, WRITE(N) converts the value to characters for the screen or printer. (On input, the task is largely the same as in lexical analysis and therefore certain routines used by the lexical analyser will commonly be found in the run-time environment.)

6.3.3   Built-in functions

Most built-in functions, such as SQRT( ), MID$( ), ORD( ), will simply be subroutines in the run-time environment. When they appear in the source, the compiler generates a procedure in just the same way as when an internal procedure is invoked. The run-time routine performs the required operation on its parameters and returns to the user program.

A good compiler will avoid generating a subroutine call for the very simplest built-in functions — for example the function ABS, available in most languages to return the absolute (unsigned) value of its argument, can be implemented on most architectures with a single machine instruction; it would thus be very wasteful if a procedure call were required for this elementary operation. Functions such as taking a substring of a character string may well also be handled with a simple skeleton.

However, the mathematical functions — logarithms, trigonometric functions, and so on — require very careful computation to provide the required accuracy, and involve many instructions in tightly nested loops. The writing of such code belongs more to the field of numerical analysis than to the normal skills of a compiler writer, and very often a mathematical library will be purchased from an outside source for incorporation into a run-time environment. Great ingenuity has been exercised over the years in writing mathematical libraries capable of computing twenty or more different functions, using elaborate iterative algorithms, in a way that only takes up very modest amounts of memory.

6.3.4   Complex operations in expressions

Whilst the code generator will happily generate instructions for addition, subtraction, and (usually) multiplication and division, other more complex operations can arise in order to evaluate an expression, for which the code generator will generate a call to the run-time environment.

Exponentiation (raising a number to a power — usually denoted by ** or an upward arrow) is usually too much to handle by individual instructions unless the power is a simple constant such as 2 or 3. A ** I will almost always be handled by a run-time environment call.

Many string operations — such as concatenating two strings to form a single longer string — require so much memory management that a run-time environment routine is essential.

Type conversions are a further instance. Many languages allow expressions such as A * J where A is a real (floating point) variable and J is an integer. In such cases, J must be converted to the corresponding floating point format (which will be done by a call to the run-time environment) before the floating point multiplication can be performed. Conversely in the assignment J := A, the value of A must be converted and rounded (or truncated) to the nearest integer.

It should be noted that on computers without hardware floating point arithmetic units, *all* floating point operations — even just adding two numbers — will require run-time environment routines.

6.4 STORAGE MANAGEMENT

In languages like COBOL, all storage is static, so storage addresses for every symbol can be allocated at compile time — there is no work to be done by run-time environment.

However, many other languages require some kind of dynamic storage allocation, for any of the following reasons.

(a) In block-structured languages, the idea is usually that storage for the variables in each procedure is allocated on entry to that procedure, and released on exit from the procedure. Where recursive procedures are allowed this is essential, as multiple copies of the variables are needed, a new set being allocated each time to procedure calls itself.

(b) The language may allow the programmer explicit control over storage allocation — this is more or less vital in a language that allows the program to create lists and other pointer-based structures — for example the directive NEW( ) in Pascal enables the program to request the dynamic creation of a storage record.

(c) Dynamic storage allocation is also needed with variable-size data, for example variable-length character strings.

6.4.1 Stack-based storage allocation

For fixed-size variables in procedure calls, the environment can just allocate variables on a stack — new variables are added to the stack on entry to a procedure and released on exit. This does have the advantage that the total storage requirement of the program may be less than if static storage were used. For example, in Fig. 6.2 below, the main routine A calls procedures B and C, but only one at a time; therefore the variables for B and C can share the same storage, and only enough space is needed for whichever is the larger.

Only if B itself called C would it be necessary to have space for the variables of all three routines together.

The compiler generates code at the start of each procedure to advance the stack as necessary for the variable space required, and to reduce the stack on exit. An area of storage is allocated for the stack, typically from the end of the program up to the end of the storage available; if the stack grows beyond its limit an 'out of storage' run-time error occurs.

The actual code to access each variable will, however, be a little more complex than in the examples of previous chapters. It is no longer possible to compile

$$X := Y + Z$$

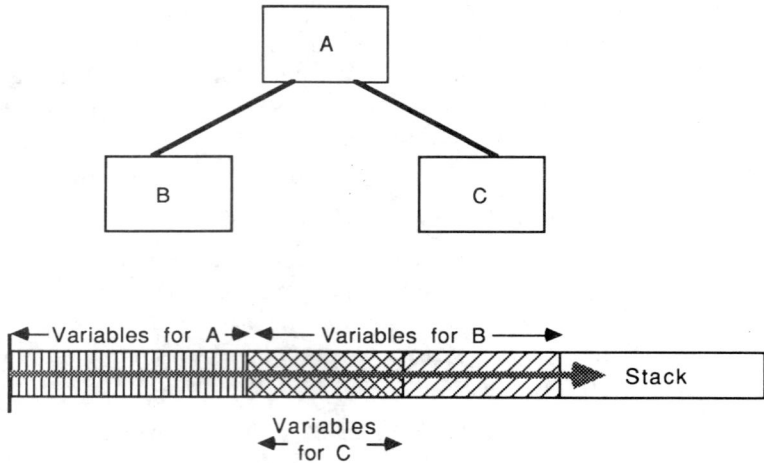

Fig. 6.2 — Storage allocation — main program and two procedures.

as

```
LDA        Y
ADD        Z
STO        X
```

because X, Y and Z no longer have fixed addresses — they are dependent upon the current stack position. If the architecture has a hardware stack the problem is not too difficult for local variables of the current procedure, as they can just be addressed relative to the stack pointer. For machines without hardware stacks an approach using index registers is required.

However, following the rules of scope (see section 2.4), procedures may also refer to variables of other procedures in which they are textually contained, and clearly the variables of other procedures cannot be allocated by reference to the current stack pointer. Global variables, that is variables defined in the main program and thereby accessible to all procedures, can be accessed by fixed offsets from the base of the stack, but access to non-local non-global data is a complex matter requiring pointer-based structures.

6.4.2   Heap-based storage allocation
For more complex cases where storage may be allocated and de-allocated at will (not just last in first out) a stack is inadequate, and storage must be allocated on a **heap**. A heap is an essentially untidy collection of storage where used and unused storage may be intermingled.

Variable-length character strings provide a good example of where heap-based storage is required. The examples are in BASIC, where string variables end with the character '$' and the symbol '+' denotes concatenation.

Variable-length strings are usually accessed by means of a **string descriptor** which contains the current length of the string and a pointer to the position on the heap where the value of the string commences. The string descriptor itself is of fixed size so it can be placed in static storage — or on the stack if the string is allocated only on entry to a procedure.

Consider the execution of the following statements: the state of the heap after execution of each statement is shown alongside, unused storage being denoted '————'; the initial position on the heap is numbered 0. (Prior to execution of these statements both A$ and B$ were uninitialised — they therefore were strings of length zero and occupied no space on the heap.)

A$ = "HELLO"   HELLO-------------------
   A$ descriptor: Length 5
       Heap posn 0

B$ = "JANE"   HELLOJANE----------------
   A$ descriptor: Length 5
       Heap posn 0
   B$ descriptor: Length 4
       Heap posn 5

A$ = A$+" "+B$ -----JANEHELLO JANE-------
   A$ descriptor: Length 10
       Heap posn 9
   B$ descriptor: Length 4
       Heap posn 5

In the third statement, A$ acquired the value "HELLO JANE" which was longer than its previous value and could not therefore be held in the same position on the heap. The storage previously occupied by A$ thus became unused and a new larger area was allocated.

In order to control this process, the run-time environment must provide heap management routines for allocating and de-allocating storage and keeping track of which portions are used and unused. As execution proceeds, the program may quickly run out of storage if new storage is always allocated at the top of the heap. The heap management therefore needs to consider storage further down the heap which has become unused, and attempt to allocate that. But sooner or later a **fragmentation** problem can arise where there may be enough unused storage in total, but it is all in pieces that are too small.

To overcome this, the run-time environment must include a **garbage collection** routine to gather up all the unused space on to one end of the heap, and re-arrange the remaining data so that it is all together — adjusting the pointers in the string descriptors accordingly.

Garbage collection is a relatively complex process and there are many different algorithms, though the more sophisticated ones are quite large and may themselves therefore restrict the maximum size of heap. The garbage collector can influence program performance significantly, especially in interactive programs, where the program may be running very well giving good response times and suddenly the heap reaches its upper limit, the garbage collector is brought into operation, and the user has to wait very much longer than normal for the program to respond.

Any language that allows haphazard storage allocation must have a garbage collection run-time environment with all the overheads this implies; there are therefore good reasons for avoiding such facilities in a language unless they are likely to be really important. In PL/I, for example, all variable-length strings are declared with a maximum length and the whole of this is allocated initially, so although this may be slightly wasteful it avoids the need for heap management in string handling.

The principles of heap management apply in many other contexts; in particular many operating system memory management functions (see Chapter 12) will incorporate such facilities. Occasionally it is possible for the run-time environment to use the operating systems memory management rather than control its own heap, but for variable-length character strings it would involve quite absurd overheads to issue an operating system call to allocate storage every time the length of a character string changed.

6.4.3 Overall storage management
Where a stack and heap are both needed, a common approach is to let one grow from each end of the available memory.

$$\text{STACK} \longrightarrow \qquad \longleftarrow \text{HEAP}$$

The storage only runs out if they meet in the middle and the garbage collector yields no free space.

Sometimes a language may need several stacks or heaps for different purposes. It is then quite difficult to allocate storage between them; some initial decisions must be made where each is to start from.

$$\text{STACK 1} \longrightarrow \qquad \text{STACK 2} \longrightarrow \qquad \longleftarrow \text{HEAP}$$

In such cases, it is possible to run out of memory on stack 2 and the heap, even though there is space left on stack 1, or vice versa. Sometimes options are provided whereby the programmer can define the initial amounts of space to allocate, in order to optimise this.

An out of storage situation must still produce an error message, and this needs helpful information to assist debugging — for example if the program was stuck in a recursive loop or a storage allocation loop, the programmer must have a chance to work out where in the program this was happening. If the problem was simply due to large amounts of user data, the program may need to handle the condition and take specific action, such as saving the excess data to a file. A good run-time environment will provide means whereby the program can check the amount of free space and take action before it is too late to be able to do anything.

FURTHER READING

Aho, A. V., Sethi, R. & Ullman, J. D. *Compilers — principles, techniques and tools* (Addison-Wesley, 1985).

Tremblay, J.-P. & Sorenson, P. G. *The theory and practice of compiler writing* (McGraw-Hill, 1985).

7

Linkers and loaders

7.1 INTRODUCTION

In Chapters 3–6 we have looked in some detail at the task carried out by language translators — both compilers and assemblers — but it would be incomplete to leave the description at the point where the language translator produces the object code. Further processing is needed to prepare and load that object code into memory in order that the program can actually *run* — and this is the function of linkers and loaders.

It is open to debate whether linkers and loaders belong with language processors or whether they are part of the operating system. Certainly it is quite common for these components to be provided with an operating system. But they are included in this part of the book because of their role in completing the language translation process.

7.2 MODULAR PROGRAMMING AND LINKAGE EDITING

In developing large programs it would be very inconvenient if the whole program — which may run to hundreds of thousands of lines — had to be recompiled every time a minor change was made; indeed many compilers would be quite unable to compile a program of this size as their various internal tables would quickly overflow. Usually large programs are written in a number of separately compiled **modules**, which are brought together for execution.

The process of bringing modules together to form a single program is called **linking** or **linkage editing**, and requires a special item of systems software known as a **linker** or **linkage editor**.

The linkage between modules is normally based on procedure calls. Most programming languages provide facilities to permit the calling of external procedures — that is procedures compiled in a separate source module. It is thus relatively simple to write programs with each major procedure prepared as a separate source file and compiled independently; these are then combined by the linkage editor, prior to execution. Some languages such as Modula-2 are designed very strongly around this concept but virtually all languages intended for serious applications provide some facilities for separate compilations.

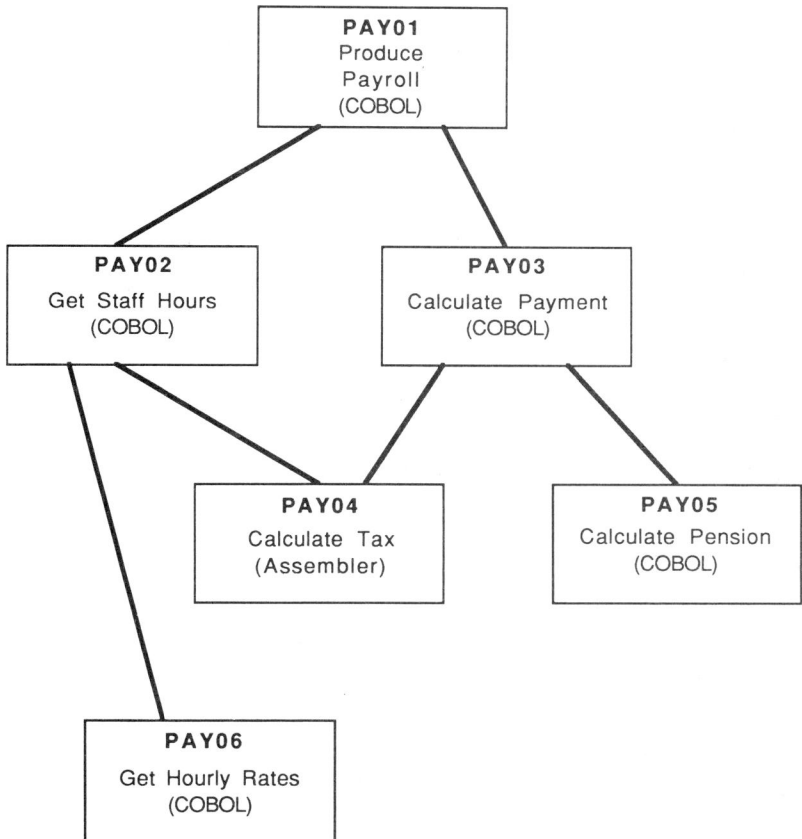

Fig. 7.1 — A modular program (each box is a module and the lines indicate external procedure calls).

The best modular structure for a program is a major software engineering design issue, and depends in part on the facilities in the language for calling internal and external procedures. In most cases there will still be internal procedures within the individual modules, but the program is helpfully structured by compiling major groups of procedures separately. In principle a major data structure could also be separately compiled — the concept is not limited purely to procedures — but only a few languages support access to external data structures.

Modular programming has many advantages; the main ones being as follows.

(a) The program is much easier to change — when a small alteration is made it is only necessary to recompile one module and then re-link the program.

(b) Several programmers can write different modules.

(c) The various functions of the program are much better isolated, with less risk of inadvertent side-effects such as where the same variable is used for two purposes.
(d) Modules performing frequently used functions can be re-used in other programs.
(e) It is possible to write different modules in different programming languages, provided all the compilers use the same linkage conventions.
(f) Debugging is assisted as the modules can be tested individually or added to the program one by one (incremental testing).

In all but the very simplest environments, program development is thus a two-stage process: compilation (or assembly), followed by linking. The linkage editor is thus crucial to the flexibility of the program development process.

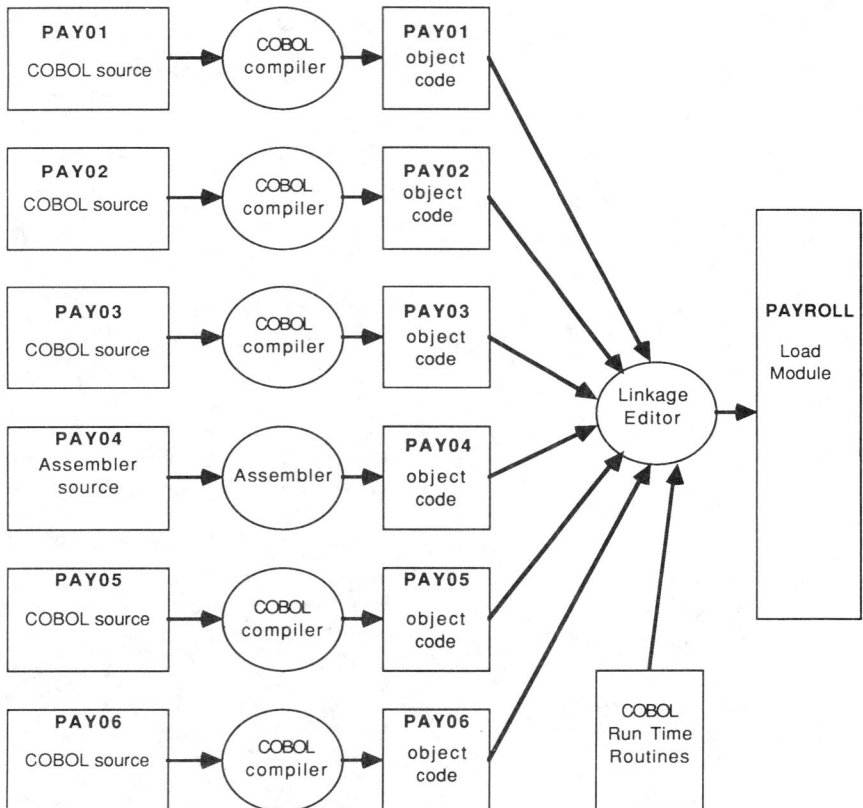

Fig. 7.2 — Production of load module.

Most translators do not therefore produce object code in the form required for a program that is about to be loaded and executed: rather they produce a form of **relocatable object code** which is in a format for further processing by a linkage editor. The final output produced by the linker is frequently called the **load module**; it is a disk file with the same layout as it will actually have when loaded into RAM for execution.

Most operating systems have ways of identifying files at the different stages of language processing; for example, in MS-DOS, source files are given extensions such as .BAS, .PAS, .COB, and so on, according to the language used; relocatable object code files have the extension .OBJ, and load modules have extensions .COM or .EXE, according to their type of memory requirement.

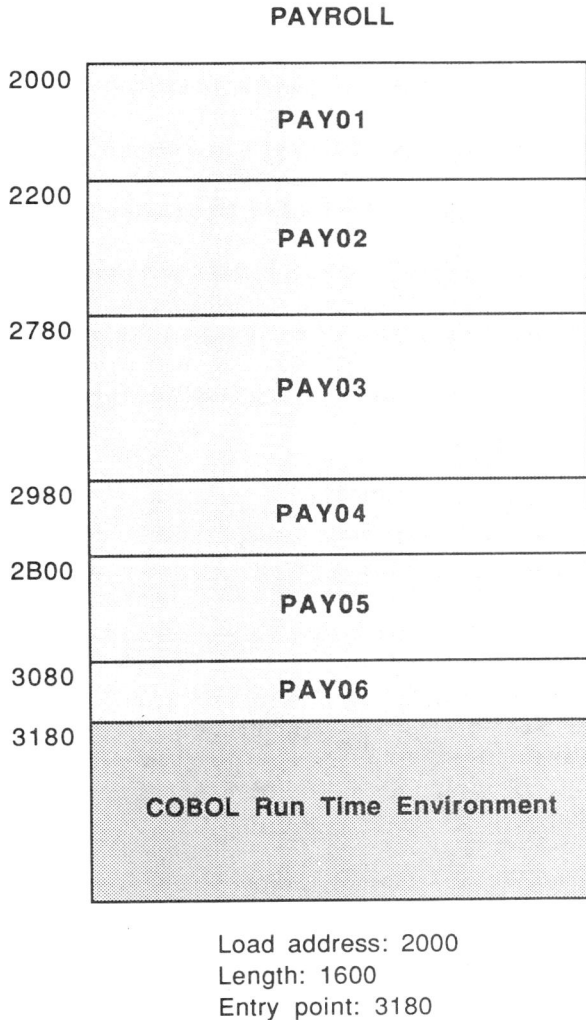

PAYROLL

2000	PAY01
2200	PAY02
2780	PAY03
2980	PAY04
2B00	PAY05
3080	PAY06
3180	COBOL Run Time Environment

Load address: 2000
Length: 1600
Entry point: 3180

Fig. 7.3 — Possible load module composition.

The linkage editor is a program which takes one or more relocatable object files and combines them into a load module. As a program, it is itself a language processor, and although its task comes after the translation stage, some of its principles (for example relating symbols to addresses) are analogous to those carried out by translators. Many linkage editors will also allow the use of special library files containing object modules, and these will be searched according to specified criteria when looking for the various modules to link into a program.

It is not usually necessary to provide a linker with a list of every module in a program — if requested to link the main module, most linkers will search the libraries for all modules called by the main module, it will then search for all lower level modules called by these, and so on, until the whole program is found or until linkage must be terminated due to a required module being missing.

One library will often contain the compiler run-time environment which must be incorporated into the load module for execution (see Chapter 6); this will be linked automatically provided the compiler included a call to the run-time environment as part of the compiled object code. One advantage of the linking process is that the run-time environment is only included once for all modules in the program. If there are modules in different high-level languages making up the program, there may have to be more than one run-time environment! Because of the complications this can cause (for example in trapping run-time errors) most designers are happy to see some modules in a high-level language and some in assembler, but multiple high-level languages in the same program are usually best avoided.

7.3 TRANSLATOR OUTPUT

In previous chapters we have stressed the role of the language translator in determining data addresses, but it is clear that when modular programming is used, the assembler or compiler will not know the actual address where the program code is to be loaded, because it will not know the size of the modules which precede the one being compiled.

Therefore, the object code produced by a translator has to be in a **relocatable** form — it is still compiled machine code, but all the addresses in the instructions will simply be relative to the start of that module. They will be subsequently relocated by the linker adding the start address of the module.

Where one module calls another, the compiler cannot possibly know the address of the other module, so it usually just puts zero in the jump address, leaving the actual address to be inserted by the linker. This is known as an **external reference**.

The relocatable object code produced by a compiler thus consists of three parts. (These may be presented in varying orders, depending on the system followed.)

(a) The major part of the object code is usually called the **text** — the compiled machine instructions and data areas (albeit with addresses only relative to the start of the module and external references yet to be inserted). Frequently this will not be in a final memory image form — for example there may be locations that will ultimately be reserved for large uninitialised areas of data; the translator will simply indicate that such addresses are to be reserved rather than supplying data for each location.

(b) Details of all **external symbols** — names of procedures to which this module needs access (external references) and name of procedures in this module which may be called by others (entry points). Usually the external symbols are just the procedure name identifiers used by the programmer in the source code.

(c) A **relocation list** specifying every place in the module where an address is used and indicating how it is to be relocated. Most addresses will be internal references to be relocated by adding the start address of this module, but jump addresses in procedure calls will be relocated by adding the address of the external reference.

7.4   TASK OF THE LINKAGE EDITOR

The linkage editor thus has three main tasks:

(a) to bring the text of all the modules together to form a load module (including searching libraries as necessary);

(b) to resolve external references;

(c) to relocate internal addresses with respect to each module's start address in memory.

With an architecture such as the GOAT, practically every instruction data address will need relocation, which makes link editing very time consuming. In many more recent architectures, the address field of the instruction just specifies an address relative to the contents of a register, so it is usually just necessary to relocate a few literals containing addresses. Programs can be written in a way that avoids use of any explicit addresses at all (that is, all addresses are determined at run time); such programs are said to be **self-relocating**.

In order to resolve the external references, the linkage editor will use a symbol table in a very similar way to an assembler, except that only external symbols appear in the table. (The remaining identifiers in the source code are no longer required after the code generation stage of the compiler.)

The load module is built using the text of one object module at a time; once the size of one module is known, the start address of the next module is determined. As each module is incorporated, an actual address can be placed in the symbol table corresponding to each external symbol. If there are any undefined symbols and the libraries have been adequately searched for all modules that may be needed, link editing is terminated with a suitable message to indicate that a procedure entry point must be missing.

Once the addresses of all modules are known, the symbol table can be used to give an address for the relocation. Internal addresses in a module will be relocated by adding the start address of that module; external references are relocated by adding the address of the external symbol concerned.

The process is quite simple for small programs, but for large programs containing tens or hundreds of modules with many references from one module to another, the task of the linker becomes comparable in complexity to the task of an assembler, and linkage editors are usually quite elaborate programs. One of the main problems is that when linking a large program whose size approaches the system limits, it is rarely possible to hold the load module in RAM as well as the linker itself, symbol tables, relocation lists, and so on. In practice therefore there may be extensive use of disk work files. If the program consists not just of a single load module, but several load modules which are loaded as separate phases during program execution, the link editing task becomes larger still, as there may be external references between the phases.

It is not surprising, therefore, that link editing can often take as long as compiling a good-sized module; although many linkers are perhaps unnecessarily cumbersome in the approaches they take. The design of linkers has not received the same attention as the design of other kinds of language processors, and many development teams have concentrated all their most able personnel on compiler development, leaving those with much less expertise to work on the linkage editor.

Once the load module is complete, with all addresses correctly inserted, it will be written to a suitable disk file from which it can be directly loaded into memory as soon as the operating system receives a command indicating that the program is to be run.

7.5   SIMPLE LOADERS

The process of taking a load module from disk and bringing it into memory for execution is carried out by a **loader**. The loader may be a distinct program or it may simply be hidden in the functions of the operating system (see Chapter 9).

Of necessity, the loader must itself be permanently resident in memory (otherwise another loader is needed to load the loader); normally it is therefore loaded when the operating system is initialised. Because it has to take up permanent space in memory it is usually designed to be as small as possible. Where there are stages in the processing of the load module which could, in principle, be done other by the linkage editor or by the loader, it is clearly advantageous for most of the work to be done by the linkage editor, thereby keeping the loader as small as possible.

A simple loader may therefore consist of less than a hundred machine instructions: it issues the appropriate operating system calls to find the disk file of the load module; reads it into memory; and then the loader executes a jump instruction to the starting address of the program. The program is then executing.

The loader is both the final stage of language processing and a component of the operating system; it may well perform other operating system functions such as memory allocation or altering the list of active processes (see Part II of this book).

7.6 RELOCATING LOADERS

The simple loader is effective for a simple single-user operating system where it is possible to determine before linkage editing where in memory the program will actually run. The linker relocates the program so that all addresses will be correct when the program is loaded at a specific address for execution.

But if for some reason the load module were loaded into memory in a different position from that envisaged when the program was link edited, all internal addresses would be incorrect. Data would be wrongly accessed and jumps would not transfer to the point intended.

With a multi-user operating system or even with a multi-tasking single-user operating system, it is necessary to be able to load programs at different addresses, according to where memory is available for the task in hand. In some early systems this was achieved by link editing several different versions of a program, each relocated for loading at a different address, but clearly such an approach is very inconvenient.

The only practical solution, therefore, is to have a **relocating loader** where the relocation of addresses is carried out as the program is loaded, rather than at link-edit time. This means the program can be loaded anywhere in memory.

Where a relocating loader is used, the linkage editor still fulfils the very necessary task of bringing together the object code of all the different modules, resolving external references, and relocating addresses within the load module (the start of the load module being taken as address zero at this stage). However, instead of dispensing with the relocation list, the details of all addresses to be relocated are actually written to disk with the load module.

When the program is loaded, the loader picks up the relocation list, and adjusts all internal addresses by adding the actual load address. This makes program loading more than just a case of reading the load module from disk, but relocation at this stage is much simpler than that carried out by the linkage editor. The relocating loader adjusts every internal address by the value of the load address; there is no question of relocating different addresses with respect to different external symbols as at link-edit time.

As at the link-edit stage, the machine architecture and the extent to which actual addresses appear in the program will greatly affect the size of task to be undertaken by a relocating loader. In a number of modern systems, all programs are self-relocating by virtue of the way registers are used, which means that a simple loader can be used even in a multi-programming environment.

7.7   MULTI-PHASE LINKING AND DYNAMIC LOADING

The approach which has been described thus far in this chapter is known as **static linking** — that is, the entire program is link edited prior to execution, and the combination of modules remains static thereafter (unless the program is re-linked). There is no facility to call in extra modules while the program is running.

Many operating systems use static linking as the main method of program development, and in most cases it is straightforward and efficient. However, there are sometimes cases where static linking is neither possible or desirable.

(a) If the program is larger than the total available memory, there must at least be some mechanism whereby the program can request separate phases to be loaded (and if necessary relocated) during program execution.
(b) In a large program where certain modules are only used occasionally (error handling, for example) but are not needed every time the program is run, it is more efficient if these can be loaded only when required. It is a waste both of memory and of loading time if these are always loaded irrespective of whether they will be needed.
(c) If a major program consists of hundreds of modules, all frequently being changed, it is impractical to re-link the whole program every time one module changes. This would apply, for example, to teleprocessing systems with many different application modules that are invoked to handle different types of messages.

To deal with such situations, most operating systems provide a facility for **dynamic loading** of modules during program execution. Where static linking is the norm, dynamic loading is rarely supported in high-level languages and is available only to the assembler programmer, but in other cases, it may be the normal mechanism whereby one module calls another. In other words, in the latter case, a call to an external procedure is compiled not as a jump, but as an operating system call requesting the loader to load a new module and transfer control to it. (This approach is used in OS/2, as described in section 13.2.3.)

With such an environment where dynamic loading is the normal means of inter-module linkage, there is no need for static linking, and the linkage editor becomes redundant, or serves merely to reformat object code into load modules. All resolution of external references between modules, and relocation if required, are handled by the dynamic loader. The binding together of program modules is thus left as late as possible — right until the time one module calls another — thereby allowing the greatest possible flexibility, an issue which is considered further in Chapter 16.

However, dynamic loading also has complications, particularly in terms of performance. Time is saved through not having to link edit the program, but the tasks formerly carried out by the linkage editor have to be performed every time the program is run, rather than once and for all. (The comparison between static linking and dynamic loading has parallels with the comparison between compilers and interpreters.)

The dynamic loader also has to make the difficult decision whether to release the memory occupied by a module once it has returned to its calling routine, or whether it should stay resident. If all modules remain resident, the system may soon run out of memory, or in a virtual memory environment there may be a great deal of paging. But if modules are always unloaded at the end of their execution and re-loaded every time they are called, system performance can be cut drastically due to the time spent loading frequently used modules. Even if modules are kept resident, the first user of the day can experience very poor response times due to the time taken to load all the modules one by one.

The choice between static linking and dynamic loading is not therefore clear cut; ideally a suite of language translators, linkers and loaders would allow the programmer to choose which modules are to be statically linked and which would be dynamically loaded, regardless of the programming languages used. In practice, such flexibility in language processors is rare, and program designs will normally be influenced by the implementation available.

FURTHER READING

Barron, D. W. *Assemblers and loaders* (MacDonald/Elsevier, 2nd edn, 1972).

Gear, C. W. *Computer organization and programming* (McGraw-Hill, 1985).

8

Interpreters and fourth-generation languages

8.1 INTERPRETIVE EXECUTION

The function of a language processor is to enable a program written in some kind of programming language to be executed by compiler. The main alternative to translation of the program into machine code, as discussed in Chapters 3–7, is to achieve execution interpretively. It is also possible to mix compilation and interpretation in a single product, as discussed in section 8.5 below.

Interpreters have tended to increase in usage in recent years, partly because they are a good deal simpler to implement than compilers and linkers, partly because the overheads of interpreters are no longer such a problem with processors becoming cheaper, and partly because they can allow a flexibility in fourth- and fifth-generation languages which is difficult to achieve with straight translation. However, there is very much less written about interpreters than there is about compilers.

An interpreter can be defined as *a program that will execute a program written in a given language by examining each statement in turn and performing the action that the statement requires.* (If the language does not divide into statements, some other convenient unit of source is taken — such as the individual function call in LISP.) The essence of interpretive execution is simply examining the source code and doing what it says.

Many people suppose incorrectly that interpreters work by translating each statement into machine code and then executing it, but this would be a very strange way to design a language processor — it would have all the complexities of a compiler but none of the advantages of a single once and for all translation.

As an example of interpretive execution, consider how an interpreter would process the statement:

C := A+B

The interpreter will initially scan the statement and determine that it is an assignment; it will then call one of its routines to evaluate the expression on the right. This routine will take the symbols A and B, determine where they are stored, obtain their current values and add them together. The interpreter will then take this calculated value and store it in the location used to hold data corresponding to the symbol C.

The actual code to execute the statement is thus contained within the interpreter itself: an expression evaluation routine, storage access routines, and so on. The interpreter contains a sufficient variety of routines to be able to execute every possible statement in the language.

Interpreting a statement is a relatively complex process, as it has to be scanned and analysed, symbols have to be searched for, and the actual demands of the statement must be carried out. It may thus involve several hundred machine instructions to interpret $C := A + B$, whereas in compiled object code, this statement would have been executed in just three machine instructions. Moreover, a crucial factor in interpretive execution is that each statement is interpreted *every time* it is encountered, so a statement in a loop may be interpreted many times.

For these reasons, it is not unusual for a program to take between ten and a hundred times more CPU time to execute with an interpreter than if it had been compiled. But there are many factors which may outweigh this: there was no compilation overhead before the program could be run; and if the program does a good deal of input/output, it may spend more time waiting for peripheral devices so the CPU overhead may be unimportant. On a single-user micro, probably no other use would have been made of any CPU time saved. Given also the greater simplicity of interpreters compared to compilers, there are many situations where interpretive execution may be desirable.

To a programmer who has been used to compilers, the use of an interpreter may seem strange. But in fact, the vast majority of commands issued, whether to humans or to machines, are normally interpreted and executed directly, rather than being translated first. If I give a friend directions to come to my home he is unlikely to translate my instructions into another language — rather, he will make sure he understands each instruction and then carry it out. If I write a program which can carry out many alternative functions, I will simply obtain the user's command and invoke a suitable routine accordingly — there would be no point in most cases in trying to translate the command into an individual sequence of machine instructions to execute it.

Interpretation is thus the simpler approach to achieving execution of a source program; it is only when an interpreter presents severe disadvantages that it is worth considering the need for a translator.

8.2 INTERPRETIVE LANGUAGES

Although it is possible to design an interpreter for almost any programming language, some languages are so complex that the overheads of interpretive execution would be so large as to make it impracticable. This can arise where, for example, the whole program (or large parts of it) have to be scanned before each statement can be correctly interpreted.

By contrast, certain languages have been designed over the years with the specific object of being interpreted. We shall briefly look at four, and then discuss some principles.

8.2.1   BASIC

BASIC is probably the most widely used interpreted language, although part of the ease of interpretation arises from its use of line numbers and its lack of strong facilities for program structuring (at least in the standard language).

BASIC interpreters are usually combined with editors, so that the program can be modified and run immediately. It is possible to write adequate BASIC editor/interpreters that occupy as little as 16 Kbytes of memory on a Z80 processor; even in as little as 4 Kbytes if a few language limitations are imposed. This means that BASIC interpreters can easily be held in read-only memory on low-cost home microcomputers without disks. However, more advanced BASIC interpreters are widely used on business microcomputers for many one-off applications that require rapid development, and to some extent on large machines too.

Much of the simplicity arises from the fact that statements begin with a keyword which immediately indicates the statement type: there is no complex syntax analysis needed to identify the statement type. Statements begin with PRINT, INPUT, DATA, IF, REM and similar easily handled keywords. Originally, even the assignment statement was identified by the keyword LET, but current versions of BASIC make this optional — any statement that does not begin with a recognised keyword is necessarily an assignment.

In addition, the fact that every statement carries a line number and that these are in ascending order not only makes it possible to have a very simple line editor, but also means that at execution there is relatively low overhead in searching for destinations of branches. In languages which allow symbolic identifiers for labels, the interpreter will often have to scan the whole program looking for a given label whenever a branch is encountered.

The popularity of BASIC has led to the development of BASIC compilers on many machines, to allow the production of applications where performance is more critical, but there are some important differences between compiled and interpretive execution.

When the program is run interpretively, there is no initial symbol table or variable storage — this is built as execution proceeds. Thus the array dimension statement:

20 DIM S(100)

would be taken by the interpreter as a request to allocate storage (dynamically) for 100 array elements whereas the compiler would take this as a declarative statement and allocate static storage accordingly, prior to execution. As a consequence, the interpreter will generate an error ('array already dimensioned') if processing comes back to this statement, whereas the compiler would be unconcerned, since no machine code is generated for a DIM statement. But the interpreter, because it allocates storage at run time, has no problem with:

```
10 INPUT N
20 DIM S(N)
```

whereas variable dimensions may be unacceptable to the compiler, as they cannot be handled with static storage.

8.2.2   APL

APL (A Programming Language) although written as a procedural language, with assignment statements and so on, is in concept quite close to the functional programming languages. Through provision of a large number of special operators (many denoted by Greek letters or other special symbols) a wide range of functions can be invoked, particularly powerful for processing entire arrays in a single operation. It is thus brief to write and very powerful for programs involving manipulation of tabulated data.

APL can be interpreted efficiently for several reasons. The first reason is that the use of special symbols for different operations means that operations are immediately identified by a character code; the extensive lexical analysis needed in other languages is greatly reduced. A second reason is that because operations are so powerful, performing what would take several statements in a loop in many other languages, the interpretation overhead is much lower as a great deal of execution is achieved for the effort of analysing each statement. There are also factors such as the scope rules in APL which are dynamic (dependent on which procedures are being called at run time) rather than based on the static format of where procedures are placed textually — this means the interpreter does not have to scan the whole source program to sort out issues of scope (one of the major problems that arises in attempting interpretive execution of many block-structured languages).

Some manufacturers have even built facilities into the CPU hardware to assist the rapid execution of APL operations, thereby making interpretation of APL very efficient indeed.

8.2.3   LISP

LISP (LISt Processing language) is a functional language widely used for artificial intelligence work. It can be used to process a wide range of pointer-based list structures; in fact a LISP program is itself written as a list — the function calls to be executed are defined by means of a list structure, denoted using many levels of parentheses.

The LISP interpreter is called EVAL (short for evaluate) and a program is executed simply by calling the function EVAL with the program as an argument. All functions can be used recursively: the interpreter itself evaluates functions by recursive calls which allow it to process the list structure that makes up a program.

The fact that programs and data are both lists means that they can be used interchangeably; in particular a program can create list structures which are then submitted as arguments to EVAL (called recursively). This is the key to its use in artificial intelligence, as a LISP program can itself generate further processing which could not have been written in the first place by the original programmer.

Such an approach, where the program may be extended as processing proceeds, can be handled quite easily with an interpreter. Since the program source is simply data to an interpreter, there is no particular problem if this is modified as processing proceeds.

Where this aspect is used, it would be impossible for LISP to be compiled, as the effect of changing or extending the program while it is running would require the generation of different machine code, which is impossible if the compiler is no longer present. In practice, LISP compilers do exist, but if they allow the interchangeability of program and data then either the compiler is re-invoked at run time, or a LISP interpreter is incorporated into the run-time environment.

However, for self-modifying programs, interpretation clearly represents the straightforward approach.

8.2.4   Prolog

Prolog programming involves specifying *facts* (about objects and their relationships to one another), defining logical *rules* about the world that determine when certain properties apply, and asking *questions*. Variables are used to allow rules to be expressed in general terms, rather than only in relation to specific objects.

The language processor attempts to infer the possible answers to the questions by scanning the base of facts and rules, in accordance with certain criteria. The facts and rules are called the **knowledge base** and the program which infers the answers is known as the **inference engine**. The whole operation is usually interactive, with new rules, facts and questions being entered once the answers to previous questions are seen.

The inference engine scans the knowledge base in a fixed order, attempting a matching process, which should eventually yield values for the variables in the question.

The Prolog program itself is clearly non-procedural: one cannot talk about statement-by-statement execution. Execution is achieved by implementing the inference engine as an interpreter which searches the knowledge base as required. There would be little point in trying to compile a Prolog program, because the processing that is needed cannot be determined in advance; it is only by applying inference to the knowledge base that the required processing emerges.

Prolog, therefore, is necessarily interpreted; the only translation that may be possible is to convert the Prolog source into an internal representation that allows more efficient interpretation.

8.2.5   General principles of interpretive languages

From the above examples it is clear that there are some languages, particularly in the fifth generation, where interpretation is the *only* way of achieving execution due to the impossibility of translating the program into a fixed sequence of instructions.

For third-generation languages that could in principle be either compiled or interpreted, there are certain language features which make interpretation a reasonably efficient proposition; for others, the overheads would be unacceptable in normal use.

Interpretive languages serve to blur the distinction between declarative and executable statements which is so important to a compiler. In Prolog, the whole program would be regarded as declarative, whereas in BASIC, the whole program could be seen as executable, but in both cases the program is simply input upon which the interpreter takes action.

8.3 STRUCTURE OF INTERPRETERS

Interpreters share a number of similarities with other language processors, but there are important differences. In the following discussion we will concentrate on the operation of an interpreter for a conventional statement-based procedural language such as BASIC, as a Prolog interpreter, for example, whilst having much in common with other interpreters, will be fundamentally different in the processing it carries out.

A sophisticated interpreter will carry out lexical and syntax analysis on the source code in much the same way as a compiler, except that only one statement is considered at a time — once the statement is fully parsed it is executed and then forgotten. The fundamental difference from a compiler is that there is no code generator; execution is carried out directly from the parse tree. It is very simple to write a recursive routine, which actually *evaluates* an expression in its tree form, rather than converting it to another form such as reverse Polish.

In practice, many interpreters will not go so far as building full parse trees (except possibly for expressions) but will use more informal approaches that lead to more rapid interpretation. For example, most BASIC interpreters will consist of an initial statement examination routine which then calls one of many subroutines to handle each of the different statement types. The initial examination routine will do little more than look for the initial keyword indicating the statement type and then use a CASE type structure to invoke the required routine.

A current statement indicator is maintained by the interpreter to mark the position in the source code where execution has reached. After a statement is executed the indicator will be advanced to the next statement, except where a loop or branch statement has been encountered.

When variables are encountered in the source, the interpreter will place them in a symbol table, in a similar way to other language processors. But whereas a compiler would just use the symbol table to indicate an address corresponding to each symbol, the interpreter may actually put the *value* of a variable in the table (or at least a pointer to the actual value).

Thus, for example, when the interpreter encounters the BASIC statement:

10 X = 1

then if X has not been encountered previously, it is placed in the symbol table. As the interpreter executes the statement, the effect is to store the value 1 against X in the table. If a subsequent statement reads:

50 Y = X * 2

then the value of X can be retrieved from the table, multiplied by 2, and the result stored in the symbol table entry for Y.

In order to locate values of variables, an interpreter has to search the symbol table every time a variable name is encountered. If there are a large number of variables in the program, the symbol table accessing can account for the largest part of the time taken to interpret each statement. The various measures discussed on section 3.6 for improving symbol table performance are thus of even greater importance in an interpreter than they are in a translator.

It is often quite critical, too, for an interpreter to make very efficient use of the available memory, because at run time, the interpreter itself, the program source code, the symbol table, and program data, all have to be accommodated in memory together.

8.4   COMPARISON OF COMPILATION AND INTERPRETATION

The choice as to whether a compiler or an interpreter is most suited to a given task is by no means clear cut. Some of the relative advantages and disadvantages of each approach have already been mentioned, but there are other factors which need to be considered. The following summarises some of the main advantages of each approach.

8.4.1   Advantages of compilers

The most significant advantage of compiling a program is the vastly greater run-time efficiency as compared to interpretation. With interpreted programs frequently taking at least ten times more CPU time, there is very often no real choice. For most major long-term applications, a compiled program is the only sensible approach, which is one of the reasons why interpreters have achieved much less attention. However, with falling hardware costs and many applications being limited by input/output speeds rather than CPU time, this argument is not as overwhelming as was once the case, particularly with languages like APL that can be interpreted quite efficiently.

A second major advantage of compilation is that the source code is not needed at run time. This allows much better usage of memory, as larger programs can be accommodated if only the object code is required to run the program. It is also very important for software vendors who are frequently reluctant to let end users have access to the source code.

A third major advantage is that the language processor itself, the compiler, is not needed at run time; only a small run-time environment is required. But an interpreted program cannot be run without the interpreter.

The need for an interpreter to be present at run time may substantially reduce the memory available for the program data, and also limits the scope for supplying the program to other users as they must already have the required interpreter before they can run the program. Such limitations do not apply to compiled programs, when only the object code and run-time environment have to be supplied.

Compilation is also chosen frequently in preference to interpretation because of all the flexibility for modular programming that is made possible by linkage editors. It is possible to design an interpreter that can handle multiple source code modules, but the process is rather large and clumsy, and is only viable if the source of all the modules can be held in memory together, which is rarely possible in very large programs. Writing different modules in different languages would be impossible, though, unless several interpreters were used together! For all these reasons, interpretation can work well for small and medium-sized programs, but very large programs must be compiled.

Another important benefit of compilation applies at the program development stage, as a compiler will perform a syntax check of the entire source code, and issue diagnostic messages accordingly. With an interpreter, lines of source code are not syntax checked until they are executed. If there is a portion of the program that is rarely executed, there may be syntax errors in the code which are not discovered until a very late stage in the testing, or even overlooked completely if the testing has been incomplete.

8.4.2   Advantages of interpreters

We have already noted that for certain languages, particularly in the artificial intelligence field, interpretation is the only meaningful way of achieving program execution, because it would be impossible to compile the program into a static sequence of machine instructions.

However, in cases where a choice does arise between compilers and interpreters, possibly the single most important reason why interpreters are used is their greater simplicity. The fact that an interpreter does not contain a code generator, but simply contains routines to execute the source code directly, means that an interpreter is usually a substantially smaller program than a compiler for the same language. It can typically be developed in under half the time required to write a compiler for the language, given that the code generator is usually the most complex part of the compiler to write, and an interpreter has no need for a separate run-time environment.

This means that interpreters are very popular for the experimental implementation of new languages, and for provision as program development tools on machines with limited memory.

Secondly, there is little doubt that program development with an interpreter is considerably simpler than with a compiler. There is no need for the separate stages of edit, compile, link edit, and execute which are needed with most program development using compilers. With an interpreter that typically incorporates an editor, the programmer moves directly from editing to executing the program. However, the biggest gains arise in debugging, because if a run-time error occurs, the interpreter is dealing directly with the source code and can highlight the source code line and variable name where the error arose. To provide such debugging features in a compiler requires considerable extra complexity. With the interpreter, the programmer can often enter statements for immediate execution in order to display the value of a variable, or set a special value for test purposes. The program can be changed very quickly and re-executed when bugs are found.

For non-computer professionals writing their own programs, an interpreter is thus very much more convenient, and many professional programmers also prefer the convenience of an interpreter for initial program testing and for small one-off applications.

Another more subtle advantage of an interpreter is that it is potentially machine independent. We noted that a compiler could be written in a high-level language, and could therefore be compiled to run on various machines, but the code generator would probably have to be completely re-written if it had to generate code for a different target machine. This issue does not arise with an interpreter, because it does not generate code. If an interpreter is written in a suitably portable high-level language, it can simply be re-compiled on a new machine, and an interpreter for the language concerned is then immediately available on the new machine. (We assume the existence of compilers for the language in which the interpreter is written. Although one could in theory run the interpreter interpretively using another interpreter, the overheads would be colossal.)

8.5   FOURTH-GENERATION LANGUAGES AND MIXED COMPILER/INTERPRETERS

So far we have considered compilers and interpreters as totally distinct kinds of language processors. However, there are many cases where compilers and interpreters are used together, or even incorporated into the same product. Although this applies in many other contexts, such a combination is particularly important in many fourth-generation languages (4GLs).

8.5.1   Partial compilation followed by interpretation

A good compromise can often be made between the relative advantages of compilers and interpreters, by *compiling* the source into an intermediate language similar to the C-language passed to a code generator and then *interpreting* the intermediate code.

This is much more efficient at run time, because the interpreter does not have the overhead of the full lexical and syntax analysis on each source statement every time it is encountered: that has been done once and for all. But the expense, complexity, and limitation to one machine, which applies to a code generator, is also avoided, by achieving final execution through an interpreter. Moreover, the programmer knows that the entire program has been syntax checked at the pre-compilation stage.

If the intermediate code is well designed for efficient interpretation, it is possible for the execution time to be little more than twice the execution time that would apply if the code had been translated directly to machine code, sometimes even less. For example, the overheads of symbol table searching can be completely removed if the intermediate code contains an actual data address (or offset in a table) instead of a source variable name. Yet, the fact that execution is still related to the source variables, for example, means that the interpreter's advantages in debugging can be retained.

Partial compilation followed by interpretation is a very convenient way of implementing programming languages quickly on new machines.

Such an approach is also used in many 4GL products which offer an interactive program development environment. As commands, screen layouts, file formats, and so on are defined, the product translates these to internal forms which can be accessed efficiently at run time. However, the actual execution of a fourth-generation program is most often achieved by an interpreter.

When implemented well, this approach makes it possible to build efficient systems, though most 4GLs emphasise development productivity rather than run-time efficiency. In most cases it would be possible to compile a 4GL program (together with its screen formats and so on) directly into machine code, but few developers of such products have actually done so, if only because of the very high development costs this would involve.

Unfortunately though, a number of 4GL products are written with very little concern at all for efficiency, which makes them unsuitable for large applications involving frequent access to data, particularly in a multi-user environment. Some products fail to pre-compile the user's instructions to any extent, and thus have the full overheads of interpretation. The source to be interpreted may be held in disk files in a way that requires numerous disk accesses to execute a program. In a multi-user environment, many 4GL systems will load a copy of the program for every user, and sometimes even multiple copies of the interpreter, which makes huge demands on machine resources in an intensive environment.

The selection of a 4GL for the development of a large on-line system thus requires considerable attention to the implementation of the internal translation and interpretation functions that the product uses.

The use of partial compilation followed by interpretation is also very valuable in implementing many fifth-generation languages. Even though the final execution requires an interpreter, both LISP and Prolog can perform at a more acceptable level if the source is converted to a more efficient internal representation. However, the reason for using fifth-generation languages is usually to tackle problems which cannot easily be expressed in other forms, and it is accepted that there will be major demands on machine resources in execution. That is one reason why the use of hardware with parallel processing facilities is important to allow large artificial intelligence problems to be tackled with reasonable execution times.

8.5.2   Provision of compiler and interpreter for the same language

One of the ways of achieving the advantages of the interpreter in program development together with the advantages of the compiler for live execution is to use both at different times. If an interpreter and compiler can be devised which process exactly the same source language, a program can be developed and tested using the interpreter, and then when it is working, can be compiled for live use.

This is commonly used on micro-computers with BASIC programs: a program is initially used under the interpreter, but if it is seen to have long-term value it may be compiled.

The disadvantage of this is that there will normally be some small differences between the source language accepted by the compiler and interpreter. There may be one or two statements to support extra facilities in the compiler environment. Equally, features like arrays with variable dimensions may be acceptable to the interpreter, so the program is tested and working, and then the relevant statement is rejected by the compiler.

Attempts have been made to overcome this by a single software developer producing both a compiler and interpreter whose source languages are identical (except perhaps for one or two clearly documented features specific to one environment or the other). The most widely known case was the provision of two PL/I compilers for the IBM 370: a checkout compiler (actually a pre-compiler plus interpreter) for debugging and an optimising compiler for producing final highly efficient object code, but other suppliers have taken similar approaches in the microcomputer environment.

The disadvantage is that it is almost impossible for the developers to avoid some differences in the actual effect of executing in the two environments, even if it is only because the compiler and interpreter will have to have different ways of handling run-time errors. It is thus always necessary to carry out some testing of the program in its compiled form, even though it has previously been tested under the interpreter, and this offsets some of the time saved. Moreover, if there are more subtle undocumented situations where code performs slightly differently in the two environments (perhaps because of different understandings of the specification by the two development teams) the use of two language processors can be more a source of frustration than of improved productivity.

However, it is clear that both compilers and interpreters have their place in program development, and with the increasing use of fourth and fifth generation languages, the demands on different types of language processors will continue. Only by using the best tools for the job in each situation will it be possible to achieve the levels of program reliability which software engineering now requires.

FURTHER READING

Berry, R. E. *Programming language translation* (Ellis Horwood, 1982).

Brown, P. J., *Writing interactive compilers and interpreters* (John Wiley, 1979).

Martin, J. *Applications development without programmers* (Prentice-Hall, 1982).

Terry, P. D. *Programming language translation — a practical approach* (Addison-Wesley, 1986).

Part II
Operating systems

9

Introduction to operating systems

9.1 INTRODUCTION

As you will have gathered by now, the topic of language processors covers a wide range of software development activities. The same is true of operating systems. The distinction between the two themes is somewhat arbitrary, because both are necessary for successful software development. Neither, however, is sufficient for a full understanding of systems software: there is little point in having an operating system without applications to run on it (although some computer enthusiasts would disagree) and very few applications can run on a *stand-alone* basis (that is, without operating system support).

The first part of the book has concentrated on a study of language processors and associated system utilities. In invoking these, the operating system will have been made use of implicitly (for example by running a pre-written command file) or explicitly (by some interaction with the console when the editor, compiler or linker were invoked).

This part of the book will be concerned with the structure and function of the underlying operating system — what its various components are and how they work together.

9.2 OPERATING SYSTEMS — AN OVERVIEW

9.2.1 Purposes

An operating system, whether simple or complex, has a number of primary purposes.

Firstly, to provide an interface between the user and the computer system. This may be via a typed command language or a direct manipulation (windowing) system, or a combination of both. The interface should be designed in such a way that the user's intentions should be captured by the system in an unambiguous way, and the results of each operation should be signalled clearly, especially if there has been an error by the system or the user.

Secondly, to provide a range of useful services that application programs can use, such as time/date calculations, mathematical routines, memory management, specialised input/output etc. These services are accessed in a standard way by calling the system from an applications program. Most high-level languages do not provide such facilities as part of their definition, but they do provide mechanisms for accessing external routines of this kind, either by source code libraries which can be included in a program; or by the provision of a run-time library which is searched by the linker and the appropriate modules included where necessary. It is significant that the C-language, which has been designed to be *portable* across processors, has very extensive sets of source code and run-time libraries.

Thirdly, to provide a range of utilities for software development and project management. This can range from a basic provision of editor, linker and debugger through useful utilities like MAKE (which recompiles and re-links modules that have been changed at source) to a full IPSE (integrated project support environment) or even a specialised IPSE such as APSE (Ada project support environment).

For a small programming project, which can incorporate all the necessary code within one source code module, the advantages of such assistance may not be apparent; but when a team of people are producing code to a variety of specifications, at different times, and at different stages of testing, a high value is placed upon the provision of these utilities.

An important secondary goal of an operating system is to ensure that the user is presented with a clear, consistent and rational interface and is not hindered by unintelligible error messages, unmemorable syntax or unpredictable behaviour on the part of an application. This is equally important whether considering the behaviour of the user interface or the syntax of system calls embedded in an applications program.

In short, an operating system should be **transparent** to the user's intentions, and be **usable**.

9.2.2   Virtual machine

Fig. 9.1 shows how the functionality of a typical operating machine can be conceptualised — in layers. An ideal operating system could be visualised as a virtual machine that is offered to users and applications, enabling services to be accessed in a standard way which does not require an understanding of the underlying mechanisms.

Although the operating systems we will be studying range from quite simple (MS-DOS) to complex (Unix) it is important to understand that, conceptually, they are quite similar. The complexity lies generally in the range of commands and system services available. Other features such as multi-user support add their own complexity.

9.2.3   Layers
9.2.3.1   *User interface*
The first contact that most people have with a computer system is via the user interface, generally comprising a screen and keyboard, so this is where we will start.

This outermost layer is the only way that a human being can interact with the system, so it must handle all the functionality that the system can offer

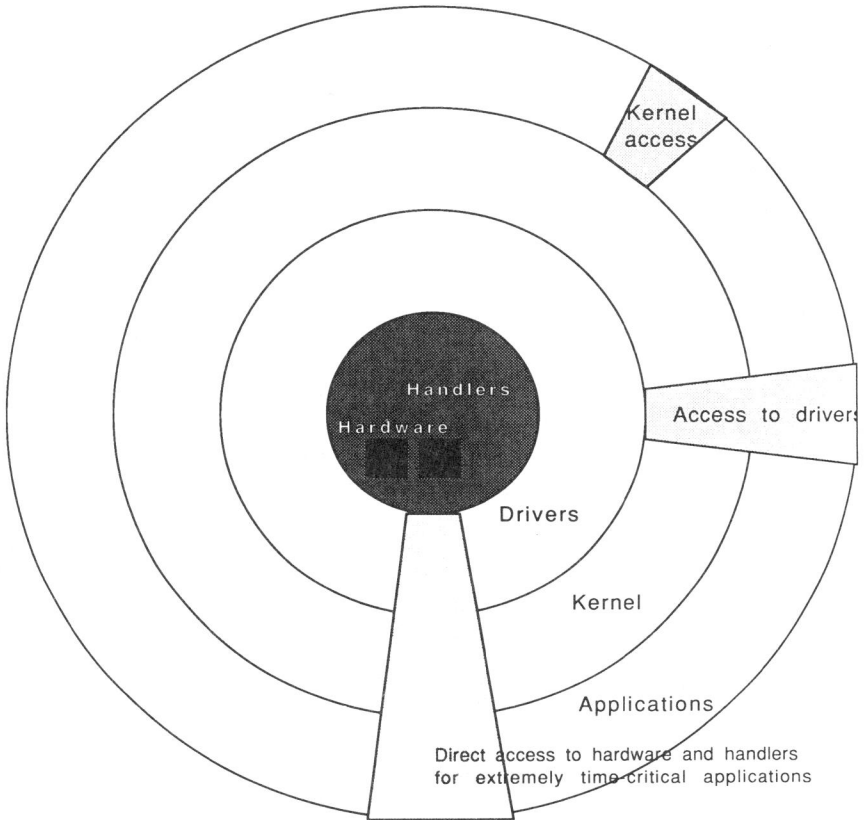

Fig. 9.1 — Operating system layers.

the user. Interaction will generally be in the form of user commands and system messages, so the **command line interpreter** (CLI) is an important component. Its function is to accept command lines (from the keyboard or from a command file), check their syntax for correctness, and make the appropriate requests to the operating system. These requests might be simple (for example, a time of day command will translate into a few system requests, not forgetting that the result has to be displayed on the screen) or complex (for example, obtaining a sorted directory listing).

In some systems, the CLI can be overwritten by an application program to provide extra memory space, as it is not used when an application is running).

As mentioned above, command lines can also be taken from a file. This facility, generally termed **batch operation**, is a useful extension to the CLI. If conditional branches and tests are included, then an application can be made to run on a **turnkey** basis where the operator has minimal intervention; this is desirable if novices are to operate the system.

9.2.3.2 Kernel

This component has some interesting constraints to work under. As the core of the operating system, it comprises a complex set of interrelated processes, particularly in a multitasking system; however, being permanently resident, it is required to be as small as possible.

It is generally accessed from the CLI or applications programs by means of a **software interrupt**, or **trap** with request parameters being passed in processor registers or on a stack. Some high-level languages (for example, DEC languages, Turbo Pascal) have extensions to allow this to be done from within the language itself, and this is a useful feature which will be exploited in the examples.

The major function of the kernel is to carry out the system requests received from applications programs in an orderly way so that they do not interfere with one another, or with the rest of the system; and also to translate logical requests for data or activities (e.g. 'Read a line from this input file') into a form which is closer to the physical reality (e.g. 'read the next 3 blocks from a diskette'). Generally, there is still a degree of hardware independence — there is little point in having to reassemble the kernel if some hardware device is changed; it is better to leave this to the lower levels.

9.2.3.3 Handlers and drivers

These occupy the two layers of software which are closest to the underlying hardware. There is some confusion regarding the distinction between handlers and drivers; often the terms are used interchangeably. We will assume that a process which deals **directly** with the hardware (that is by communicating directly with hardware ports for commands and data) is called a handler; and a process which has some degree of hardware independence (for example, switching a logical stream of data between different serial ports) is a driver.

9.2.4 Operating system commands

The syntax of operating system commands will now be discussed in more detail.

9.2.4.1 Command handling in MS-DOS

If an MS-DOS system diskette is booted, the user is confronted with the following prompt:

       A>

indicating that the default (assumed) drive for subsequent operations is the one that the system was **booted** (loaded) from.

This prompt is issued by the CLI, which has been loaded from the file COMMAND.COM. The CLI then makes a system request for a line of input from the keyboard. In other words, the system is idling — being a single-user system, there is nothing else for it to do. When the line is input, it is first checked to see whether the command it contains matches any **built-in** command (certain frequently used operations are permanently resident for speed). If it does, that command is executed. If it does not, then the assumption is made that the command represents the name of an executable program file, and that file is loaded and run. Such a command is termed a *transient command* because it does not remain permanently resident.

Some examples of built-in commands are:

> TIME, DATE, DIR(ectory), DEL(ete), COPY

Some examples of transient commands are:

> BACKUP, RESTORE, CHKDSK (check a disk), SORT

9.2.4.2 Command syntax in MS-DOS

Certain commands listed above do not make sense on their own — COPY, DEL and SORT obviously require some kind of **argument**, generally a filename. In addition, a transient command may be resident on a different drive to the default drive; or an argument may require some kind of qualifier. The conventions used to indicate what comprises a legal command line constitute the **syntax**.

Certain special symbols are used in the syntactic description of command lines:

[item]	— The inclusion of this item is optional
/item	— The / is a delimiter (separator) and the item is a qualifier
<CR>	— (carriage return) — This normally terminates command line input
item:	— The item is a device such as PRN: (printer), COM1: (serial I/O)
COMMAND	— The command itself

The full specification of the DIR command in MS-DOS, for example, is:

> DIR [d:][path][filename[.ext]][/P][/W]

thus

> DIR/W/P <CR>

produces a wide directory listing, pausing between pages, and

> DIR A:\DOCS*.BAK <CR>

produces a listing of all the files with the extension .BAK in the subdirectory DOCS on drive A. The '*' is a wildcard character (see below).

It is usually convenient to specify groups of files rather than individual files, so

> DIR *.DOC

lists all files with the extension .DOC, and

> DIR *.P??

lists all files whose extension begins with 'P'.

In the next chapter we will see how tree-structured directories ease the file-grouping problem.

9.2.4.3 Batch files in MS-DOS

As we noted in section 9.2.3.1, batch files are useful. In the simplest case, the input to the CLI is merely taken from a text file. This is adequate when it is only required to 'replay' a set of commands. The usefulness of this feature can be enhanced, however, if the CLI can interpret *meta-commands* such as IF, GO TO and so on. Using these features, simple password protection, more friendly error messages etc. can be incorporated.

Very often, a specially named batch file (AUTOEXEC.BAT in MS-DOS) is looked for when the system boots. This can be used to set up 'favourite' environments, perform simple housekeeping (such as deleting all .BAK files older than three months), or to improve system security by performing an automatic tape backup after a particular application is run.

To complete the overview of operating systems, it is necessary to look in greater detail at the services offered by the system — at the kernel level, and also in terms of the software utilities provided with the system.

9.2.5 Kernel services

9.2.5.1 Character I/O

Input/output to and from character devices such as screens, printers and keyboards is a very common requirement. A range of services looks after single-character I/O, edited (line) input, line output and so on.

These devices can be accessed at a number of different levels by appropriate services; for example, there is a high-level service which treats the screen and keyboard as a single bi-directional device (CON:), which could be logically redirected to a serial port; and a low-level service which writes characters specifically to the video display.

9.2.5.2 Filing system I/O

Although devices and files can be considered logically equivalent in certain respects, it is convenient to treat disk file access and maintenance services separately. Services exist to open, close, create and delete files on disk; to change certain attributes of files (such as whether they are protected from deletion); and to perform certain operations on the file directory, such as searching it. These topics are treated in more detail in Chapters 10 and 11.

9.2.5.3 Command line services

In certain situations, it is useful for an application to be able to access the command line which invoked it. It can then check for any additional arguments that the user has input (the text following the command, if any, is known as the **command tail**).

More advanced operating systems will **parse** the command tail into its constituent parts for convenience, and will provide a system service to access these **tokens**.

9.2.5.4 Resource allocation
Sometimes a specific device (such as a tape deck) or facility is required by a user, or an application may need exclusive use of a device in order to avoid multiple access to that device. This problem will not generally occur in a single-user system unless it is also a multitasking system.

9.2.5.5 Memory services
In a simple system such as MS-DOS, a normal application will not need to reserve memory for itself, as only one application runs at a time. The exception is that applications which terminate and stay resident (TSR) — for example, pop-up utilities — must indicate to the system how much memory they need so that they are not overwritten by the loading of subsequent applications.

In more complex multitasking and multi-user systems, memory access is not such a simple activity. Allocation will have to be arbitrated between users of different priorities, and there are additional requirements such as the protection of blocks of memory from certain kinds of access. In a multi-user system, the kernel code itself must be protected from any kind of write activity, and the data areas from reading or writing by any process but the kernel itself.

9.2.5.6 Process control
In a multitasking system (for the detailed discussion see Chapter 12), there must be a facility for an application to create new processes (tasks), to stop or remove processes, and to arrange for communications between processes. This is a job which can only be performed by the kernel, as it is the only element which has a global knowledge of all the processes in the system and how they are interacting.

9.2.5.7 Error trapping
A large number of system- and processor-related events, which would normally disrupt system activities, or indeed crash the system, should be intercepted, or **trapped**, and passed back to the process which caused them, in an orderly way.

For example, an attempt to run a program which contains an illegal (or corrupted) instruction should not result in the halting of the system when that instruction is encountered. Instead, a hardware interrupt is caused, which is vectored to an error-handling routine in the kernel. This routine will look up the appropriate error message and display it on the user's screen. The faulty program or process will be aborted.

Other situations which are handled in a similar way include: addressing errors (a page fault in a virtual memory system may be regarded as a special, recoverable case of this), floating point calculation errors (such as an attempt to divide by 0), input/output errors, and so on.

The process of error trapping illustrates very well the intimate and orderly relationship that must exist between hardware and software if an operating system is to work reliably.

9.2.6 Utilities

The third area of functionality that an operating system offers comprises a range of utilities for such activities as software development, document preparation and inter-user communication, in addition to the normal complement of editors and compilers. In larger systems, on-line mail, instant communication (*phone*) utilities and conferencing services may also be offered.

Many utilities become standard facilities after a period of use and improvement: notable examples are the text processing programs for the Unix system: nroff (a text formatter), troff (a text formatter capable of driving a phototypesetting machine), style (which produces various measures of writing style), and so on.

9.3 CONCLUSION

Operating systems offer a rich set of resources to help users make best use of the underlying machine. The basic elements are: a command line interpreter, or other user interface, which provides a means to access the facilities of the system at the user level; a kernel, which offers various facilities and services to the CLI and to applications; and a set of utilities to assist in software development and document preparation.

FURTHER READING

Lister, A. M. *Fundamentals of operating systems* (Macmillan, 3rd edn, 1985).
Barker, Peter J. *System software* (Blackie, 1980).

10

Files and directories

10.1 INTRODUCTION

Files, and the way in which they are stored and accessed, represent one of the most important topics in a study of operating systems. All the permanent data storage within the system resides in files, and both the system and the user have an interest in their reliable maintenance.

10.2 FILES

Logically, a file can be quite simple (such as a stream of text) or quite complex (a file of complex records, each of which can be directly accessed). A stream file may also take the form of characters from a physical device, such as a page scanner or a modem. In physical terms, all files spend their lives as a collection of sectors on a diskette or hard disk. A file from a device, of course, does not exist in any physical sense until the stream is opened.

The way in which the *user* view of a file is translated into a *system* view is shown in Fig. 10.1. It should be noted that the user view of a file as described here is becoming increasingly adopted due to its simplicity. The only concept that the user needs to understand is the file pointer, which gives an addressing resolution of 1 byte, and a theoretical capacity of 4 Gigabytes when 32-bit pointers are used. This scheme is used, for example, by the Unix operating system and by current versions of MS-DOS.

It is interesting to note that this scheme, whether by accident or design, is suitable for true virtual memory systems in which no distinction is made between main memory and mass storage.

The discussion of file storage and access will centre on the MS-DOS operating system, for the following reasons: it is simple in concept and operation; the structures and processes can be investigated without risk to other users (there are none); and the file system has been adopted without change in the recently released OS/2 Standard and Extended Editions.

10.2.1 Types of file

It is convenient to group files in terms of the purposes for which they are used. In certain situations these distinctions are ignored, as, for example, when a text file is loaded by a debugger for inspection at the byte level. This

User Level

" *I Wandered lonely as a cloud*........."

String

DOS Kernel level

File Buffer (s)

BIOS level

Sector Buffer

Driver
(Low level routine)

Sectors on disk

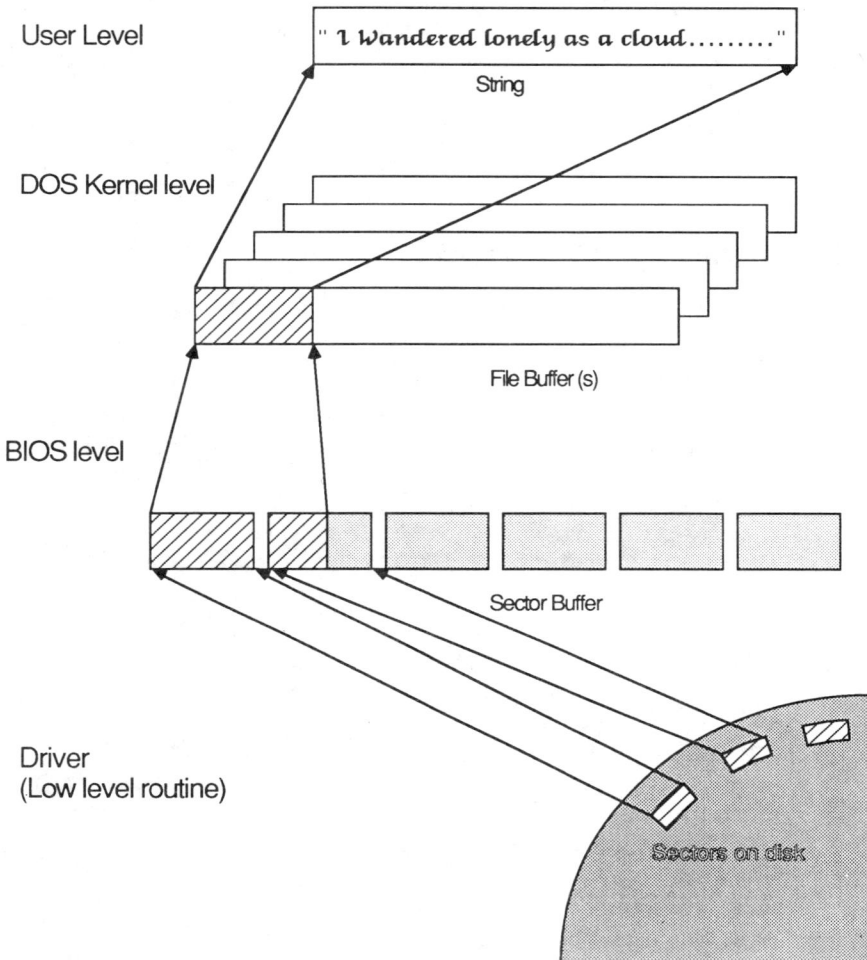

Fig. 10.1 — Levels of file processing and logical to physical mapping.

cannot be done, however, when a file is to be loaded and run as a program. Even the simplest operating system will check the file extension and refuse to load and run it if it is the wrong type.

Generally speaking, two broad types of file can be distinguished, whether structured or not. **ASCII** files consist of characters, both printable and control, which make up the ASCII character set. As there are 128 defined characters in this set, all the characters can be represented by using seven bits (0–127) in each code. A normal ASCII file can thus be typed on a console or printed on a printer without producing bizarre effects. The term *ASCII* has increasingly been used to indicate a 'pure text' file, whether the character codes are ASCII or some other code such as EBCDIC (extended binary code for digital information communication) which is used, among others, by IBM.

Binary files contain all possible eight-bit combinations (0–255) and no character has any special significance with regard to how the file itself should be interpreted. Program code files will therefore always be binary files. Note that the Extended character set for the IBM personal computer uses the eighth bit to identify 128 *graphics* characters which are used to construct boxes, lines etc. It would not, however, be correct to identify a file of such characters as a *binary* file: the control characters would still be meaningful.

Some operating systems distinguish between file types by including information within the file itself; others do not. One consequence of this is that, in the latter kind of system, a file could be renamed with the wrong extension and loaded. The consequences are generally fatal to a simple system.

The main types of file in MS-DOS are listed below. Note that these types are not specified formally by Microsoft, but represent a convenient distinction. Additionally, there are very many third-party software products which improve or enhance standard system programs, and which have their own file types.

(a) Text files, which have no particular structure; the file is interpreted as a stream of ASCII characters which can be sent directly to a screen, printer or disk file. The end of the file is signified by the ASCII EOF character (CTRL/Z, 26 decimal) and the final physical sector of the file is generally filled to the end with EOF characters. There are thus two ways of detecting the end of a text file: logically, with EOF, and physically, by 'running off the end' of the file.

(b) Absolute program files (*.COM) which load at a fixed address in memory, normally just above the operating system itself. Most system transient commands reside in files of this type, as (i) the files are smaller (see Type (c) and (ii) only one can be resident at a time, so there is no benefit to be obtained from making them relocatable. The command line interpreter (CLI) in the MS-DOS system is such a file and is called COMMAND.COM. The first block (256 bytes) of each .COM file comprises a header known as the program segment prefix (see next item).

(c) Relocatable program files (*.EXE). The code that these files contain has to be relocated by the operating system loader (see Chapter 7), and some other housekeeping has to be done, before the program can run. The relocation information is contained at the beginning of the file, in a section known as the program segment prefix, or PSP.

This is a block of information comprising the first 256 bytes of the program image. The PSP consists of several fields, some of which are described below:

(1) A software interrupt instruction which terminates the program.

(2) The memory requirements of the program in 16-byte quantities.

(3) The address of the program's termination routine.

(4) The address of the program's error handling routine.

(5) The address of a routine which handles breaks (i.e. panic buttons).

(6) A pointer to the *environment strings*, which are useful variables shared by the operating system and the program — for example, a default directory name.

(7) A pointer to any string entered on the command line which invoked the program (for example, SORT FRED).

Most application software to be found on MS-DOS systems is of this type, as no guarantee can be given by the system about where the application will run.

In the multitasking OS/2 system, the normal method of running a program (which is always of the relocatable type) additionally involves linking system references to actual system service addresses. This **dynalinking** process has been discussed in Chapter 8.

(d) Object files (*.OBJ) produced by a language processor. If an application is developed in a modular fashion (as it should be unless it is trivial), then the values of certain labels in the program will be unknown because they are declared in other modules. It is the function of the **linker** to resolve all the inter-module references (see Chapter 7).

An additional feature often found is an embedded command within the .OBJ file which instructs the linker to search a particular library.

(e) Library files (*.LIB) are maintained by a **librarian** program, and consist of collections of object modules, associated relocation information, and an index to the module names. This makes the linking process more convenient when large numbers of object modules are involved; it is also possible for the linker to include only the modules referenced by other modules, thus avoiding wasted space. The structure of a library file can be quite complex, as they are often highly compressed to save space and interpreted as a bit stream. The logic behind this is that, if only one bit of information is needed at a particular point, then this is all that will be used.

A fuller explanation of how file types (d) and (e) are used will be found in Chapter 15.

In addition, many specialist file structures are supported by certain application programs like spreadsheets, but these do not concern the operating system. They will be 'seen' by programs other than the application that generates them as text files or record-oriented files. Here is a list (by no means exhaustive) of file types commonly used in MS-DOS systems and applications:

System files:

File type	Assumed usage
*.COM	Absolute program code
*.EXE	Relocatable program code
*.SYS	System drivers or information
*.BAT	Batch command files (See Chapter 9)
*.OBJ	Relocatable program code

Language processor files:

*.BAS	BASIC interpreter code
*.COB	COBOL source code
*.MOD	Modula-2 source code
*.FOR	FORTRAN source code
*.PLI	PL/I source code
*.PAS	Pascal source code
*.INT	Intermediate code (for run-time interpreted code)

Application-specific files:

*.WKS	Lotus 1-2-3 Worksheet file
*.DBF	dBASE II/III database file
*.IDX	dBASE II/III index file

General file types:

*.DOC	Word processor text file or general documentation
*.BAK	Backup file
*.TXT	ASCII text file
*.ASC	Alternative to above

There are, in addition to the above, a number of *universal* file types used, for example, by applications which translate between application-specific data formats and an industry standard format such as the Data Interchange Format (*.DIF). This is a format which can be used by a number of different application packages such as spreadsheets and databases.

10.2.2 File operations

All files are affected by standard system commands like DEL, COPY etc. Evidently it does not make sense to TYPE a program file, or to RUN a text file. Certain system utilities assume a particular type of file, and attempt to interpret the contents accordingly: the linker expects object format code, and EXE2BIN (a utility which converts .EXE files to .COM files) assumes that its input file contains relocatable runnable code.

10.2.3 File attributes

In certain circumstances, it is desirable to protect files from writing or deletion, while making them available for reading. Often an operating system will keep a set of *hidden*, or *system*, files which are not listed by any directory operation and are hence invisible to the user. In the IBM PC-DOS operating system, for example, two files which contain low-level routines (IBMIO.COM and IBMDOS.COM) are hidden from normal directory listings.

The set of attributes that a file possesses is especially important if it must be shared by more than one user, either in a multi-user system or because it is available over a network. In this situation, the option must be available to the user to be selective about which other users are permitted to read, write, execute or delete the file.

In addition to the *static* attributes described above, which an application cannot alter, various types of **file** or **record locking** may be applied by the operating system on a dynamic basis. For example, there is generally no problem if more than one user wishes to open a file for reading, but if multiple users wish to write to the same file then a number of options must be considered. Should the file be locked to all users but the one who opened it, until it is closed (file locking)? Or could it be locked only for the writing of a record (record locking)? As an example, think about the file access problems which might occur in an international airline reservation system.

An additional complication is that some operating systems distinguish between privileged and non-privileged users, and deny certain types of access to users depending on their status (in an administrative sense).

10.3   FILE ACCESS MECHANISMS

This topic illustrates very well the relationship between logical and physical data structures and procedures. The user is only concerned with a file as a logical object which can be manipulated by the system or accessed by an application program. In the latter case, typical operations would include creating a new file, opening a file, closing a file, reading and writing a file etc.

The logical structure and procedures should be independent of any physical variables in the system, such as whether the files exist on a floppy diskette or hard disk, the size of the media, or (on a networked system) its geographical location.

At some stage, of course, a translation has to be made, and normally a component in each layer of the system (handler, driver, kernel, shell) will play some part.

10.3.1   Handler

The handler, which is only concerned with reading and writing physical tracks and sectors, may nevertheless have its own 'private' scheme of caching sectors in memory so that an unchanged sector is not read twice from disk even if the driver is 'dumb' enough to request it. Sometimes, the caching may take the form of a *track buffer* in which entire tracks are stored. This has an advantage in addition to rapid access of sectors within a track: it means that all the physically sequential sectors in a track can be read in one disk rotation without needing an *interleave factor* which staggers the sector numbering so that slow CPUs can keep up with the incoming data. Many flexible and hard disk controllers now have *read track* commands; some have several megabytes of on-board memory in which full tracks can be stored, which means that the handler can be simpler.

It should be borne in mind that the disk handler in a virtual memory system may also be involved in such activities as page swapping (see Chapter 12); this requires some very close co-operation between handlers and *intelligent* controllers. For example, it would be wasteful of time to move the disk head to an inner track just to pick up one sector — a *queue* of sectors to collect would be sent to the disk controller, and it would calculate its own access order to give the least head movement. Obviously system processes would be given priority over user processes. It is evident that designing efficient systems software requires active collaboration between hardware and software engineers.

Most handlers can deal with incoming and outgoing information *concurrently*, that is, they can initialise and 'prime' a hardware channel so that the actual data transfer occurs asynchronously and does not affect the main processor (via, for example, direct memory access (DMA)). The only interrupt in this case would be from the DMA controller to signal that the requested transfer had finished.

10.3.2   Driver
The driver has two tasks: to present the appropriate data and commands to the handler, in a form it expects; and to provide data to the kernel in an appropriate format. Thus a request from the kernel for 'read the next 2 clusters' would result in accesses to the file allocation table (see section 10.4.3) to determine the location of the clusters, followed by several requests to the handler for sectors at specific track and sector locations, followed by a repackaging of the data into clusters and a return to the kernel.

10.3.3   Kernel
The kernel maintains one or more file buffers, which may be regarded as a further stage in caching the data that an application uses. For each file that is opened, a buffer is reserved. If more buffers are available than are needed, they are appended together to provide more buffer space for large files.

The data in the file will be returned to the application as a string of the required number of bytes from a particular *byte-addressed* location, the byte pointer then being updated. The only 'knowledge' that the application has of the file is a handle number and a pointer.

To understand this process, refer to Fig. 10.1. The application program, written in Pascal, has requested a line of text from a file via a *readln* statement. We can now trace the resulting sequence:

The Pascal compiler generates the code to invoke a *read file*: system call, passing as its parameters the file handle and a 32-bit-long integer variable representing the number of bytes required.

After the software interrupt has been performed, the kernel copies the correct number of bytes from the appropriate buffer into the variable. If there is enough data in the file, the kernel will just return to the calling application.

If more data is required to satisfy the request, then the driver will have to be asked for the next **cluster**, or block, of data (see section 10.4.2). In a simple sequential file, this will just be the next available cluster. The driver (which is a **block-structured** driver in this case) is passed a cluster number and a pointer to an area into which the data should be deposited. The driver may have its own buffer, in which case the data can be supplied and a return made, or it may need to make a further request to the handler.

The handler is the lowest level of access, and only 'understands' physical track and sector numbers. The call from the driver will therefore be in the form of a request for, say, four sequential sectors. If a track has to be changed, then the call will have to be made twice.

A fuller discussion of driver and handler interaction will be found in the next chapter.

10.4   DIRECTORIES

The discussion of files assumed that we had some mechanism for accessing the files and for extracting attribute information. This is largely the concern of the file directories.

10.4.1   Simple directories

Fig. 10.2a illustrates a simple directory structure which has sufficed for such operating systems as RT-11 (a small, real-time operating system for DEC PDP-11 minicomputers) and microcomputers such as the BBC.

It will be seen that the directory is a list of paired filenames and disk locations; each file is assumed to consist of a number of **contiguous** sectors.

The advantage of such a scheme is that file loading is fast, as the sectors can be loaded without interruption until the end of the file is encountered. File access is also fast, as the file pointer can be advanced without having to calculate whether it is necessary to access a new area of the disk.

The major disadvantage is that, on deletion of a file, the space cannot be re-used unless the new file is shorter than the deleted one, otherwise the start of the next file would be obliterated. A result is that an arbitrary restriction has to be placed on the size of a newly-opened file, generally half the available free space; or, in the absence of such a scheme, a new file always has to begin at the end of the last file in the directory. To deal with this, some form of **compaction** is used, where the free disk space is made contiguous by moving all the files around.

A more advanced structure is seen in Fig. 10.2b. The file can be physically distributed over the media, and the directory entry will indicate a

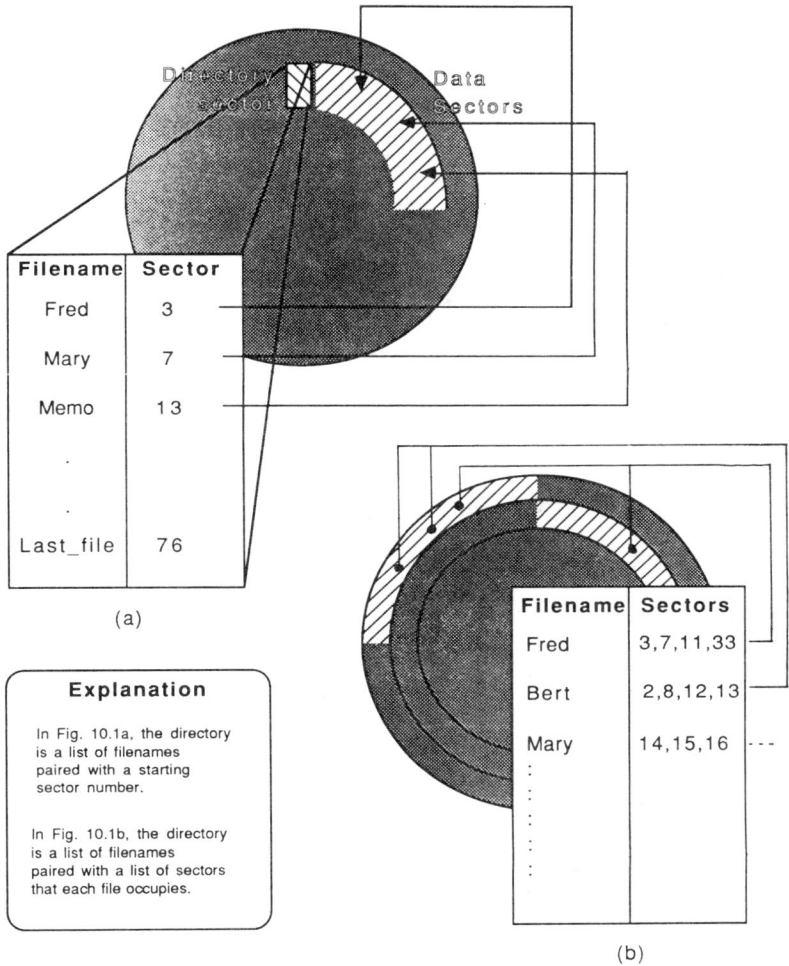

Filename	Sector
Fred	3
Mary	7
Memo	13
.	
.	
Last_file	76

(a)

Explanation

In Fig. 10.1a, the directory
is a list of filenames
paired with a starting
sector number.

In Fig. 10.1b, the directory
is a list of filenames
paired with a list of sectors
that each file occupies.

Filename	Sectors
Fred	3,7,11,33
Bert	2,8,12,13
Mary	14,15,16
:	
:	
:	

(b)

Fig. 10.2 — Directory structures.

list of sectors rather than a single starting sector. It can be seen that any file
can be extended as long as free space is available somewhere on the disk.
However, as files are created and deleted, gaps will appear. In a disk which is
heavily used, it can be seen that **fragmentation** will occur. In extreme cases,
this can noticeably impair performance. Additionally, the overhead of
maintaining a list of so many sectors could be unacceptable.

One solution to this problem would be to re-organise the disk periodically, but this would take time and it is not clear on what parameters this re-
organisation would be based if it were to be left to the operating system.
Presumably a 'fragmentation factor' could be maintained.

10.4.2   Clusters

An acceptable alternative, which has the merit of simplicity, is to group sectors together in **clusters** of 1,2,4 or more. A cluster of sectors is always dealt with as a unit by the operating system. A large cluster size reduces the problem of fragmentation (because the file is maintained in fewer, larger, chunks) and overhead (because fewer clusters need to be tracked). On the other hand, the minimum file size is then forced to be the cluster size, which could be a drawback if many small files are to be created. The ideal solution would be to vary the cluster size at the discretion of the user, generally at system installation (build) time.

There is a further advantage in the adoption of this scheme: reference to each cluster can be made by its offset from the first cluster on the disk, so the kernel need not concern itself with track and sector numbers but merely reference the relative cluster number. These are passed to the low-level drivers which finally carry out the translation to track, head and sector numbers.

This is the solution adopted by MS-DOS, and it is now time to consider the file access mechanisms in detail.

10.4.3   File allocation tables (FATs)

Fig. 10.3 indicates the structure of the first few sectors of a typical diskette. These contain all the information necessary to maintain the files on the disk.

The **root directory** consists of a list of 32-byte entries. If an application wishes to access a particular file, then the appropriate system call is issued. The system first attempts to match the required filename, in the form of a string of bytes, against each entry in the directory.

If this match is successful, the **starting cluster number** is looked up. This indicates both the relative location of the first cluster in the file **and** the location within the FAT. (At this point, the 'open' system call would return to the application with a **file handle** which is a unique number by which the file is referenced from now on. In the event of an error, the appropriate code would be returned.)

If a 'read' system call is now issued, then the first cluster is read into the internal buffer, and a note made of the value in the FAT entry. If only a few bytes are required by each 'read' call, then the data in this buffer will suffice for à while. Eventually, however, more data will have to be obtained from disk, and it will be in the next cluster.

The location of this cluster is the value that was noted when the previous cluster was accessed. This also gives us the next FAT entry number to reference. The process continues by stepping through the FAT until either an end-of-file value (FFFF Hex, −1 decimal) is seen, or a 'close' system call is issued, in which case the buffers are released for further use and the file handle made available for re-use.

Fig. 10.4 illustrates two examples — (a) is the structure of a short file on a new disk, and (b) a larger file in a more fragmented state. Note how the FAT entries are not contiguous. Their precise location is immaterial as long as the chain is unbroken.

Root Directory Entry   Bytes

BOOT RECORD	
FAT 1	
FAT 2	
ROOT DIRECTORY	
DATA	

Root Directory Entry	Bytes
Filename (FILE)	0 - 7
Extension (.DAT)	8 - 10
Attributes	11
Reserved (RFU)	12 - 21
Time	22 - 23
Date	24 - 25
Start Cluster	26 - 27
Size	28 - 31

FAT   Entry Number

1
2
3
4
5
6
7
8
9
10
11
12

41
42
43
44
45

KEY

Used
Unused
Last Cluster

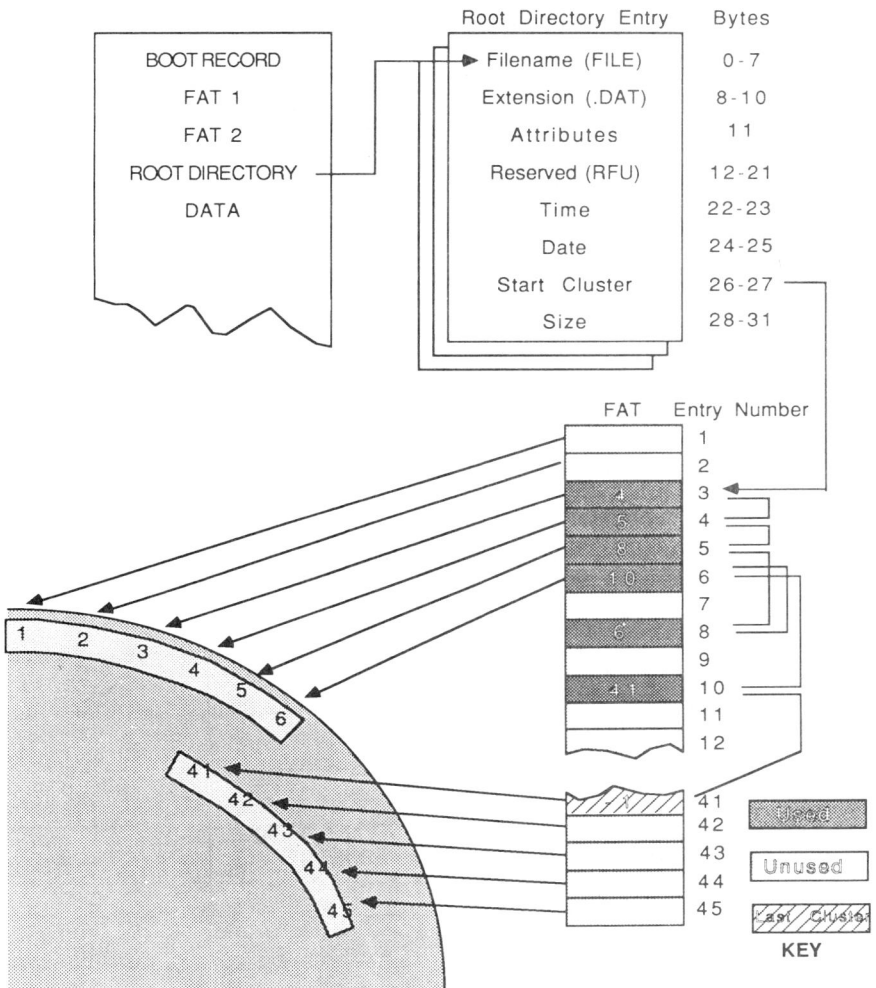

Fig. 10.3 — File allocation tables.

The type of data structure used by the FATs is known as a **linked list** and is used very commonly in operating systems and in computer science generally.

10.5   CONCLUSION

Files are central to operating system activities; they are used to store data, programs and temporary data. The way they are viewed logically is generally quite different to the way they are organised physically. It is one function of the operating system to make this transition, and offer a 'transparent' file service.

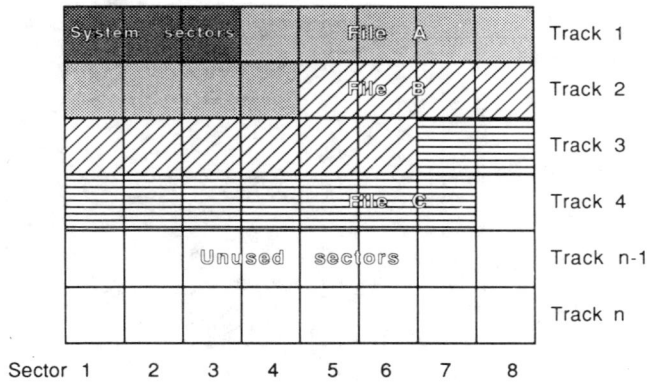

.. after some use (copying, extension, deletion)..

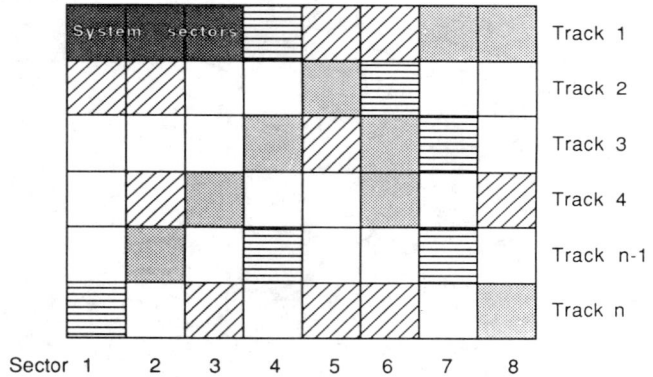

Fig. 10.4 — File fragmentation.

FURTHER READING

The Microsoft Press publish a number of books which explore the technical aspects of file access in MS-DOS: the books by Peter Norton are recommended, specifically:

Norton Peter *A Programmer's Guide to the IBM PC* (Microsoft Press, 1985).

11

Input and output

11.1 INTRODUCTION

You will recall that it is convenient to regard an operating system as comprising a number of layers, with the outermost layer being designed to work with the human user, and the innermost layer looking after the hardware. This layering helps to ensure that the operation of the system is 'transparent', that is, its workings do not get in the way of the users' intentions. In the previous chapter a useful distinction was made between **logical** and **physical** operations on files; this distinction is even more important when considering other kinds of input and output. Logically, the user would like to divert (or redirect) the output to any appropriate device (disk file, printer, modem etc.) without needing to know about the particular physical characteristics of the device.

For example, the command requirements and data formats for pen plotters, dot matrix printers, text scanners and fax machines are very different, but the user would expect to be able to communicate with all of them using normal operating system commands such as COPY, PRINT etc.

11.2 HARDWARE INDEPENDENCE

It has been said earlier that one important aspect of an operating system is to shield the user from the hardware. This implies more than just shielding the user from dealing with the input/output registers involved in, say, accessing the serial port. All accesses to the system kernel should be as **transparent** as possible to the calling application, and this includes coping with the possibility of directing output to more than one device of the same type (or different types) simultaneously.

11.3 USER LAYER

Many input/output operations can be initiated from the console by the user. These range from simple **print** operations to requests for entire sets of resources such as mag. tape drives.

11.3.1 Device assignment

A logical device may be 'mapped' onto a physical device in a transparent manner, so that, for example, printer output may be sent to a high-speed draft printer or a high-quality laser printer using the same commands. In the MS-DOS system, this may be achieved by a command such as

MODE LPT1: = COM1:

which assigns the first serial port to the LPT1 driver. Within the operating system, there is an assignment between PRN: (a logical device) and LPT1: (the physical device) so that any output to PRN: is routed to the appropriate destination.

11.3.2 Redirection and piping

This capability is one of the hallmarks of the Unix system, and is also implemented in VAX/VMS and, in a simplified form, in the MS-DOS system. Apart from the command names, the syntax is similar in MS-DOS and Unix.

11.3.2.1 Redirection

It is sometimes convenient to alter the destination to which information is routed; for example, a directory listing might be more conveniently stored in a disk file for certain purposes. The following command will achieve this:

DIR > AFILE <CR>

The output of the DIR process has been redirected to a file called AFILE. The normal (default) redirection is to the screen.

Similarly,

SORT

issued as a command will take lines of input from the keyboard (terminated by a CTRL/Z combination, the standard end of file character) and produce them in alphabetical order on the screen, and

SORT > AFILE

will redirect the output to a file.

The process works both ways, so

SORT < AFILE > BFILE

takes input from AFILE and places the result in BFILE.

11.3.2.2 Piping

It is sometimes inconvenient to open explicitly named files when redirecting I/O; the same effect would be achieved by a memory-resident file which was written by one process and read by another. Such a file is called a pipe (sometimes FIFO, for 'first in first out').

In Unix and MS-DOS a pipe is indicated by the vertical bar character (|). For example,

DIR | SORT

'pipes' the output of the DIR process into the SORT process. This is more convenient than the 'non-piped' version:

DIR > TEMP
SORT < TEMP > TEMP2
TYPE TEMP2
DEL TEMP
DEL TEMP2

Note that in MS-DOS, a pipe is implemented as a temporary disk file; in Unix a shared memory buffer ('true pipe') is used.

11.4   KERNEL-LEVEL I/O: HANDLERS AND DRIVERS

The user is concerned with input and output at a logical level, either directly (via the CLI) or as a writer of applications programs that make system calls. The kernel must, at some stage, make the distinction between the logical and the physical layers. There is a trade-off which must be observed: the main kernel should be as hardware independent as possible to ensure **portability** between different systems; and this is fairly costly in terms of design and development time. Generally, though, it is considered worthwhile to invest in this feature.

It is achieved by the following things: a **modularity** of kernel components, so that changes can be made cleanly; appropriate definition of data areas (**local** or **global**; and the provision of an appropriate set of **protocols** so that system requests can be made in a well-defined way.

Although some translation is made in the kernel (for example, the maintenance of file buffers), the main logical–physical translation is made in the module that the kernel calls with the request for I/O. Unfortunately, there seems to be no standardisation about whether this is called the **driver** or the **handler**. We will use the convention that the process closest to the hardware is called the handler; and that the process shielding the kernel from the handler is called the driver. To make things difficult, the functions of handler and driver are often conflated in simple I/O situations, but we will maintain the distinction.

The driver will perform operations such as mapping a logical device name to a physical; translating virtual I/O to actual data streams (as, for example, a plotter driver); and returning meaningful (device-independent) error codes. In a system with various levels of protection, the code will probably run at a higher priority than user programs, so that any attempt to access it directly would result in a privilege violation and an orderly recovery.

The handler will contain private information about device registers, and will run at the same, or higher, priority as the driver. It will also perform such activities as setting hardware interrupt enables on devices and dealing with interrupts.

A good illustration of the distinction to be made between drivers and handlers is found in operating systems that permit networked file servers to be accessed as if they were additional disk drives on the local machine, for example:

NETWORK D:\Server\C

sets up drive C on the file server 'server' to appear to the local machine as drive D. In this case, the driver would make no distinction between the different kinds of device until it needed a block of information, at which point it would call either the disk handler (for drives A to C) or the network handler (for drive D). The request would be for a block of data referenced by a relative identifier; the hardware dependence would be deferred until the decision to call the appropriate handler, and is consequently minimal.

The network handler in such a configuration would service the requests for networked disk drives, but might also be concerned with requests for remote printers or displays, in which case it would handle data in the form of character streams as well as blocks.

11.5 AN EXAMPLE: TIME OF DAY CLOCK

This simple example, summarised in Fig. 11.1, is really an 'input only' function, but it demonstrates the interaction between kernel, driver and handler. The kernel is called by the application with an assumption that the data will be returned in a particular area; for example, in a processor register or in a data area pointed to by a register. The kernel will, in turn, call the driver which will access the 'raw' data maintained by the handler, generally by reading a shared data area in memory. The handler is called by two processes: the driver, as described above; and the asynchronous interrupt from the hardware (which, in the case of our real-time clock, could be generated by the mains frequency of 50 Hz).

At each hardware interrupt, the handler will (i) save the processor registers, (ii) increment a memory location (generally a doubleword of 64 bits), (ii) restore the processor registers and (iv) return. In a more sophisticated system, other checks would be made (for example, in a multitasking system, checking if a time-slice has expired). For precision, a 'lock' might be set to prevent access while the register was being updated.

The main task of the driver in this simple example is to reformat the raw data into something more acceptable; whereas the value in the handler's 64-bit register is a measure of, say, fiftieths of a second past January 1st, 1980, it would be more appropriate to divide it into the year, month, day, hours, minutes and seconds. These values are the ones that are returned by the driver to the kernel, and by the kernel to the calling application. The application would then perform the final reformatting from integral values to a useful string such as

Saturday 24th September 1988 4.32 p.m.

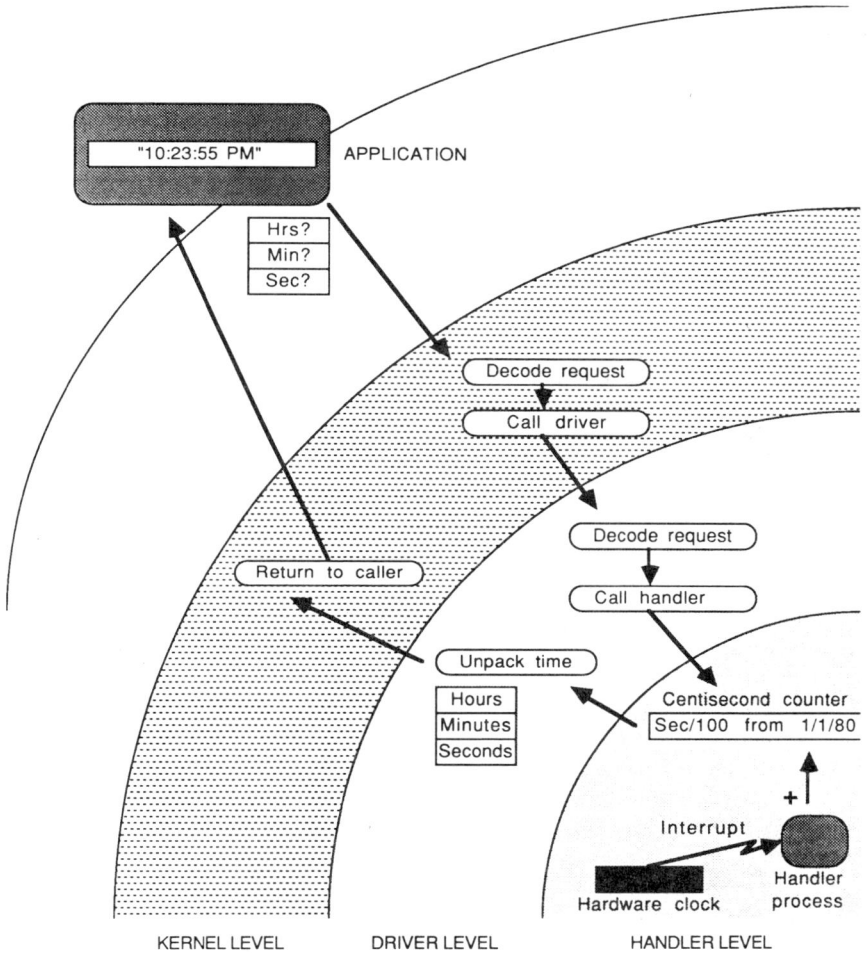

Fig. 11.1 — Real-time clock driver and handler.

The time of day clock would of course require initialisation. On system startup, the driver would be called to initialise the clock. It would do it by (i) setting the time-of-day register to the appropriate base value (by prompting the user) and (ii) calling the handler with an 'initialise' code which would cause it to set up the appropriate hardware registers and enable the interrupts.

The test of a well-organised operating system would be to change the hardware from a mains-frequency interrupt to a battery-backed clock chip: no part of the driver should need rewriting, and only a small part of the handler.

11.6   REAL DRIVERS

11.6.1   Anatomy of a typical driver

There appears to be an emerging standard in how drivers are organised: the example we are going to study would be familiar to both MS-DOS and Xenix systems programmers (Xenix is a Unix 'look-alike'). We will not consider any code, but will discuss the anatomy of the driver using pseudo-code. The driver is for a simple stream-oriented device (such as a printer or modem) rather than a block-structured device (such as a disk drive).

MS-DOS implements a convenient mechanism for the installation of a device driver: if its name is present in the startup configuration file, CONFIG.SYS, then it will be linked on to the end of a chain of drivers in memory.

Each driver is then immediately called with the initialise code. It takes this opportunity to call the appropriate handler (which may be in the ROM BIOS) to initialise the device; it also sets up any interrupt vectors which it will need to intercept. The reason for the immediate call is that, if the handler indicates that the end of its memory requirements are located just before the initialisation routine, then the system can load the next driver at this point, overlaying part of the previous driver. This saves on overall memory requirements.

In normal service, the driver is called in the usual way, via the software interrupt which was set up in the initialisation routine. The kernel ensures that a pointer is provided to a data area called a **request header**. This contains all the information that the driver needs to return the correct data. The first task of the driver is to establish why it is being called — in addition to its normal I/O task, it may be expected to perform a control operation such as initialising a printer (which can be quite complex) or 'cleaning up' after file operations. This information is provided in the **request code**.

Pseudo-code listings
The driver

```
Driver_Entry_Point: (* Pointed to by software interrupt vector *)
        Save processor registers,
        Analyse command code and
        Jump to appropriate routine
                or
        Indicate an error and
        Go to Driver_Exit

Read_A_Char:
        If there are characters in the input buffer then
                Place as many as required in the data area,
                Update the buffer pointers,
                Return the actual byte count and
                If there were fewer bytes than required then
                        Return end of file indicator and
```

                              Go to Driver_Exit
                    Else if there is some fault then
                              Return an error
                    Go to Driver_Exit

Driver_Exit:
          Restore processor registers and
          Return

Initialise:
          Call Handler_Initialise
          Return

The handler:

Handler_Initialise: (* Called from driver *)
          Disable processor interrupts,
          Set up the hardware interrupt vector to point to Handler_Entry,
          Set up hardware device
          Enable processor interrupts
          Return

Handler_Entry:
          Check status of device and (* Receive or send a character? *)
          Go to Reading or Writing as appropriate

Reading:
          Get character,
          Put in input buffer,
          Update buffer pointers and byte count and
          Go to Exit

Writing:
          If there is at least one character in output buffer then
                    Get the character,
                    Update buffer pointers and byte count,
                    Output character to device and
                    Go to Handler_Exit
          Else go to Handler_Exit

Handler_Exit:
          Enable processor interrupts and
          Return

11.7 MULTITASKING

Drivers which are expected to operate in a multitasking environment are
basically the same anatomically, but must have extra features to handle such
conditions as mutual exclusion and synchronisation. These would normally
be handled not by primitive operations coded within the drivers themselves,
but by system calls for such activities as testing and setting semaphores.

The following listing indicates how a device driver might be written for a multitasking operating system in Modula-2. It is a driver for a simple character input device such as a serial port or a keyboard. The exact details of the coding are not important, but you should ensure that you understand the principle of the listing.

Serial device driver

```
MODULE SerialIn [5];

FROM SYSTEM IMPORT Semaphore, NewProcess, Process,
                   IOTransfer, Signal, Wait;

EXPORT ReadChar;

CONST BuffSize=64;
      Interrupt_Vector=60H;
      TriggerDevice=20H;

VAR S : Semaphore;
    Main, Handler, ReadChar : Process;
    ByteCount, InPointer, OutPointer : CARDINAL;
    Buffer : ARRAY [1..BuffSize] OF CHAR;
    DeviceStatus [3F8H] : BITSET:
    DeviceData [3FAH] : CHAR;

PROCEDURE ReadChar (VAR ch : CHAR);
BEGIN
    WAIT(S);
    ch := Buffer[OutPointer];
    OutPointer := (OutPointer+1) MOD BuffSize;
    DEC (ByteCount);
END Driver;

PROCEDURE Handler;
BEGIN
    LOOP
       IOTransfer (Handler, ReadChar, Interrupt_Vector);
       IF
         ByteCount < BuffSize
       THEN
         Buffer[InPointer] := DeviceData;
         InPointer := (InPointer+1) MOD Buffsize;
         INC (byteCount);
         SIGNAL (S);
       ELSE
         Beep;
       END; (* IF *)
    END; (* LOOP *)
END Handler;
```

```
BEGIN
   ByteCount:=0; InPointer:=0; OutPointer:=0; S:=0;
   NewProcess (Handler);
   NewProcess (ReadChar);
   INCL (DeviceStatus, TriggerDevice);
   TRANSFER (Main, Handler);
END SerialIn;
```

The driver works in the following way. The main body (*SerialIn*) is executed just once, as it is not needed again. It initialises the pointers *InPointer* and *OutPointer*, and sets up the new processes *Handler* and *ReadChar*. The *INCL* statement sets the appropriate bits in the device's control/status register.

Next, control is transferred to the *Handler* process. Its first task is to set up the address of the statement *after* the IOTransfer as its entry point in the device's interrupt vector, and then it transfers control to the *ReadChar* process. As nothing has happened yet, the driver merely 'hangs' at the WAIT statement. In a real system, it would now be suspended.

On arrival of data at the device, control passes to *Handler* (at the IF following the IOTransfer) and the data is inserted into the buffer (unless the buffer is full, in which case the data is ignored and an error message given — a 'beep').

Finally, the semaphore S is notified of the event, which allows *ReadChar* to continue. *Handler* now loops round and sets up a new *IOTransfer* ready for the next character.

The module *SerialIn* is incorporated into a user program by IMPORT-ING it:

FROM SerialIn IMPORT ReadChar;

and the driver is used by simply issuing a

ReadChar (ch);

statement.

FURTHER READING

Lister A. M. *Fundamentals of operating systems*   (Macmillan, 1985).

12

Controlling the machine

12.1 INTRODUCTION

The set of resources that an operating system offers is considered here from the point of view of the central processor itself. The shortcomings of the physical machine itself, such as its limited memory capacity and the serial nature of its program execution, are encapsulated and translated into a more suitable virtual machine which offers unlimited memory space and concurrent execution of processes.

In this chapter we will consider three topics: multitasking, the sharing of processor time so that an apparent concurrency of process execution is achieved; memory management, and how a logical, or virtual, addressing space is mapped onto whatever physical resources the CPU possesses; and finally an examination of a real processor and how these activities can be carried out by a combination of hardware and software resources.

12.2 MULTITASKING

The topic of multitasking is of central importance to operating systems. An appreciation of it is necessary to the understanding of such activities as concurrent I/O, resource management, multi-user operation etc.

In this section we will examine the development of multitasking in an incremental way, starting with simple polled systems, then foreground/background processes and finishing with a discussion of the problems of mutual exclusion and synchronisation in a full multitasking system.

12.2.1 Need for multitasking

The architecture of most CPUs is of the **von Neumann** type, that is, the fetching and execution of a single stream of instructions from memory. Theoretically, most (some would claim any) computational problems can be solved by programming such a machine in the appropriate way. For large, compute-intensive tasks (such as those found in aeronautical engineering), this is adequate; and if the CPU power is found lacking, more processors can be added. However, general-purpose computing systems must also perform other tasks, such as the input and output of data, responding to various events in the real world, and so on; and they must do this without being halted or 'hung' by their associated peripherals, as might happen for example with a paper-out or ribbon-out condition on a printer.

12.2.2   Polled systems

Not so long ago, personal computer systems were based on fairly simple eight-bit microprocessor chips, and the operating systems were correspondingly simple, being vehicles for merely supporting the running of applications programs and the maintenance of a file system. For a while, users of these microcomputer systems were happy to have access to a personal computer system supporting word processing, database and spreadsheet operations.

Eventually, however, users began to ask questions: why was it not possible to edit and print at the same time? Why did the screen 'freeze' when the disk was being accessed? These were reasonable questions, as fielding (say) 10 keypresses a second is not an onerous task for the processor. The reason, of course, was that the operating system was not intended to support such activities, and if the processor was held up servicing a device, then there was no way of rescheduling it.

As a consequence of this, the applications vendors began to build a simple form of multitasking into their products. A **polled** method was adopted, which avoided any complication with interrupts etc., and we will now examine this in detail.

Fig. 12.1a illustrates a possible sequence of events over time in a simple single-tasking system running (say) a wordprocessor. At occasional intervals, the user wishes to print out some work. As will be seen from the diagram, the 'attention' of the CPU is diverted to this task; as there is no provision for multitasking, the printer can be allowed to 'hang' the processor when it is not ready to print a character — after all, there is nothing else for it to do. The tasks thus run serially rather than concurrently.

This simple system is enhanced by the addition of two **polling** routines which enable the processes of keyboard input, screen output and printer output to proceed at the same time. The pseudo-code for the resulting **polling loop** would look something like this:

```
repeat
        if a key has been pressed
        then
                input a character
                process the character
        if we need to output to screen
        then
```

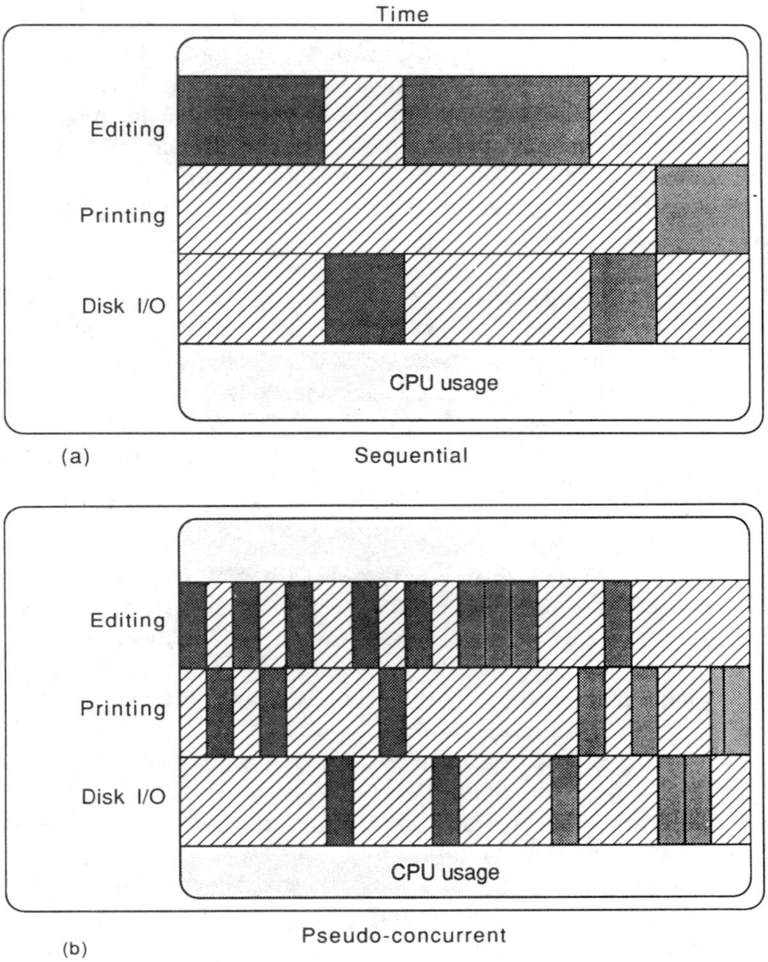

Fig. 12.1 — Task sequencing.

```
            if screen is ready
            then output a character
        if we are printing
        then
            if the printer is ready
            then output a character
        forever . .
```

Note that the main application is no longer held up when a device is not ready, and that due to the relative speed of the CPU compared with the other devices, all the activites will **appear** to execute concurrently (Fig. 12.1b). Such polling loops are adequate for the very simplest systems; the major disadvantage is that the application would probably have to be customised for the particular system it was intended to run on, unless system calls were available for all the particular I/O operations listed. Despite these drawbacks, this scheme has many of the features of a true multitasking system: the CPU **resource** is **despatched** to one of a number of **processes**, and this is carried out in an orderly fashion.

12.2.3   Foreground/background processing
There is a major drawback with the simple polling scheme discussed above: the multitasking process is maintained by the application rather than the operating system.

If the printer hardware can interrupt the processor then the application need not poll the printer periodically. A **background** process could be set up by the application itself, or by the operating system. The latter is more desirable, as the operating system could present the same interface as far as the application is concerned. One way would be to **redirect** the printer output to the buffer belonging to the background process rather than the printer driver itself. Meanwhile, the **foreground** task, such as a word processor, would run as if it had exclusive use of the processor.

This is the method adopted in the MS-DOS system, in which a PRINT utility is loaded which re-points the hardware interrupt vector associated with the printer device driver so that the output is sent to a buffer. The new driver code remains resident in memory.

Note that there are major constraints in such a scheme: all I/O processing must take place as quickly as possible once the printer interrupt routine is entered, as the operating system or the application may 'miss' the processor if it is away for too long. Additionally, the hardware interrupts must be disabled throughout the service routine to avoid the possibility of the routine re-interrupting itself — a fatal occurrence in a system which does not contain re-entrant code (the problem of re-entrancy is discussed more fully later in this chapter). Finally, and for much the same reasons, an interrupt routine cannot call an operating system routine. It is this last aspect which really distinguishes a foreground/background system from a true multitasking system.

This scheme has been used in successful commercial systems, such as the RT-11 system which runs on DEC PDP-11 minicomputers. A time-critical task (for example, data acquisition from a measuring instrument) would run under interrupts while a non-time-critical task (such as analysing the data) would run in the time remaining. Such a system would also incorporate convenient ways of sharing data buffers and ensuring synchronisation between tasks.

12.2.4   Mutual exclusion
The background printer process described in section 12.2.3 is adequate for one application requiring a print-out, and it might be thought that true

multitasking could be achieved by running multiple background tasks. However, several difficulties arise if, for example, more than one task wishes to access the printer. This can happen even in a single-user system if, for example, a 'pop-up' utility is in use and some print function has been selected. If the kernel is using a single print buffer, the outputs could be mixed together by line or, worse, by character. This can be amusing, irritating or disastrous depending on the circumstances.

It is evident that either (i) some kind of protocol would have to be developed to resolve this situation which all applications must observe, or that (ii) the operating system itself would have to incorporate procedures which handled the situation.

Any operating system which undertakes to offer multitasking facilities adopts the latter approach. A set of system services is made available which handle these problems.

12.2.4.1   *The mutual exclusion problem — a solution*

It might be thought that quite a simple mechanism, for example the setting and testing of a flag, might be adequate to cover the mutual exclusion problem outlined above. When one task required use of the printer, it would set a flag which the other task could examine, and either wait or continue as appropriate.

It might be interesting at this point to study a real-life example of the mutual exclusion problem — the maintenance of an efficient rail service over a single track.

Safety procedures were devised to cope with a variety of situations, such as trains stopping in the middle of a section, travelling in the same direction but at different speeds, and travelling in opposite directions; but despite the fact that flouting these procedures meant instant dismissal for a driver, fatal accidents still occurred. The reader may like to study Figs. 12.2 and deduce why accidents occurred in spite of the signals available.

The solution to this problem was devised in 1878 by Edward Tyer, and is still in occasional use on railways today. Although the permission to enter a single-line section was still conferred by the possession of a token, the mechanism of releasing and restoring the tokens was far more complex (see Fig. 12.3).

A signal box at each end of the section would be equipped with a **tablet** device. A tablet consisted of a labelled metal disk with a unique pattern. Once a tablet had been released, it would only fit the device at the other end of the section. The two devices were connected electrically, and each could release a lock on the other device, but not on itself. Once a tablet had been removed from an instrument, no further tablets could be removed from either instrument until the first had been replaced.

When a train was anticipated at a single-line section, the signalman and his colleague would exchange bell signals in a primitive kind of communications protocol. The result was that the tablet would be released from the machine by the signalman at the other end of the section.

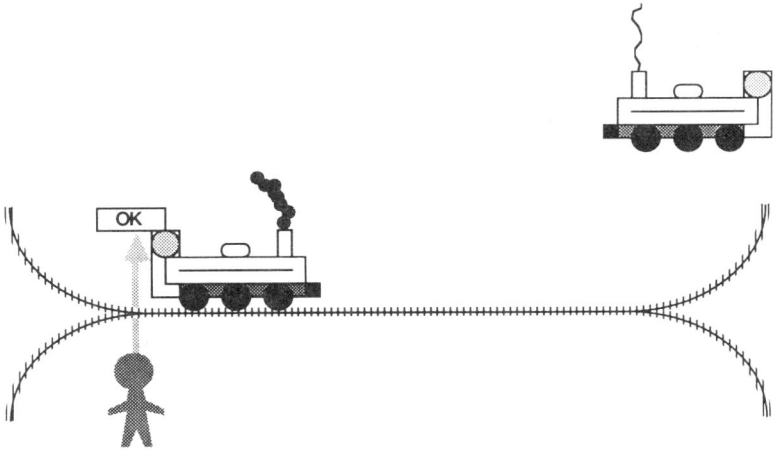

Fig. 12.2 — Mutual exclusion on railways.

Explanation

1   On approach of a train, signalmen exchange bell signals
    to synchronise operations

2   Signalman B releases tablet from Machine A

3   Signalman A hands tablet to driver

4   Driver proceeds and hands tablet to Signalman B

5   Signalman B inserts tablet into Machine B.
    Machine A inoperative until this is done.

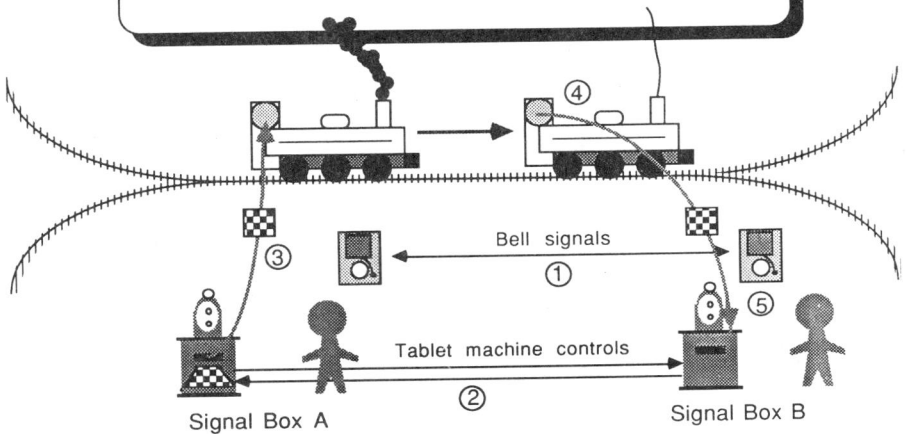

Bell signals

Tablet machine controls

Signal Box A   Signal Box B

Fig. 12.3 — Single-line working by tablet transfer.

The train driver would collect the token from the signalman and proceed. At the other end, the driver would hand (or, more generally, throw) the tablet to the signalman. Various complicated mechanical devices were developed to enable the exchange of the tablets at high speed.

After the introduction of this system, fatal accidents virtually ceased (there was, of course, no protection against malice or disobedience).

The important point to note here is that this is the **simplest** system which would ensure error-free operation. Thus we can see that the mutual exclusion problem is of general interest. We will now examine the situation that obtains in an operating system. (Readers may wish to consult the discussion of kernel and driver interaction in Chapter 11).

Fig. 12.4 illustrates a typical system call sequence. In a single-tasking

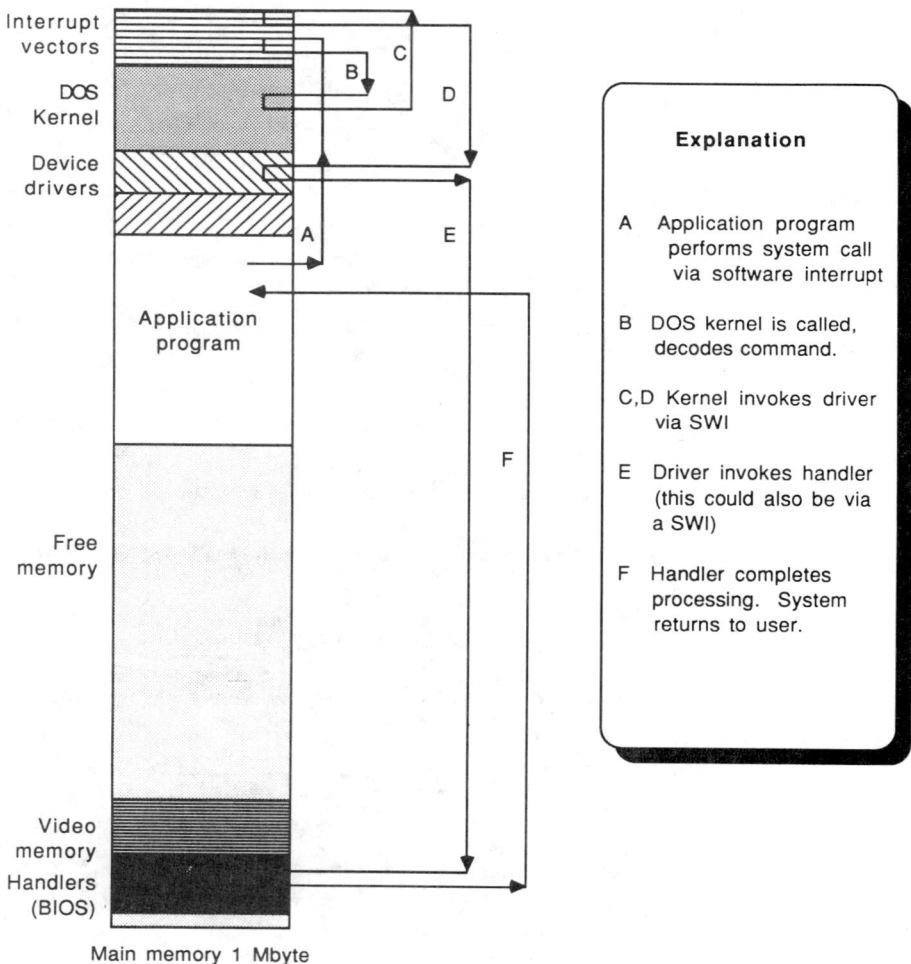

Explanation

A   Application program performs system call via software interrupt

B   DOS kernel is called, decodes command.

C,D Kernel invokes driver via SWI

E   Driver invokes handler (this could also be via a SWI)

F   Handler completes processing. System returns to user.

Fig. 12.4 — System call sequence in MS-DOS.

system, or a system with background processing in interrupt time only, there is no problem as long as the correct calling protocols are observed. All the procedures involved are locked correctly in synchronisation because there is no possibility of anything happening **asynchronously** or unpredictably.

Fig. 12.5 illustrates a situation, only possible in a multitasking system,

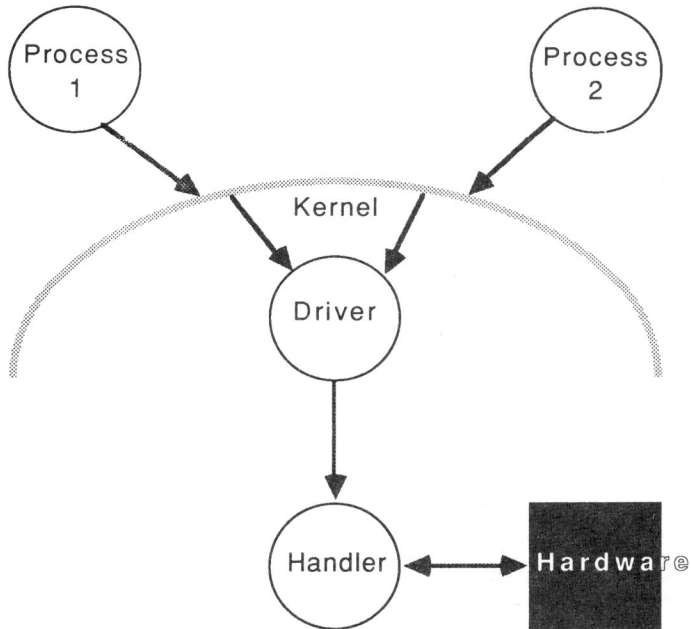

Fig. 12.5 — The mutual exclusion problem.

where two application processes have requested the same operating system service. This could happen in a single- or multi-user system. Somewhere along the line, the implication is that a single piece of code (probably a driver routine) will be involved in both requests, and a decision will have to be made about which one should have priority.

It might be thought that a simple **flag** would be an appropriate control device; but this would occasionally fail for much the same reasons as the single-line railway occasioned fatal accidents, in spite of having an apparently foolproof mechanism (the token). The pseudo-code for a typical flag process might be:

```
while flag = FALSE do
        null
    else do
```

```
flag = FALSE
:
critical code
:
flag = TRUE;
```

Sooner or later, a situation would occur when two processes entered the above procedure simultaneously and found the flag FALSE. The result would be that both these processes would permanently 'hang' unless some kind of time-out were arranged.

(We will make a slight digression at this point: it may be helpful, in visualising the fairly complex processes we are discussing, to look at the system from a 'process-centred' point of view; that is, as a number of independent tasks which occasionally need the assistance of some resource, whether it is I/O, memory, or a CPU. This is in distinction to the traditional 'computer-centred' point of view, in which a CPU executes a stream of instructions, some of which are located in different logical processes.)

12.2.5   Semaphores

The concept of semaphores was proposed by Djikstra in the 1960s, and represents a general solution to problems of the kind we are considering. It is a good example of the way in which a theoretical concept (from computer science) and a practical problem (from operating systems practice) have been combined to provide a useful solution.

There are two basic semaphore operations (**wait**, **signal**), and one data type (**semaphore** (an integer)). These operations are defined as being **indivisible**, that is, the operation must not be interrupted during its execution. A wait will be executed by a process waiting for a resource, and a signal will be executed by a process that has just released a resource. This resource may be I/O, memory, or code.

The signal operation merely increments the semaphore. The wait operation decrements the semaphore and continues *as long as decrementing the semaphore would not take it below 0, i.e. negative.* Thus if a resource were free to be used (semaphore positive), a process could immediately use it. If this resulted in the semaphore being decremented to 0, any other process would have to wait. In a practical implementation, the wait operation would merely 'hang' the calling process until it could continue. Every shareable resource in the operating system has its own semaphore, and, by definition, all these semaphores are 'known' to the operating system, although not to user processes. The operating system will, however, make semaphore operations available as a system service (See Chapter 14).

We can now examine the **mutual exclusion** problem illustrated in Fig. 12.6.

The pseudo-code for a solution is as follows:

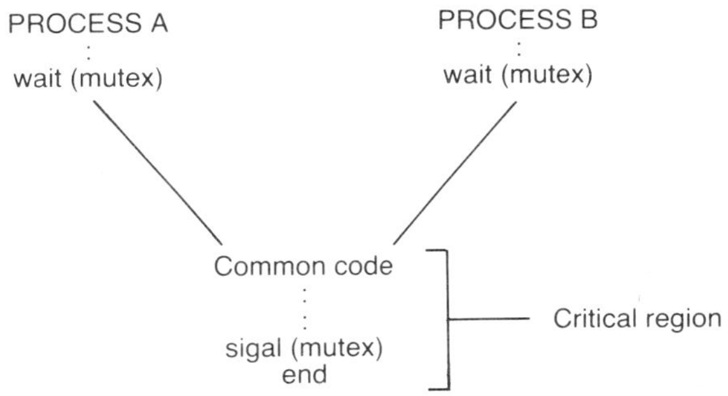

Fig. 12.6 — Mutual exclusion.

If you study this listing, you will find that it is only possible for one process, A or B, to be executing the code in the critical region, as each process has to wait for a signal to continue. A different problem arises when two processes share a common data item, such as a buffer. In this case, the two processses are both dependent upon the correct operation of the buffer, and are said to be coupled.

12.2.5.1 An example in Modula-2

Modula-2 is a development of Pascal which incorporates provision for separately compiled modules, data hiding and access to low-level process control primitives. The listing below represents an implementation of the outline above.

```
MODULE Mutex;
    FROM SYSTEM IMPORT Semaphore, StartProcess, Pro-
    cess, Signal, Wait;

    FROM Kernel IMPORT Critical;

    VAR S : Semaphore; P1,P2 : Process;

    PROCEDURE P1;
    BEGIN
        LOOP
            Wait (S);
            Critical;
            Signal (S)
        END
    END P1;

    PROCEDURE P2;
    BEGIN
        LOOP
            Wait (S);
            Critical;
```

```
              Signal (S)
        END
      END P2;
      BEGIN
        S := 1;
        StartProcess (P1);
        StartProcess (P2)
      END
    END Mutex.
```

Note that processes P1 and P2 perform their own signal operation on the semaphore, unlike the pseudo-code example. A little reflection will show that this does not make any difference to the logic of their operation — the semaphore does not need to 'know' which processes operate on it, and P1 and P2 do not 'care' how it got set.

It is evident that Modula-2 is a good language to use for writing operating systems (see also Chapter 15).

A different problem arises when two processes share a common data item, such as a buffer. In this case, the two processes are both dependent upon the correct operation of the buffer, and are said to be **coupled**.

12.2.6   Synchronisation

It is time to consider how an operating system may be made truly multitasking, that is, capable of running more than one independent process so that there is no interference between these processes, either directly or through procedures that they share. In order to do this, a degree of **concurrency** must be introduced into the system. This will enable processes to run 'at the same time'. The concurrency can be in the form of multiple **parallel** processors, or via a constant rescheduling of the currently running processes. For our purposes, there is no logical difference between these methods; there is a physical difference, the speed at which things happen. We will consider the case of a **uniprocessor** system.

What 'drives' the multitasking in such a system is a process called a **scheduler**. This process has a number of tasks, one of which is to establish which of a number of candidate processes is most deserving of the CPU resource, and to **dispatch** that process (that is, give it the CPU). After a while, one of several things will happen. The process will need to perform some I/O (from a file or device); or a higher-priority process will become ready to run; or it will run out of the **time-slice** of CPU time allocated to it. Note that in this chapter the discussion will consider multitasking from the kernel point of view — that is, the procedures that the kernel uses to provide multitasking services to a higher-level interface. Chapter 14 includes a discussion of this interface as a system service.

If a user process is interrupted by some external event, the first task of the interrupt routine is to establish whether the interrupt signals a very brief event, which would not warrant the rescheduling of the interrupted process.

An example would be the updating of a time-of-day clock. If this is the case, then only the CPU registers are saved. Otherwise, it is necessary to save the **context** of the process that has been interrupted. This includes the values of all the CPU registers (including the program counter), the privileges and priorities and all the data areas which are local to the process. This is most easily accomplished if each process keeps all its data in one contiguous **workspace**; all that then needs to be saved is a pointer to this workspace.

All this information is bundled together into a **process descriptor** record and referred to with a single pointer. The process descriptor also contains a unique **process identifier**, or PID, generally a simple integer.

The aim is to ensure that, if all the information in the process descriptor is loaded into the CPU registers, the process would continue as if nothing had happened.

Control is then passed to the scheduler, which in the simplest case will place the process descriptor pointer at the end of a queue. The scheduler will then select a process from the front of the queue, load all the information from the process descriptor into the appropriate areas and give the process the CPU resource — generally by executing an indirect jump.

This simple case is illustrated in Fig. 12.7 and would be adequate to run a simple 'round-robin' system in which each process had equal priority.

The situation is more complicated if the context switch was due to an I/O request by a process: in this case, two things must be done. Firstly, the scheduler must make a request to the appropriate device driver by placing the PID onto a **waiting** queue. The scheduler has a number of additional tasks to perform: it has to constantly check if a queued I/O request matches up with I/O actually performed; and it has to move the PID of a process from a waiting queue to a **runnable** queue when such a match is successful. Finally, it has to dispatch the process at the top of the runnable queue. Figure 12.8 illustrates this arrangement.

In a real system (such as VMS, discussed in Chapters 13 and 14) the mechanism of process scheduling is abstracted to a higher level, and primitive operations such as dispatching are hidden from the user process. Instead, two concepts are introduced which provide an easy interface to process-control primitives.

Logical event flags (LEFs) are 32-bit words in which a set bit indicates that a particular event is being waited for; this may be I/O, a real-time event, or a message from another process. The associated system service, a 'flag wait', returns to the calling process when the appropriate bits match.

Asynchronous system traps (ASTs) are context switches 'primed' in advance by the calling process and delivered when the appropriate event occurs — such as a 'break' key combination being typed on the keyboard, or the occurrence of an I/O error. Additionally, processes may **hibernate** themselves and be **woken** by other processes. A particular example is discussed in Chapter 14.

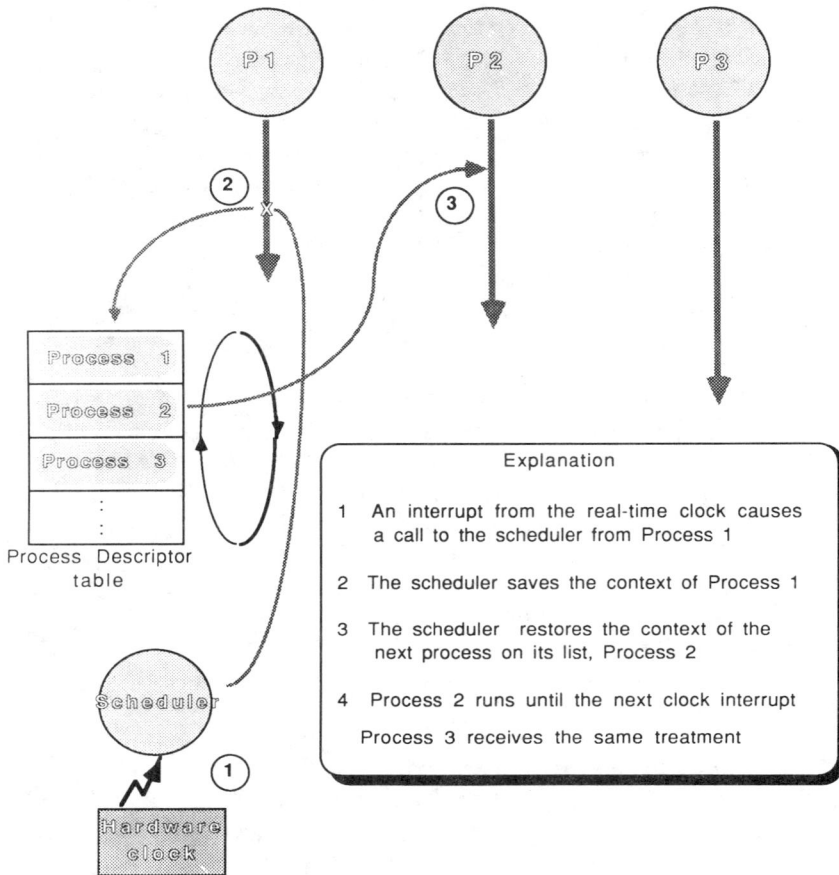

Fig. 12.7 — A round-robin system.

12.3 MEMORY MANAGEMENT

In this section we discuss the historical development of memory allocation schemes and move on to an explanation of virtual memory management.

12.3.1 Allocation

In a simple, single-tasking system there is rarely a memory allocation problem. Programs are loaded at a fixed address, and their memory requirements (such as arrays) are fixed at link time. Programs that need dynamic memory allocation facilities (such as those written in Pascal) just ascertain how much physical memory remains to them, generally via a system call, and use memory up to this limit.

Operating systems which allow relocatable programs to be loaded,

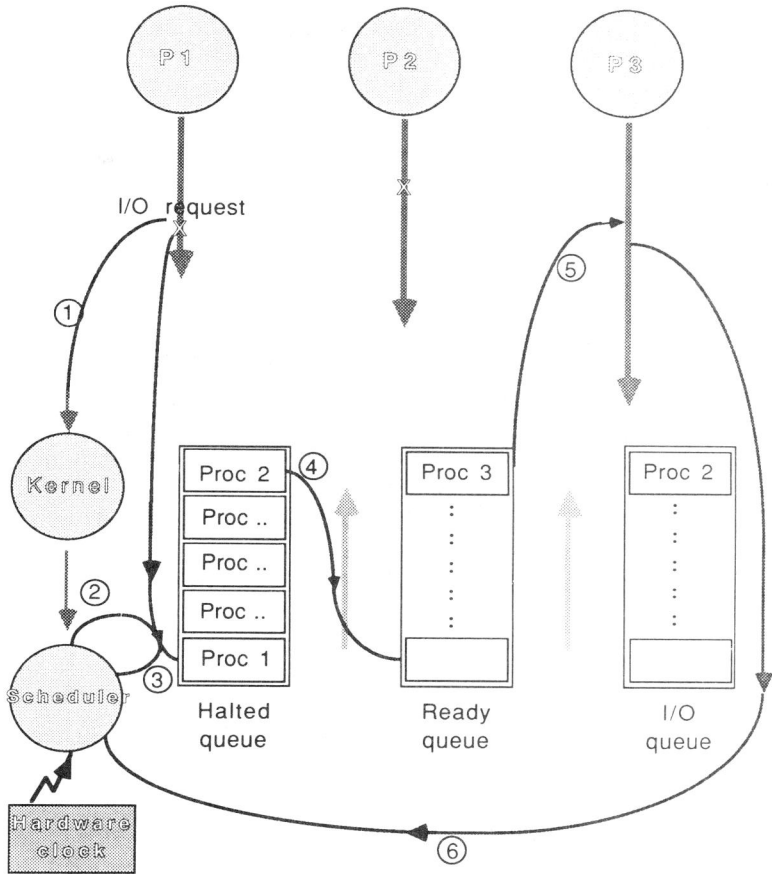

Fig. 12.8 — Typical multitasking arrangement.

especially those programs which **terminate and stay resident** (TSR) with existing programs, offer more sophisticated facilities to allocate and release blocks of memory on request; the limit, however, is still bounded by the physical addressing capacity of the CPU.

There are two situations in which such schemes are inadequate: when programs are written which require more space for code or data than the system physically possesses; and when multiple users are involved, and the total demand for memory is likely to exceed capacity. It is useful to consider now the solutions which have been developed.

12.3.2 Overlays

Not so long ago, the typical memory size for a small system was 64 Kbytes. With the size of the resident operating system taken into account, the usable space was reduced to perhaps 48 Kbytes. It was inevitable that this limit would prove inadequate, and ways had to be found of circumventing the problem.

If a program can be split logically into a **main** section which is often accessed, and a number of **sections** (modules) which are accessed alternately, then the size of program in residence at any one time can be reduced by having only one module in memory. The others are kept on disk, and accessed when needed. If all the alternative program sections have the same start address, then an **overlay area** can be defined at link time.

The simplest overlay schemes have just one overlay area, while more complex schemes have a nested structure in which several modules can share one section, and several sections are defined. To ease the programmer's task, some language processors can work out their own overlay scheme.

A well-designed overlay scheme can work quite well, but there are disadvantages: if alternative overlay modules are called frequently, then an undue amount of disk activity will take place, slowing the program; and there are restrictions on how overlay modules can call one another. The major disadvantage from the systems software point of view is that an overlay scheme cannot be managed by the operating system: all the allocation is accomplished by the langauge processor and the linker between them.

12.3.3   Bank switching

The method of overlays, described above, introduces the concept of several program sections sharing a common memory area and using the same addresses. The same effect can be accomplished by keeping several physical 'banks' of memory which share the same address, and switching between them by placing a value in a hardware register. The procedure which does the switching, of course, has to be located in a 'non-switchable' memory bank.

This scheme has several advantages: the bank switching can be managed by the operating system; program or data sections, once loaded, can be kept resident in a bank; and any number of banks can be defined. For example, up to 256 48-K memory banks can be selected using an eight-bit register. There is no restriction on what the memory is used for, so disk storage could be emulated or large data caches implemented. This scheme is used in small eight-bit personal computers such as the Amstrad PCW series, and demonstrates how a reasonable amount of functionality can be conferred on a low-cost system by virtue of intelligently written systems software.

12.3.4   Windowing

This may be regarded as a 'cleaner' form of bank-switching, and is used for much the same reason — the desire to extend the apparent addressing capacity of a CPU. Rather than switching almost the entire address range, a small **window** is selected, generally 8–16 K in size. This window is **mapped** onto a section of a much larger physical memory by setting the appropriate bits in a hardware register. The addresses in this window are all **virtual** addresses because they are logically correct for the program which uses them, but the **physical** addresses they correspond to can vary.

A typical example is found in the PDP-11 range of minicomputers, where the processor's addressing range of 64 Kbytes is mapped onto a physical address space of 4 Mbytes. Memory management is handled by calls to the RT-11XM (extended memory) operating system.

12.3.5   Virtual memory

If the windowed memory concept described above is taken to its logical conclusion, then the entire logical memory space could be mapped to an arbitrary amount of physical memory. If the mapping were properly managed, then the virtual address space would be independent of the physical address space. Furthermore, this mapping could be managed transparently to the user program.

A system which fulfils all these requirements is a **virtual memory** system. Several major operating systems have been built around a virtual memory architecture: MVS (Multiple Virtual Storage) for IBM mainframes, and VMS (Virtual Memory System) for the VAX range of minicomputers.

The operation of a virtual memory system is as follows. Memory is considered to be divided into a number of **pages**, generally of 512 bytes each. Each page is mapped onto a portion of physical memory by a **memory management unit**, or MMU. The physical memory could be main memory or fast mass storage. As far as the user program is concerned, the address space available to it is a linear array of pages, the page boundaries being 'invisible' to the program. The VAX offers 4 Gbytes, or 4000 Mbytes of virtual memory and from 4 to 32 Mbytes of physical memory, generally with several hundred megabytes of mass storage.

If the system is lightly loaded, then a user program (task A) will occupy consecutive page slots as shown in Fig. 12.9, and its memory map will form part of its context. If this task is now suspended, for example by a normal context switch, its space will become a candidate for replacement as needed. Task B is now loaded, replacing part of task A, and runs for a while. The overwritten pages of task A are first saved on disk if any change has been made. Eventually task B will be rescheduled, and task A will resume. As it comes to the end of page A2, and attempts to execute the first instruction in page A3, the hardware in the MMU detects that page A3 is no longer in memory. A **page fault** (interrupt) is generated, and the task suspended until the appropriate page is loaded. When this has been done the instruction which caused the page fault is **restarted**.

It might be thought that this is a particularly inefficient way of running a system, but it should be remembered that (i) a large proportion of programs spend most of their time within a 512-byte page boundary, and (ii) while a task is suspended by a page fault, another task can run.

Eventually, after a certain period of time, the pages belonging to the

(a)

(b)

(c)

Swap area

Mass storage device

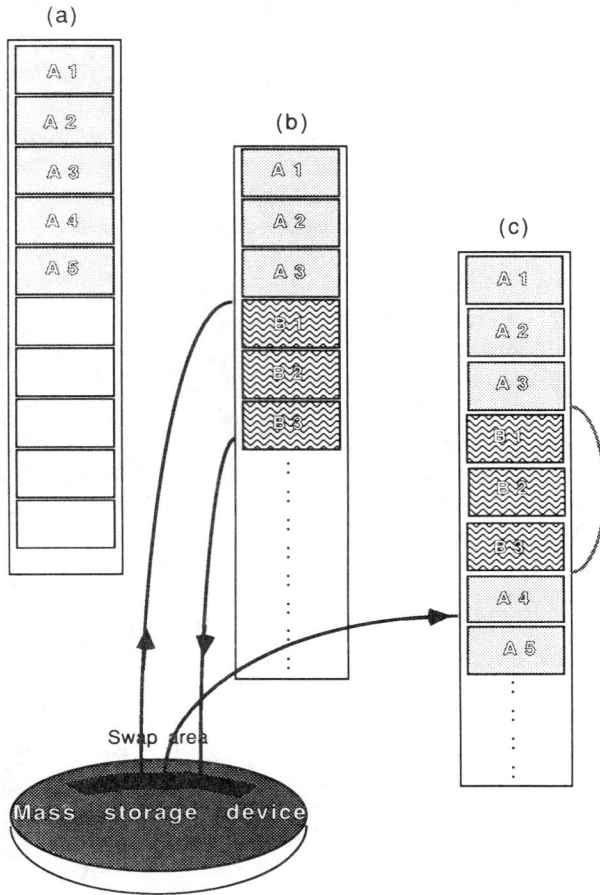

Fig. 12.9 — Virtual memory paging.

various tasks will be fragmented throughout the system; this makes no difference to the programs themselves, which still 'see' a contiguous address space.

12.3.6 Protection
Even in a well-managed application, a process can occasionally run amok, attempting to address illegal areas of memory. In this situation, unless protection is applied, the operating system will crash.

The final enhancement, therefore, in a virtual memory system is to associate each task with a priority, and to mark each block of virtual memory used by that process. The MMU will then detect if an illegal access is attempted, and generate an error which can be trapped.

12.4 AN ADVANCED MICROPROCESSOR — THE INTEL 80386

Although this book does not address hardware topics in any depth, it is worth discussing one example of the new generation of CPU chips in a little more detail, as the systems programmer or language developer will want to know the details so that improved products can be developed. The Intel 80386 is likely to be the mainstay of desktop business computing for some time, and has also been used in applications which have previously been the preserve of microprocessors such as the Motorola 68020, for example the Unix Workstation market.

The discussion will restrict itself to those aspects of the design which have consequences for the systems software specialist.

12.4.1 Speed

The processor has a performance of 4–5 MIPs depending on the clock speed of 16–25 MHz, and achieves this speed by having 32-bit wide address and data paths, and a high-speed cache memory which stores the most-used instructions and data. (The cache memory is actually located outside the processor, so that the designer has a choice between speed and cost. Generally, memory with 40–60 nanoseconds access time is used.)

12.4.2 Memory management

Readers may wish to refer to section 12.3.5 in conjunction with this section.

Although the address width of 32 bits implies that 4 Gbytes (4000 Mbytes) of physical memory can be accessed, it is still an expensive proposition when more than, say, 8 Mbytes of main memory is considered. Consequently, full virtual memory is implemented, in which there is a choice between a segmented scheme (where the segment register is used to calculate the location of some data) or a paged scheme (where pages of 4 Kbytes are maintained either on disk or in main memory as described in Chapter 12). Alternatively, a paged scheme can be implemented to run invisibly **under** a segmented scheme; or the segmentation can be ignored and a 'flat' memory model of 4 Gbytes used, which eases the implementation of operating systems such as Unix. As a matter of interest, the virtual address size is greater than 32 bits, and offers a total addressing range of 64 Tbytes (64000 Gbytes). It has been calculated that one copy of every book ever printed would occupy such a space.

In addition to the virtual memory feature described above, there are hardware memory **protection** checks which will only permit access to an area of memory if a process has the appropriate privilege.

In this way, the operating system can manage memory resources effectively without having to spend time calculating privileges. It only needs to take action upon a privilege violation, which will generate an interrupt.

12.4.3 Multitasking in the 80386

The process of context switching has migrated into the hardware, which renders multitasking extremely reliable. All the processor registers are automatically saved into a **task state segment** (TSS) belonging to a task, and reloaded for the new task from a similar area. In addition to the processor registers, a TSS contains 'privilege' information about what areas of memory the task is allowed to access, and indeed what instructions it is permitted to execute.

A task normally invokes another task via a special structure, located in a known position in memory, known as a **task gate**. Before one task invokes another, a privilege check is performed. Consequently a low-level (user) task cannot directly invoke a high-level (kernel) task, but may do so via an intermediate 'gateway' which first checks the status of the calling process. Similar data structures also exist for data areas in memory.

In conjunction with an operating system specially written for it (such as OS/2, which is discussed later), it is evident that extremely robust systems can be built.

12.4.4 Multiple virtual machines

An interesting extension to the 'virtualising' philosophy is that it can be applied to all areas of CPU operation, including registers, I/O ports and interrupts. The consequence of this is that the 80386 can support multiple virtual 8086 processors (the 8086 being the simple 'base' model around which most personal computers are built).

The virtual machines are handled by a piece of systems software known as a **hypervisor** (one level up from a supervisor) which ensures that the real 80386 registers and memory are accessed in an orderly manner. This is very important when it is remembered that each virtual machine will 'see' the same address space of 1 Mbyte. Given this facility, there is no reason why an entire operating system (such as a copy of MS-DOS) should not run on each virtual machine. This is the approach in IBM's VM/370. The hyperviser could be embedded within a conventional operating system such as Xenix or OS/2. Each system call from a task running in a virtual processor is trapped by the hyperviser and either performed directly or emulated. The Sun 386i is a workstation that uses this method, and comprises a Unix system (SunOS) with a windowing interface (SunView) which supports multiple MS-DOS processes on virtual processors. One interesting consequence of this method is that an error which would crash a 'real' MS-DOS system (such as an unimplemented opcode, or a hardware fault) would only result in a termination of the offending process in the 'virtual' system.

12.5 CONCLUSION

By an orderly co-operation between hardware and software, systems can be made resilient and reliable, and the physical realities and limitations of the hardware made more amenable to the needs of applications.

In certain instances the design of hardware can run ahead of software solutions, as in the area of virtual memory management and protection.

FURTHER READING

Ben-Ari, M. *Principles of concurrent programming* (Prentice-Hall).

13

Some real systems

13.1 INTRODUCTION

Considering their perceived role as vehicles for running applications and performing housekeeping tasks, operating systems often seem to inspire great loyalty (or sometimes more negative attitudes) in their users. It is generally advisable for normal people to conduct a discreet withdrawal when a Unix 'power-user' confronts a VMS 'power-user' in the coffee room unless they want a crash course in the human psychology of buzzword usage.

Whatever the reasons for these strong feelings, there is no doubt that the various operating systems discussed in this chapter demonstrate a great variety in what they offer the user, and in the services offered to application programs.

We consider three systems of quite different 'character' and undoubted power: OS/2, a new multitasking operating system for personal work-stations; VMS, a proprietary operating system for the VAX range of minicomputers; and Unix, a well-developed system popular in academic institutions. We do not have the space to attempt a full description of each system, but the important features and facilities will be examined.

Although these are very different systems in 'flavour', they are not that dissimilar in the generic facilities they provide; consequently, three main aspects will be considered: the command interface (and any facilities for 'batch' commands); the range of system services; and the utilities on offer.

13.2 OS/2

13.2.1 Introduction

This recently released operating system, jointly developed by IBM and Microsoft, is a suitable candidate for discussion, partly because there is so much information available for it.

Fig.13.1 shows the relationship between the various components of the system. Normally, the end user would operate with the presentation manager and it is anticipated that applications would make full use of the windowing facilities available.

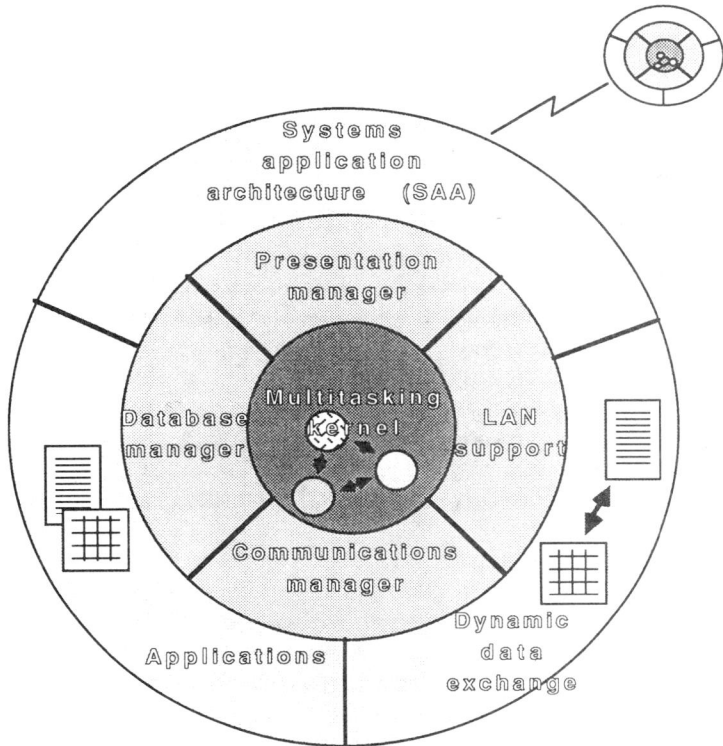

Fig. 13.1 — OS/2 architecture.

13.2.1.1 Basic features

OS/2 is a virtual memory pre-emptive scheduling multitasking single-user operating system for workstations. (The precise meaning of these terms is explained in Chapter 12.)

User programs can be run in a DOS (i.e. MS-DOS) compatibility mode (one task) or as full tasks in protected mode. The reason for this is that the software base for true OS/2 applications is, as yet, small, and most users will want to run their existing software at first.

13.2.2 User interface

The main starting point in the system is the program selector, which is a shell process from which tasks can be started. Running tasks are displayed as a list, and the user can switch between them as appropriate. The program selector can be called up at any time with a 'hot key' (Ctrl-Esc); alternatively, another hot key chord (Alt-Esc) will cycle between the running tasks.

What the user 'sees', therefore, is the current task, and any output it may have produced.

Help is available at most stages in the form of a single line status display and a 'Help' command which expands the displayed error number.

13.2.3   Tasks

In OS/2, a task consists of one or more **threads**, each of which has a set of associated resources. Tasks are protected from one another.

There are four task classes: time critical, foreground, regular, and idle. Within each class there are 31 priority levels. The time-critical class would be used for such tasks as communications or network interfaces; the foreground task is the one currently using the screen. Idle class tasks run when nothing else is happening in the system.

Tasks may be started from a batch file or indeed from other tasks; quite a complex system could therefore be started up on a 'turnkey' basis.

Certain tasks can be defined as containing code which is shareable between other tasks at run time; runnable programs can be dynamically linked to these tasks at load time by OS/2, which maintains a symbol table containing the name of each shareable entry point in the system and, while the tasks are running, keeps a track of resources claimed and released. If the shared module is not in memory, it is loaded by the kernel and the addresses fixed up accordingly. This form of late binding has been discussed in Chapter 7.

13.2.4   System calls

All system calls in OS/2 are in fact dynamically linked calls. This has the advantage that the internal architecture of the system can be changed at any time without affecting the system call syntax. Note that the MS-DOS technique of performing a software interrupt could not be used, as user tasks should not be able to access sensitive areas such as interrupt vectors. These are now the exclusive preserve of the kernel process.

System services (numbering approximately 200) exist for all the facilities discussed in Chapter 9, and are grouped for convenience into DOS calls (I/O, process control, etc.), VIO calls (keyboard and screen I/O), KBD calls (keyboard-specific) and MOU (mouse-specific). Additional system calls (some 500 in number) are available for presentation manager calls (discussed below) and for the relational database in IBM's OS/2 Extended Edition.

All calls are performed by pushing parameters onto the stack and calling an externally defined symbol which passes on the call to the applications program interface (API) which is in fact a **task gate** as introduced in the discussion on the 80386 processor. (Note that this mechanism effectively makes the API processor-independent.)

One implication of this mechanism is that all language translators in the system must 'know' about the API symbols, either implicitly or via libraries.

13.2.5   Extended edition

The basic OS/2 system is enhanced by the addition of three modules: the file manager, the database manager and the presentation manager. Apart from their obvious utility, they are offered as exemplars of applications that work with IBM's proposed **systems application architecture**, in which the 'virtual machine' supporting applications is defined to an international standard. Two other enhancements are a communications management facility and a range of 'built-in' terminal emulations.

13.2.5.1   File manager
This comprises a visual display, in tree form, of the subdirectories and files in the system. Files are accessed by pointing and selection with a mouse or cursor keys. Most common housekeeping operations can be carried out using this interface, which in other systems of this kind has been termed a **desktop.**

The program selector, as described above, is accessible as a **window** in this desktop. Alternatively, the program selector can be dispensed with and all functions selected from the presentation manager.

13.2.5.2   Data manager
This comprises a full relational database management system with **SQL** (structured query language) interface, and can be 'driven' from the user interface or accessed from system calls.

A report generation facility is also provided.

13.2.5.3   Presentation manager
The presentation manager provides a windowed, multitasking environment in which multiple applications can run and make use of *virtual workstations* which provide a hardware-independent interfere for text and graphics I/O. Each application can create its own threads, which are time-sliced, and applications can pass messages between themselves via a *clipboard.*

The basic operation of the system is similar to the description in Chapter 16. Applications are written so that a number of *events* are anticipated and acted upon where appropriate. These events are concerned with the behaviour of the keyboard, mouse, or timers in the system.

A major advantage of making the operating system as hardware-independent as possible is that correctly written applications only need to be installed once, for the virtual interface: any change of hardware only occasions the installation of a new system driver.

13.2.5.4   Dynamic data exchange (DDE)
There is a trend in applications programs towards the integration of information between, say, database, spreadhseet and graphics modalities. One drawback is that each vendor tends to use a 'private' format for internal data storage and so data is not portable between applications. This is ultimately counter-productive, as it impedes the free flow of information between users.

DDE provides a protocol for sending messages between applications. The messages generally consist of data such as text, *rich text* (text with embedded formatting commands), graphics or commands. Messages can be directed to specific destinations, or be broadcast. An example of a broadcast message would be a random number generator, which a spreadsheet could use for testing purposes, or a time of day clock which any application could read or use for synchronisation.

The ultimate implication of such a facility must be that integration of functionality need no longer be a primary aim of applications; no compromise would need to be made between power and data compatibility. In other words, a likely consequence is the 'dis-integration' of packages such as Lotus 1-2-3 and Framework because the component parts could co-exist quite happily as separate threads in an OS/2 system.

13.3 VMS

13.3.1 General features

VMS (virtual memory system) is a multi-user multitasking system designed to run specifically on the DEC VAX (virtual address extension) minicomputers. The system is upward-compatible from smaller to larger systems, and may be run on small workstations. It is a general-purpose system, being suitable for commercial and real-time applications, and for end users and software developers. An interesting feature is its ability to run in an environment of **clustered** machines — that is, to run as a **distributed** operating system.

13.3.2 User interface

13.3.2.1 General

The standard user-level interface is a command line interpreter. A command will invoke either a program or a built-in function. Commands can be 'batched' together in **command** (.COM) files. The syntax of the commands in command files is enhanced by the addition of such facilities as conditional tests, loops error handling, etc., and this comprises the Digital Command Language (DCL).

13.3.2.2 Syntax

The system prompt is normally a '$'. The command line syntax is:

[label:] command [/qualifier [/qualifier...[/qualifier]]][−]
         [parameter-1 [qualifier]] ... [parameter-n [qualifier]]

As can be seen from the above, the command (optionally prefixed by a label, which is used in a command file) may be modified by one or more **qualifiers**. Each of the optional parameters may be followed by a parameter. A line that is too long can be physically (but not logically) split into any number of input lines.

13.3.2.3 Features

While the command line is being entered, a variety of editing features are offered. Previous command lines can be recalled from a stack and modified or combined with new input.

An important feature of the system is the **on-line help** facility. This takes two forms: an explicit HELP command, which takes the user into a tree-structured help system, with main topics and subtopics, and which is offered by both the CLI and applications; and a prompting facility, which suggests further action if a command line looks incomplete. For example, the normal syntax of the COPY command for files is:

COPY FILE_A FILE_B <Return>

but an entry omitting the parameters (two filenames) produces the sequence:

COPY <Return>
−From? FILE_A
−To? FILE_B

13.3.2.4   Commands

Various commands are available for the following activities:

program development,
resource alllocation,
environment control,
process control,
file maintenance,
utilities.

Finally a range of commands is available to monitor the progress and performance of the system as it runs, which is useful during the development of complex applications.

13.3.3   Processes

Each task running in the system is termed a **process**. A process comprises an **image context** and an **image** which represents the executable code and data areas. The image context indicates the **state**, **privileges** and **quotas** appropriate to the process. Part, or all, of a process may be resident in memory (the **working set**) or **swapped out** onto mass storage (the **balance set**).

13.3.4   Services

A wide range of system services is offered. For a detailed discussion see section 14.5.

13.4   UNIX

13.4.1 Introduction

In the mid 1970s there was little choice of operating systems for the user. Systems were generally tied closely to the hardware available; the large systems were daunting and complex, while the small systems (generally running on laboratory minicomputers) were inadequate to support collaborative software development. The particular problems with regard to small systems were:

They had no convenient file structure.
They were not multiuser systems.
Devices were hard to handle.
Not many utilities were provided.
There was no unified language.
There was no communications capability within or between installations.

As a result of this, the process of software development was made difficult for the new group of people who wished to use small computers — scientists, engineers and academics.

Unix first appeared as a 'model' system, written ('over a weekend') by Thompson and Ritchie, running on a DEC PDP-11, and quickly became popular as a result of the features it offered:

hierarchical file structure,
I/O redirection,
Pipes,
Multitasking,
Scripts.

13.4.2   Files
13.4.2.1   Directory structure
Fig. 13.2 shows the typical file structure for a small Unix system.

Conventionally, the topmost directory is called the **root** and identified by '/'. System utilities are held in the **bin** (such files were at one time called 'binaries'), and important user files in the **usr** directory, which is also the master directory for user accounts. The **etc** directory is generally used for installation-specific programs and some applications programs.

13.4.2.2 File types
It may be useful to read this section in conjunction with Chapter 10.

There are three major types of file in Unix: **ordinary**, **special** and **directory**. Ordinary files cover all disk files such as programs and text files. They are characterised by a **name**, a unique identifier (**inode** number), **size**, **create** and **modified** timestamps, and a set of **permissions**.

Special files are in fact devices, which are treated in the same way as files under Unix.

Directory files, which are not normally accessed by users, contain information about subdirectories.

13.4.3   User interface
13.4.3.1   Commands
The basic set of commands comprises 'built-ins' and program names. Most commands are characterised by their terseness, which novices find unfriendly and experienced users report to be time-saving. They comprise

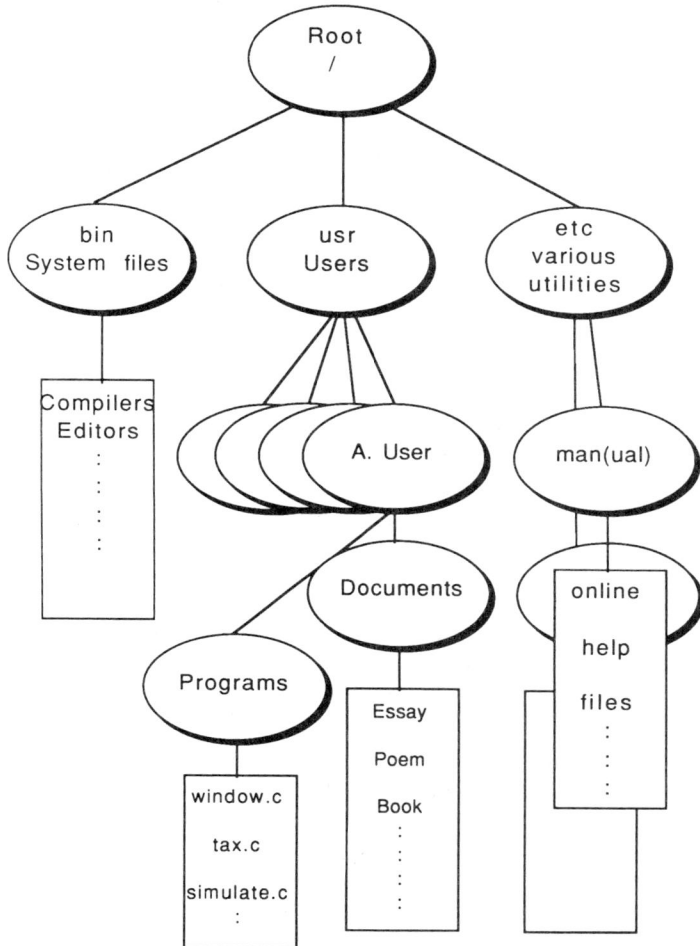

Fig. 13.2 — File structure in a small Unix system.

meaningful mnemonics of activities which are initially arcane but ultimately useful.

All commands are executed from a **shell**, which is a process created for the user to interface with upon logging in to the system.

Some examples follow:

cat — (catenate) a printable file to the output device (by default, the screen): logically, 'type' or 'print' might seem a better choice of name, but these have device-specific connotations.

ls — list segments (files) on the default device: the name is a throwback to the **multics** system which inspired the 'feel' of Unix.

13.4.3.   Command syntax

This is consistent throughout the system:

command [switches] [arguments] [filename/s]

A **switch** is a flag which is toggled on or off to indicate some variation on the normal command, for example:

ls −l   (produce a long listing of all file attributes)
ls −r   (produce a listing in reverse alphanumeric order)
ls −lr   (do both)

An **argument** is a value to be supplied to the command, and the **filename**, where appropriate, represents the file on which to carry out the operation, for example:

grep 'word' textfile

finds all occurrences of 'word' in textfile and lists each line. The command name is a contraction of 'General Regular Expressions Pattern Matcher'.

13.4.3.3   Other features

Commands can be concatenated on a line by terminating each one with a ';'; and multitasking can be simply initiated by terminating each command with a '&'. The command thus invoked executes independently as a **child** process of the user's shell, and will execute in the background until it terminates. For processes which do not need terminal I/O (such as compilers and file maintenance utilities) this represents a convenient boost in system functionality. The child task **inherits** much of the environment of its parent, such as privileges, quotas and so on. If the shell is exited (by using the standard key chord CTRL/D), which amounts to a request to logout of the system, then the user is prompted to kill off any child processes still running, as they are dependent on the parent.

Redirection
Input and output can be redirected from and to ordinary files or special files, thus:

ls > list_file

redirects the output of the ls command to a file called list_file, and:

ls > lpr

redirects the output to a file which has been designated a special file — the system printer. Multiple redirection may also be achieved:

mail arthur brian craig < letter

places the contents of the file 'letter' in the mailboxes of three users.

Piping

The principle is the same as described in Chapter 11, but the process can be extended to invoke multiple pipes. Thus:

uniq the_book | sort | more

produces a sorted listing of the unique words in the file 'the_book' on the terminal, pausing between pages. Pipes can also be tapped into, by using a 'tee', and information drawn off by a number of processes.

Shell scripts

The Unix system implements a shell script feature which goes far beyond the usual 'batch file' facility. It represents a redirection of the input to the user shell, in a similar way to a batch system, but a comprehensive command language is supported, with conditional tests, looping and so on.

It is important to understand what is happening when a shell script is executed: the shell is a process, like any other, and consequently its input can be redirected:

sh < command_file

for convenience, the permissions on the script file can be modified so that it is made directly executable:

chmod 755 command_file

The number 755 is a representation, in octal (base 8) of which bits are set in the file attributes.

13.4.4   System services

Many system services are available directly via commands, but in addition there is a wide range of system calls and subroutines available. They are all available in a standard form as C-language headers and library references. The system calls result in accesses to the kernel; the subroutines include extra code to provide a more convenient interface to some system services, and also provide access to system libraries for such activities as driving terminal screens. The distinction is similar to that made in the VAX/VMS system between system services and the system subroutine library.

13.4.4.1   Brief overview of system services

The services are accessed from a C program in the following way. For an example we will examine the fseek service, which repositions a pointer in an input or output stream. Firstly, the appropriate source library is included in the application program:

```
                      :
        #include <stdio.h>
                      :
```

and a declaration made of the data types:

```
                      :
        int fseek (stream, offset, ptrname)
        FILE *stream;
        long offset;
        int ptrname;
        |
```

The service can now be invoked from the application:

```
                      :
        fseek (stream, offset, ptrname)
                      :
```

Timer services
    alarm — set an alarm clock for a process
    ctime — convert date and time to ASCII

Mathematical services
    bessel — perform a Bessel function
    exp — exponential
    trig — various trigonometric functions

Database routines
    dbms — perform database functions
    bsearch — search a binary tree
    qsort — perform quicksort

File system operations
    chdir — change directory
    chmod — change permissions on a file or directory
    close — close file
    creat — create a file
    fseek — set file read/write pointer
    ioctl — control I/O device (e.g. reset)
    open — open an existing file for reading or writing

Process control operations
    creatsem — create a new semaphore
    exec — execute a program
    exit — from a process
    fork — create new process
    kill — a process
    lock — a process in memory
    nice — sets priority for a process
    ptrace — control execution of a child process
    sigsem — signal a process which is waiting for a semaphore

sleep — hibernate for a given time
ssignal
wait
waitsem

General I/O
curses — cursor control routines
printf — character output function used by C

13.4.5   Utilities

A very wide range of utilities is available for software development, text processing, document preparation, and interpersonal and intersite communication.

13.5   OTHER SYSTEMS

These will not be discussed in any detail, but are included because they offer alternative approaches to conventional operating system architecture.

13.5.1   Pick

This system was developed, by Richard Pick, to fulfil a need for the growing number of users who wanted to develop their own applications but who did not want to use a conventional programming language nor have to learn too much about 'driving' operating systems. Its main features are as follows.

It is a multitasking system using a 'virtual memory' technique to manage many processes. Note that this is not a true virtual memory system as discussed in Chapter 12, but emulates the technique on processors without memory management units.

There is a flexible database system integrated into the kernel of the system. All information is held in database files which are either data files or dictionary (index) files. There is a central master file, the system dictionary. The important feature of the system as far as the user is concerned is the ability to alter record lengths and formats, even when a file is 'live'.

The 'Plain English' interface, ACCESS, enables quite naive users to make meaningful enquiries after a short familiarisation period. Relational operators (greater than, less than) can be used together with logical operators (AND, OR, NOT).

The Pick system is popular with certain types of user, notably local authorities in the UK.

13.5.2   Hypercard

This high-level software, arguably just as much a piece of systems software as an application, is offered by the Apple Corporation to users of its Macintosh personal computers. Although not a full object-oriented language by strict criteria, it contains a programming language (HyperTalk) and a windowing interface.

The problem is conceptualised as a number of **stacks** of cards; each card

contains information in the conventional way. The power of the system lies
in the way in which fields of information can be cross-indexed between the
cards, and from the fact that certain areas of a card can be designated as
'active' (i.e. hypertext). The hypertext areas can 'trigger' whatever information the user regards as appropriate — pictures, text, or sounds.

The windowing interface operates in much the same way as described in
the discussion of the OS/2 presentation manager.

13.5.3 Helios

The new generation of RISC machines, such as the Fairchild Clipper, Acorn
ARM and Inmos Transputer (which is not technically a RISC chip, but very
fast) have been used primarily in speeding up compute-bound activities as a
co-processor to a traditional system with its own I/O facilities; in this role,
little has been needed in the way of operating system support; indeed it
would only serve to slow the process down.

More recently, these processors have been used as system CPUs in such
applications as advanced graphics workstations. Traditional operating
systems, however, are not capable of exploiting the most significant feature
of these chips: their multiprocessing capability. Even a distributed operating
system is not working at a level appropriate to the central activity of an array
of (say) Transputers, firstly because such a system is set up primarily to deal
with file access protocols between fixed processors; and secondly it could not
cope with the extremely rapid dynamic behaviour of processes running on
different chips and passing data between themselves. In the extreme case, a
process may not always continue to run on the same processor it was first
targeted to, and there is no concept of a 'master process', or supervisor.
Furthermore, many RISC chips do not possess the hardware protection and
memory management necessary to run a kernel.

The strategy, therefore, is to distribute the system itself over the
component CPUs, and to ensure that communication between processes is
only achieved by means of a secure message-passing protocol.

The interface has been designed to look like the Unix C-Shell, and
system calls have a compatible format. Internally, the system is very
different. Each processor has its own mini-kernel which manages a number
of tasks; a task may be distributed over a number of processors. Thus a pair
of 'piped' processes may communicate via a real, not a notional, link; or a
process may be 'shared' by several client processes. A shared process is
known to other processes by maintaining a 'server name' which is searched
for by potential clients.

13.6   CONCLUSION

A wide variety of operating systems is available, each with its own range of
services and utilities, and new systems continue to be written. They cater,

collectively, for all kinds of application. Each one attracts loyalty or disapprobation from large numbers of people.

FURTHER READING

Duffy, C. An Introduction to the Unix operating system (Chartwell-Bratt, 1987).

14

System services

14.1 INTRODUCTION

Practically all aspects of operating system usage, whether through the CLI or by a language processor, involve system services: file I/O, housekeeping and so on. There are also many occasions when a programming language lacks the facilities to perform certain operations, such as data conversion routines, time and date functions and event timing. Many real applications, however, need such features. For example, a payroll program or timetabling system would clearly need the support of date and time routines. Similarly, a standard language facility (such as dynamic memory management in Pascal or Modula-2) has to be organised so that it will operate without change on a variety of system architectures.

In both these cases, building these services into the language itself renders the compiler implementation-dependent, not always a desirable state of affairs.

The ideal solution is for the operating system itself to offer a range of services which can be accessed in a standard way. There is an additional advantage in that, once tested, the maintenance of these services is the responsibility of the operating system vendor. Moreover, they can be shared between different languages.

In this chapter we discuss the kinds of system service available, how they are invoked, and their operation and effects. After this, some real examples in the MS-DOS, VMS and Unix systems are examined.

14.2 TYPES OF SYSTEM SERVICE

There are two basic types of system service: those which make a kernel routine available at run time, and those which enable library routines to be incorporated at compile or link time. Unfortunately, there does not seem to be a standard nomenclature for these services. In this chapter we will distinguish between **kernel** services and **library** services. In both cases, access will be via a **macro** or **procedure** which the language processor expands to in-line code, containing either a trap (in the case of the kernel call) or code performing the function (in the case of the library routine).

Certain services exist as shared modules outside the kernel itself, but for our purposes they will be treated as kernel services. Similarly, extended source libraries and documentation are often offered, sometimes by third-party vendors. These may all be regarded as library services.

The exact range of services offered depends on which operating system we are considering; larger systems such as Unix or VMS will offer a more extensive range than small systems like MS-DOS.

14.2.1 Kernel services
These comprise:

> Time and date routines — time of day, elapsed time, date calculations
>
> Data conversion routines — numeric strings to binary
>
> Process timing, scheduling and synchronisation — scheduled wakeups, hibernation

14.2.2 Library routines
Formatted I/O routines — text and graphics.

14.3 CALLING SYSTEM SERVICES

There are generally two stages involved in accessing, or invoking, a system service. The first stage, common to both kernel and library routines, is to specify the service in the chosen source language. It is unusual for a high-level language to extend its set of keywords to include service calls; generally, the service name is prefixed by a special character sequence, such as 'sys$' or '$'. The library to handle such calls is automatically included by the compiler. Alternatively (as in the case of most C libraries), a **header** file is included and referenced so that the service name can be used transparently. Finally the appropriate code is generated.

The second stage occurs at run time. Firstly, references to any parameters included in the invocation are passed (usually by pushing onto the processor stack). Then in the case of a kernel service, a trap or software interrupt is made; for other services the code is either called as a normal procedure (if it has been included at compile time) or as an external (possibly shared) procedure.

There is no reason, of course, why the second stage could not be used directly, and the call made directly. In simple operating systems (such as MS-DOS) a language vendor will often extend the language by the inclusion of a 'DOS' keyword.

14.4 MS-DOS SYSTEM SERVICES

Two levels of service are offered: DOS calls, which provide a logical level of access; and calls to the basic input–output system (BIOS), which access the system at the driver level. The difference is evident when considering file handling, for example: DOS services consider a file as a contiguous string of bytes, managed by a single **pointer** and accessed via a **handle**; while BIOS services only 'understand' disk sides, tracks and sectors. This distinction between logical and physical levels is explained in detail in Chapter 10.

In both cases, the service is accessed via a software interrupt after loading the processor registers with the appropriate values.

14.4.1   An example: time of day

This is one of the simplest facilities, but illustrates the principles (and problems) quite well. The mechanism which maintains the time of day was discussed in Chapter 11.

The following commented listing is in Turbo Pascal.

```
program TOD;
type
      registers = record
            AX,BX,CX,DX,BP,SI,DI,CS,DS,ES,Flags  :  Integer;
            end;
var
      regs : registers;
begin
      regs.AX := $2C00; (* Place the function number for TOD
                              service in the pseudo-register AX*)
      Intr ($21,regs); (* Implementation-dependent — software
                           interrupt to MS-DOS*)
      writeln ('Hours: ',regs.CX div 256,
            'Mins: ',regs.CX mod 256,
            'Seconds: ',regs.DX div 256)
end.
```

14.5   VAX/VMS SYSTEM SERVICES

The VAX/VMS system offers the applications and system programmer a wide range of such facilities. There are two major groups, consisting in each case of a collection of routines which can be incorporated into programs written in Macro or a high-level language.

The VMS run-time library consists of routines suitable for mathematical or text applications.

In addition, services that the VMS system uses in its own operation have been made available to the programmer and are known as system services. They include services for I/O below the Record Management System (RMS) level, for process communication and control, real-time event handling and timing. They can be extremely useful where, for example, a high-level language does not offer the facility required.

The calling interface for both facilities has been made quite simple, and conforms with the VMS conventions for parameter passing. Additionally, the macro definitions for invoking them are 'built-in' to all the standard

VMS language processors, so that the services can be called from Pascal, FORTRAN or COBOL main programs. These routines are contained in the 'language-independent' library; thanks to the consistent structure of the VMS language processors it is also possible to call 'language-specific' routines so that, for example, a programmer working in COBOL can use the run-time facilities of the Pascal library. Some of these services, of course, are only available to privileged users so that the integrity of the system is not compromised.

Let's discuss how the facilities are called up before we look at them in detail. We will use a simple example written in Pascal. Read the comments carefully, as they indicate how the parameters are passed to the routines.

The example we have chosen is useful enough for you to include in your own Pascal program library. It enables you to perform cursor positioning operations on a workstation independent of the type of device — in other words it should perform the same functions whether your terminal is a VT100 or VT52. The example as it stands is a simple application which tests the terminal — it prompts for two co-ordinates (line and column), displays an asterisk and then exits.

LISTING OF PROGRAM 'SCREENER'

```
program screener (input, output);
const
        Number_of_columns = 80; (* Number of lines and *)
        Number_of_lines = 24;    (* columns on terminal *)
var
        x,y,line_wanted,column_wanted,result : integer;
(*
The line below informs the Pascal compiler that the scr$set (screen set)
function is contained in a system subroutine library.
The actual screen manipulation routines, called at run time, are found
by the kernel in the terminal driver process
*)
        function scr$set_cursor (line,column : integer) : integer external;
(*
The scr$set_cursor function is passed the line and column parameters
by value and returns an integer result indicating success or failure — we
do not check this here, although a full implementation would do so
*)
        begin
(*
Output the line and column numbers as a frame
*)
        for x := 1 to 6 do write('1234567890');
        writeln;
        for y := 2 to max_lines do writeln(y);
(*
```

Now place the cursor at line 5, column 24 and collect new line and
column values from user
*)

```
        result := scr$set_cursor (5, 24);
        repeat
              write ('Please input line and column positions ');
              write ('as Line (1-',Number_of_lines,')');
              writeln (', Column(1- ',Number_of_columns,': ');
              readln (line_wanted,column_wanted)
        until (line_wanted in [1..Number_of_lines]) and
              (column_wanted in [1..Number_of_columns]);
(*
Place cursor at the required position and write an asterisk
*)
        result := scr$set_cursor (line_wanted, column_wanted);
        write ('*')
    end.
```

14.6   UNIX SYSTEM SERVICES

The range and scope of Unix system services is detailed in Chapter 13. We
concentrate here on a more detailed examination of a particular service.

14.6.1   The fork

A major feature of the Unix system is the ease with which applications can
be multitasked. From the terminal, it is simply a matter of suffixing the
command line with a '&'. What this action does, in effect, is to cause the shell
process to create a 'clone', or duplicate, of itself which executes the desired
command independently until it terminates. It would not be sufficient to just
run a program from disk: the cloned, or **child** process must run in the
environment that the shell is working with — that is, the files which are open,
the privileges of the user and so on.

On calling the **fork** system service, a copy is made in memory of the
parent process; control is returned to the parent process with either the
process identifier (PID) of the child or an error; and a result of 0 is returned
to the child process at exactly the same point — that is, after the fork call.
Each process then takes the appropriate action on the basis of this returned
value. For example, the parent process might test for a non-zero value in the
returned variable and branch around a piece of code; the child, finding a
zero value, would just execute the code. Generally, the child's action would
be to find and run (**exec**) another program.

In addition to the file information, various other parameters are 'inher-
ited', such as the timers indicating CPU used, timeslice value and so on.
These are set to 0. While the child process is running, it produces its
messages (if any) on the user's console. On termination, the child process
executes an **exit** system call which terminates it and closes its files.

The 'near-Pascal' code follows of a typical situation in which a **fork** call might be used:

```
begin (* Parent is executing code *)
    :
    :
returned_id := fork;
case returned_id of (* Both parent and child do this test *)
    0 : begin
            :
            :       (* This is the child's code *)
            :
            exit (child_status) (* Child terminates here *)
        end;
    -1 : error_procedure;
end otherwise (* Not 0 or error, must be parental code *)
begin
    : (* Parent code executes *)
    :
    : (* It could be something useful *)
    :
    wait (child_status) (* Wait for this signal from child *)
    :
    : (* Clean up files *)
    :
end;
end. (* Parent now exits *)
```

14.7 CONCLUSION

All operating systems offer a range of system services which render some of their kernel operations usable by applications. The names may differ considerably, but the principles are very similar.

FURTHER READING

Milenkovic, M. *Operating systems — concepts and design* (McGraw-Hill, 1987).

15

System utilities

15.1 INTRODUCTION

We have concentrated so far on the inner workings of operating systems, but in many ways the picture is incomplete. The 'look and feel' of a particular operating system is determined just as much by the kind of utilities that it offers for such activities as software development, document preparation and so on.

In this chapter we discuss the basic set of utilities such as editors, language processors, linkers and librarians; and then more advanced ones such as project maintenance utilities and IPSEs.

15.2 THE SOFTWARE DEVELOPMENT PROCESS

Traditionally, applications software development has followed a classical edit–compile–link–test–edit cycle, and the fact that there are many interesting new tools such as 4GLs, IPSEs etc. does not alter this underlying cycle: it is merely made more transparent to the development process. Moreover, editors are still needed to provide the source code, even in an object-oriented system. From the programmer's point of view, a richer and more interesting set of facilities has been provided.

The system programmer is just as much concerned with a good development environment, but the nature of the software produced means that more traditional activities are appropriate. Systems software development still offers opportunities for hand-crafted code, self-modifying code, and innumerable tricks for extracting more performance from a processor.

15.3 SOFTWARE DEVELOPMENT TOOLS

15.3.1 Editors

15.3.1.1 *General purpose editors*

The operation of an editor can be conceptualised as providing an active 'window' within a file, with text being read into the window from the existing file as input and written to a temporary file as output. At the end of the session, the remaining contents of the input file are copied to the output file, and this file is then renamed to match the original. Generally a copy is also taken of the original file and renamed as a **backup** file.

The set of operations that an editor is capable of performing always includes basic operations such as character, word or line deletion, cursor movement, text insertion and so on. Some are capable of recording **macros** of keystrokes, and some have an underlying command language; some (for example EMACS — 'editing macros') allow keys to be redefined (**bound**) to different functions.

Often, a 'junior' version is offered which possesses a useful subset of the full features. The junior edition of EMACS is MINCE ('MINCE Is Not Complete Emacs'), and various versions have been developed to run on microcomputers ('MicroEMACS').

Editors often attract a loyal following, and approximately equal numbers of vociferous detractors, which is puzzling in view of their limited application. It may well be due to the fact that an editor, at some level, is a vehicle for capturing human thought and the essentially intimate nature of such an activity, and how it is managed, is likely to interact with peoples' attitudes and 'cognitive set'. Indeed there is a great deal of research on users' interaction with editors.

15.3.1.2 Special-purpose editors

A very wide range of special purpose editors is available, and more continue to be written. Posssibly the most useful to the software developer are the **language-sensitive** editors (LSEs). In the simplest case, these might just offer advanced tabulation facilities where a language (such as FORTRAN or COBOL) is sensitive to the column in which source text is placed. Often an extensible editor such as EMACS will cope with this.

More advanced LSEs offer an 'intelligent' set of functions: **folding** editors can compress all the text between, say, the **begin** and **end** of a Pascal procedure so that less redundant information is available on the screen. Another useful feature is for the editor to perform elementary checking so that syntactic or typographical errors can be trapped at an early stage (they are notoriously difficult to spot later). For example, the editor provided with most LISP systems will check for well-formed expressions, correct bracketing and so on. The commission of errors can also be reduced by the intelligent use of macros for commonly used text such as 'procedure'.

15.3.2 Language processors

Part I of this book has covered the inner working of language processors in detail, and this section should be read in conjunction with Chapter 2. We are concerned here only with those features of a language which render it particularly useful for writing systems software rather than applications software, and on broad issues of suitability which might influence the choice of language for a particular project.

15.3.2.1 Assemblers

Assembly language will now be the choice only when the desired effect can be achieved in no other way — many high-level languages now offer low-level facilities. The choice of assembly language is often mandatory when writing new languages, or when working with a new processor or a co-processor.

Some high-level languages attempt to span the gap between low-level and high-level applications.

15.3.2.2 C

C offers structures, dynamic memory allocation and pointer types, but is also optimised to produce efficient code for loops and conditional tests. Variables can be declared as 'register' type, in which case the compiler will attempt to keep them in the processor registers to improve speed. Systems programming is assisted by the ability to write interrupt handlers, device drivers and so on. Another major advantage of C is that it is portable between different processors. Extensive libraries of functions are available for different operating systems. The language has achieved something of a 'cult' status, possibly because the very compact and terse source code that can be written can be a source of admiration for those who have developed it from those who cannot understand it. A major drawback of C is that it is not strongly **typed**: a range of data types (char, int, float etc.) can be nominally declared, but the compiler will not check their inappropriate use. Thus, for example, a floating-point variable (four bytes) can be nibbled away a byte at a time if an array of four 'chars' is declared at the same location. This is quite deliberate, but is a strength of the language which can trap the unwary.

15.3.2.3 Modula-2

In contrast, **Modula-2** (a successor to Pascal) is a very strongly typed language which will not permit the use of a variable type in any circumstances other than the context in which it was declared. The name of the language derives from its primary feature: modularity. A module is a self-contained process which implements data hiding — that is, its internal data and procedures can be kept private or made public by **exporting** them. Exported objects can be **imported** by other modules. A module which exports objects comprises two parts, a **definition** section (which defines the module to the outside world: the names of its procedures, their parameters and so on), and an **implementation** section, which comprises the procedures themselves. The growing importance of a modular approach to project development cannot be overestimated: Systems are becoming more complex and interdependent, and the consequences of error are more profound. If development and testing is done in a modular fashion, then error-prone processes can be isolated and revised. Moreover, developed modules can be held in a library, catalogued and documented, and be re-used by other projects. This so-called **software chip** approach is one of the strengths of Modula-2. The parallel is quite apt: just as the inner workings of a hardware chip are not amenable to inspection, and do not need to be, the inner workings of Modula-2 modules are not visible. Only their definitions are made public, and are the sole points of access to their functionality, in the same way as the pins of the hardware chip.

Modula-2 also offers low-level facilities such as co-routine support (Transfer), device-level support for writing drivers (IOTransfer), concurrency (StartProcess) and fast arithmetic (INC, DEC). It is therefore suitable for both systems and application level programming.

15.3.3   Linkers
The relocatable code that is produced by any native-code language processor is not yet in a runnable form. The actual run-time addresses of local and global labels and variables are not known. Even with position-independent code (and in many newer processors the code is inherently position-independent) there are inter-module references to resolve, as described in section 7.4. In addition to building the component modules together into the load module, the linker may be required to produce a **load map** of actual addresses or a **symbol table** for the use of the debugger. Many linkers can respond to special requests for such facilities as **shared modules** (whose procedures and data can be shared by more than one process in the system) and **automatic library search**, where the linker works in conjunction with a library of precompiled modules (see next section). Special code can be incorporated to satisfy particular requirements — for example, a debugger could be incorporated automatically into the load module, or a special interface for dynamically linked procedures. Most linkers have the facility of allowing a 'batch' file input if the command lines would otherwise be long.

15.3.4   Librarians
A project with large numbers of separately compiled modules can result in numerous object modules, the names of which must be recorded somewhere (hopefully not in the programmer's memory). In these circumstances it is often helpful to be able to combine, or archive, together all the modules which relate to a particular portion of the project. This is the function performed by a librarian. A simple librarian will be able to compile libraries of object modules, permit replacement and deletion of these modules, and supply copies on request from the linker. A more advanced librarian will be able to handle other kinds of file, such as the on-line help text libraries in the VAX/VMS system.

15.3.5   Debuggers
However careful the design process has been, a program may have faults at run time. These may be subtle or striking in their effects, especially if it is a piece of systems software. It is also possible that unforseen conditions will occur in an otherwise well-designed system, particularly if there are complex, non-deterministic (unpredictable) interactions between events.

In these circumstances the use of a low-level debugger is appropriate. In essence, this will operate in a similar way to the high-level language debuggers discussed in Part I. The principle is simple. The program under test is monitored in a controllable way, and information about its performance is made available to the user via the debugger. The monitoring is achieved by software or hardware methods. A software debugger ensures that each instruction executed by the CPU is trapped, either by temporarily inserting software-interrupt instruction in the program or (more commonly) by taking advantage of a facility of the CPU which results in an interrupt after every instruction. In either case, the interrupt is vectored to an entry point in the debugger. The context of the test program is saved (much as in a context switch in a multi-user system) and displayed on the console. A hardware debugger acts by monitoring the CPU data and address buses and interrupting the processor when it detects certain conditions, such as an address being accessed or a particular kind of instruction being accessed.

In operating the debugger, the user can set one or more **breakpoints** (addresses to trap), set **pass counts**, **disassemble** the machine code into meaningful mnemonics, request a **symbolic backtrace** of the recently executed code and so on. The more advanced debuggers provide statistics of instruction usage, graphical displays and so on. Memory locations and registers can be individually examined and modified.

15.4   PROJECT MANAGEMENT

In recent years the approach to software development has become more professional; the discipline of software engineering has become established. A report for the Department of Trade and Industry in 1985 revealed that, in the UK, there were 84,000 software engineers working on 42,000 major projects. Although there is no breakdown of numbers of engineers per project, it would be reasonable to assume that the average project had from four to eight people, each person working on two to four projects. Thus there is a requirement for good management by both project teams and individuals. An engineer may have modules which are common to more than one project, or which are different in detail. Each module may be in a variety of states: source code, compiled with errors, object module, untested, tested and so on. Additionally, there may be several versions of each module: a version may represent a functional difference or a revision to a previous version. Fig. 15.1 illustrates the typical situation that presents itself to the project manager.

It should be evident at this point that, however advanced the utilities provided, their use via a standard command line interface is hopelessly inadequate. Some higher-level interface is needed, which can automate the activities of version control, test reports, linkage to documentation versions and so on.

15.5   PROJECT MANAGEMENT SOFTWARE

Many products are available, ranging from simple version control utilities to advanced computer-assisted software engineering (CASE) tools and integrated project support environments (IPSEs). We will discuss some now.

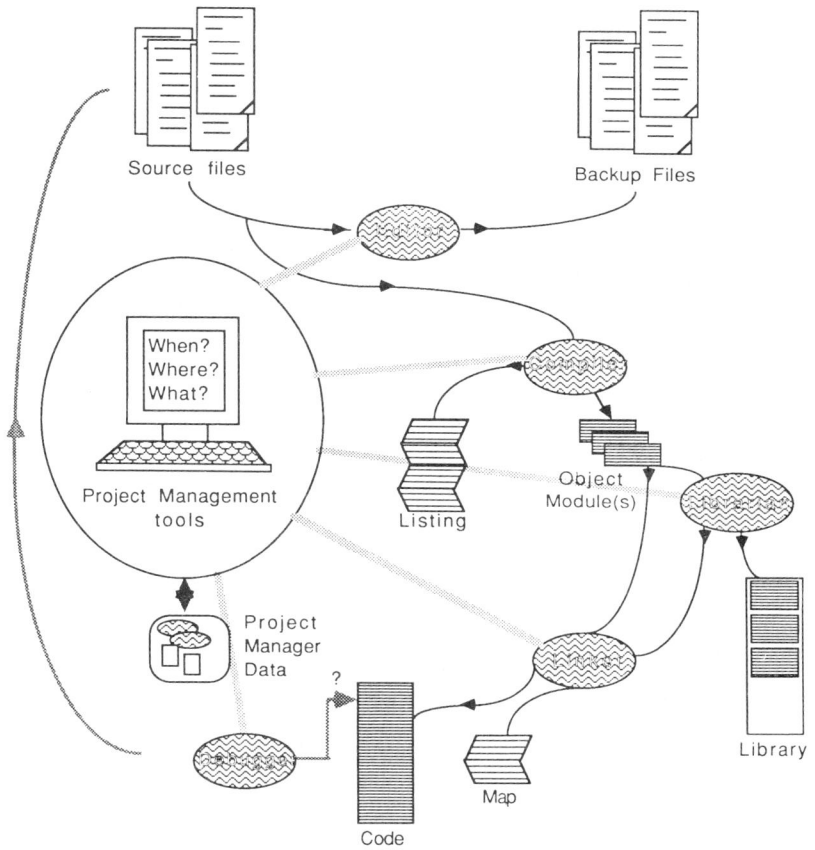

Fig. 15.1 — Project management.

15.5.1   Version control

15.5.1.1   Make

The **make** utility is available for a number of systems, from Unix (where it originated) to MS-DOS, and is also provided with a number of the increasingly popular integrated compiler packages for such languages as C, Pascal and Modula-2. It is invoked simply by typing

       make

in response to the system prompt. No arguments are necessary if a file called 'makefile' exists on the system. This file should contain lines of the following form:

```
        prog.exe: module1.o module2.o module3.o    (Dependency line)
              link module1.o module2.o module3.o     (Command line)
        module?.o: module?.c                                (Ditto)
```

cc module?.c

The lines in the file are arranged in pairs. The first line in each pair is a **dependency** line, which indicates which resources are needed to produce the object on the left-hand side. Thus in line 1 of the file above, 'prog.exe', the load module, needs the three object modules module1.o, module2.o and module3.o. The other line of the pair indicates **how** the desired result is to be achieved: in this case by issuing a command line which invokes the linker. The process is still not complete: we have not indicated how the object modules were produced. The second pair of lines indicates how this was done. 'Module?.o' (wildcards are permitted — the resulting rule is known as an **implicit** rule compared with the normal **explicit** rule) is dependent on 'module?.c'; and the C compiler (cc) is invoked on the command line.

The significant feature of the make facility is that, if any module is changed, then all modules which are dependent on it will be updated as necessary to reflect the changes. This is done by scanning the revision date of all the objects and comparing them with the date of the last **make** operation. If any are different, then they must be dealt with. For example, if changes have been made to the source of module2.c, then a check will be made of those modules which are dependent on it, and the appropriate command invoked. This process 'ripples through' until all the dependencies are satisfied. If at any time an individual module needs to be recompiled (even if the source has not been changed) then an accompanying utility, **touch**, can be used to achieve this by forcing the revision date on the module to be current. The make utility is then invoked in the normal way.

15.5.1.2 Source code control system (SCCS)
The SCCS, and its associated utilities, is generally found on Unix systems, and provides a way of maintaining upgrade information on source code and documentation. Every time a file is edited, an SCCS file can be automatically updated (using the **admin** command) to provide **delta** (difference) information. All the deltas are retained so that, in principle, a lost file can be recreated from the original plus the delta information.

In addition to the 'delta' information, version numbers can be automatically calculated. The following information is maintained in an SCCS file:

Module name

SCCS identification

Release number   ——————————+
Level number   ——————————|–+
Branch number   ——————————|–|–+
Sequence number ——————————|–|–|–+
                (e.g. 'Version 3.5.6.A')

Current date
Current time

Date and time newest delta was created

15.5.2   Integrated environments

These comprise an integrated package of editor, compiler and linker. Given adequate space, programs can be developed and tested in memory. Run-time errors can be referred directly back to the source code and messages displayed as the user scrolls through the source file. A **pick file** facility is often provided, which keeps information about the context of the last few files edited, and restores the package to the same situation the next time it is invoked. This is an increasingly popular 'packaging' for language processors, and products are available for such languages as C (Borland, Zortech), Pascal (Borland), Modula-2 (JPI) and Prolog (Borland, LPA).

These packages, although falling short of true CASE status (see below), offer productivity benefits at the level of small group software development.

15.5.3   CASE and IPSEs

Two major advances in software engineering tools, far in advance of the *programmer's workbenches* we have discussed, are the complete development environments offered by independent vendors or 'bundled' with language processors.

15.5.3.1   CASE

CASE is a rapidly growing area. A useful set of tools (such as a 4GL and associated utilities) is provided (sometimes called a **workbench**), and for straightforward applications a great deal of traditional design and coding work is avoided. Indeed, a number of writers have predicted the demise of traditional programming tasks within a few years, the emphasis shifting towards design and information requirements analysis.

15.5.3.2   Integrated project support environments

As mentioned earlier, there is a considerable project management load on any non-trivial project. Version control utilities, such as make, help considerably but are generally used in conjunction with other software such as graphical design tools, automated structured design methodologies (such as SSADM or MASCOT), document management systems, communications with other sites, interface design tools, and so on. An IPSE combines all these functions, and more, within a single **desktop**. Generally, the IPSE is run on a powerful stand-alone workstation, and would have a WIMP interface. There are a number of specialised 'language-oriented' IPSEs, such as the one for the Ada language — the Ada Project Support Environment (APSE).

15.6   CONCLUSION

Operating systems vendors are becoming increasingly aware that they must do more than offer just a basic system, a compiler and a set of basic utilities. A system which supports advanced tools, such as the ones we have discussed above, is a system which will be preferred. Ultimately the performance of these tools is constrained by the functionality and power of the operating system on which they must run.

Conclusion

16

Current and future developments

16.1 INTRODUCTION

We have seen how systems software can be regarded as providing a 'virtual machine' which shields the user from the complexities of the underlying hardware, whether the user's interaction is via a language or via an operating system command interface. However, nothing stands still, especially in the computing world. The systems that made headlines and quickened the pulses of enthusiasts a year ago are now commonplace, even obsolescent. We need to ask whether our model of systems operation also needs modification. The answer, fortunately for us, is that the model has sufficient generality to cope with the developments discussed here.

Although the world of mainframe computers is undergoing a great transformation due to technological developments, the experience of many readers will be with smaller personal or distributed systems: much of the discussion therefore centres on this area. It is also more likely that anyone wishing to experiment in a practical way with the concepts introduced by Part II of this book will achieve safer progress using a small installation, unless he/she has access to a well-protected system such as IBM's VM.

16.2 HARDWARE

There is no reason to suppose that the rapid growth in speed and addressing capability of hardware will slow down. Economic factors in production such as high packing density and extremely high volumes make for low unit cost, while desirable usage characteristics such as low temperature dissipation and low power consumption enable more reliable and powerful systems to be built.

There is some evidence that physical limitations are being approached, such as the minimum width of connecting traces (due to the essentially optical nature of the chip-making process) and the speed of the devices on the chip (due to the finite speed of electrons in metal). Although current devices have a trace width of two micrometres or so (a micrometre being 1/1000th of a millimetre), the latest 16-Mbit memory chips have trace widths of 0.15 micrometres. This is approaching the wavelength of light.

Equally well, there is evidence that new technologies will come on stream just as (or hopefully just before) the 'old' ones run out of steam. Experimental chips have been constructed using **gallium arsenide** rather than silicon, which gives an increase in speed of at least one order of magnitude (10–100 times). An experimental device developed by Bell Northern Research operates at 5000 MHz, which gives it a bandwidth sufficient to transmit the entire text of the Encyclopaedia Britannica in less than one second.

Experiments have also been carried out with **optical** processing units, which can achieve very high speeds and high packing densities, partly due to the fact that coherent light beams can pass through one another without interference. Finally, early studies on **biological** devices have shown some promise. These devices use the natural properties of certain types of biological molecule to store information by absorbing light of a certain colour and changing state. There is no particular advantage, apart from handling convenience, in making these devices any larger than a single molecule, so the potential is obvious for mass storage applications.

It is likely that, in the future, types of computing machine other than the classical **von Neumann** architecture, with which we are familiar, will be developed. In all probability, these machines will be characterised by a highly **parallel** type of architecture. This kind of architecture has attracted great interest from the artificial intelligence (AI) community, mainly because the human brain itself is thought to be organised in a similar way.

If these kinds of capabilities seem far-fetched now, then it might be interesting to imagine the response of a data processing manager in, say, 1982, on being informed that the power of his installation would, in five years, be available on a piece of silicon a quarter of an inch square; or that whole encyclopaedias would be packed on to an optical disk.

In spite of these interesting possibilities, there is plenty to discuss given the current state of the art: conventional CPU architectures have been made small and fast but possess mainframe functionality; peripheral controller devices have been made 'intelligent' by virtue of their embedded CPUs; improved methods of connecting and controlling subsystems such as hard disks are available; more reliable communications technologies have been developed for both local and global communications; and most importantly, there is an emerging set of international **standards** regarding the specifications of such systems and their interfaces.

There does not seem to be a performance problem, at least for a while: conventional CPUs possess an adequate performance, and expected demands can be met by adopting parallel solutions. The significance of systems software in such systems will be evident — for example, see the discussion of the Helios system in Chapter 13.

There are several consequences of this trend, which has been termed 'technological push':

(a) Functions which were formerly performed by software can now be performed in hardware, such as memory access and protection. The advantage is that a software malfunction does not crash the system.

(b) Applications which took 'short-cuts' by directly accessing the hardware to avoid a speed penalty can now use 'legal' system calls.

The load on systems programmers has also been reduced by the migration of many important functions onto the hardware. In addition to all this, the whole development process has been eased by the provision of such tools as CAD (computer-aided design) for integrated circuit layout and automated manufacturing processes.

16.2.1   Central processors
The developmental thrust has been generally along three directions: increasing word size to 32 bits; incorporating hardware multitasking and memory management facilities; and matching instruction sets to the requirements of high-level languages. This last development has received wide attention recently, as a rigorous analysis of the machine instructions that were actually used by compilers and programmers revealed that only a small subset was regularly used, and some instructions were not used at all. To the extent that even unused instructions require decoding, which requires logic, a new range of reduced instruction set computers (RISC) was developed. Complex operations that were previously handled by a single instruction are handled in RISC machines by a sequence of instructions. There is still an enormous saving in time.

In some cases, it has been considered worthwhile to implement a language interpreter in hardware; this is useful if the language is normally slow to run. One example is the Texas Instruments Micro-Explorer chip, which is optimised to run the LISP language, widely used in artificial intelligence and expert system applications. There are also chips optimised to run the FORTH control language.

16.2.2   Other hardware
Equal advances have been made in the design of associated hardware found in computer systems. We will restrict ourselves to a brief discussion of the major types.

16.2.2.1   Specialist processors
Increasingly, CPU chips are designed to work together with an accompanying floating point unit (FPU). Until recently, applications programs accessed these devices directly, but increasingly these operations are being offered as system services. An FPU can speed up arithmetic-intensive applications by an order of magnitude (10–100 times). This is a significant factor in compute-intensive applications such as spreadsheets, engineering calculations or graphics generation.

Graphics displays have become increasingly demanding of resources, with higher clock speeds and more memory being necessary to sustain the high resolutions and number of colours now regarded as essential; graphical output is an increasingly important part of systems operation, and applications such as CAD make heavy computational demands when calculating shapes, rotations etc. The logical step was taken to embed these functions in hardware, and, fortunately, systems software development has kept pace so that a familiar interface can be retained so that applications will run unchanged.

16.2.2.2   Other specialist devices
Other functions which have benefitted from a hardware implementation are: local area network interfaces, text string processors, voice input and output processors, serial communications processors etc.

16.2.3   Convergent technology
An important consequence of the increasing functionality of devices is that there is now no restriction upon the **type** of information that can be captured and transformed into a digital form suitable for processing in a variety of ways. For example, an auditory waveform such as speech can be digitised, stored and recalled at appropriate times, or transmitted around a network. This capability has been exploited in **voice store-and-forward** systems, which digitise an incoming message and enable it to be indexed and relayed in a form suitable to the recipient. This trend has been termed **technological convergence**; the phenomenon it renders possible is termed **data fusion**.

More advanced forms of data fusion are to be found in the emerging **multi-media** systems such as electronic encyclopaedias. In these systems, certain areas of text (termed active text, or **hypertext**) can be made to index and access files of graphic or auditory information. These files can be displayed or replayed through a loudspeaker.

Later in this chapter we will discuss a commercially available system which exploits this concept.

16.3   SOFTWARE

In the previous section we saw how hardware has improved in both speed and functionality. All this power is of little use if it cannot be harnessed. The cost of writing all the code for a new operating system (or to 'port' an existing one), if all the work must be done in assembly language, would be prohibitive. The vendors of a new CPU, therefore, generally pay attention to the provision of an adequate set of development software, probably in the form of a C compiler and linker. As C is now the lingua franca of systems software, the rapid evolution of the software base is assured.

Perhaps as a result of this stimulus, compiler development has been considerable over the past few years: compilers now produce highly optimised code and some have separate front and back ends so that the appropriate code generator can be used. This is particularly true when the target is a RISC machine.

Finally, conventional high-level languages themselves are making low-level facilities available to the programmer, either through extensions in the implementation (for example, Borland's Turbo Pascal, C and BASIC products) or via an extension to the language specification itself, as in the Modula-2 language. Devised as an extension to, and improvement on, Pascal, Modula-2 incorporates such low-level process handling facilities as StartProcess, Transfer (from one process to another), and IOTransfer (which enables asynchronous device handlers to be written). In this way, operating systems and associated software can be written entirely in a high-level language.

16.3.1   Languages — 4GLs

A 4GL is a popular solution for users who feel competent to develop their own application; their scope and use has been discussed in Chapter 8.

Their main feature is that they are more 'domain-specific' than a conventional language (3GL); their syntax and features are more directly related to, say, commercial activities than even COBOL. Within this restricted domain, a certain flexibility is offered to the applications developer.

16.3.2   Languages — 5GLs

As we have seen in Part I, there is a rich variety of ways in which a problem may be formulated and expressed using a programming language. As the requirements of users become more sophisticated, it is incumbent upon software vendors to provide languages which offer a high degree of functionality and reliability in spite of new requirements. It would seem that, increasingly, the traditional procedural languages are giving way to new kinds of language in applications of the type which have been termed 'knowledge-based'. This does not mean solely the maintenance of a fixed database which can be interrogated by a 4GL such as SQL; the implication is that new facts can be inferred from existing ones, and the knowledge base updated accordingly.

Fig. 16.1 illustrates two methods of tackling the same problem: that of printing out the possible routes from a given city to the other cities which are connected to it by road, together with the distance in each case. The listing in Fig 16.1 is in PL/I, a powerful procedural language. Even without knowing the language, it is evident that it is working quite hard to represent the data. The network of cities (which is quite a simple concept) is represented by complex data types and pointers. The resulting program (of which the listing is about one-tenth) is arguably opaque to the non-expert eye. It is quite likely that such a listing would also be opaque to the person who wrote it after some time had elapsed.

The basic problem is that the knowledge present in the original data, which had to do with the way in which the cities were connected (the **what**) has been translated by the programmer into a set of imperatives about **how** to locate each city.

Fig. 16.2 lists a solution to the same problem in the Prolog language. The simplicity of the syntax hides the underlying complexity of the

```
declare
    1 city_node based,
        2 city_name char(city_size) varying,
        2 total_dist fixed,
        2 investigate bit,
        2 city_list pointer,
        2 route_list pointer;
    .
    .
    .

print_all:
    proc;
    dcl
        (p,q) pointer;
    do p = city_head
        repeat(p→city_list) while(p ≐null);
        put skip list(p→city_name,':');
        do q = p→route_head
            repeat(q→route_list) while(q ≐null);
            put skip list(q→route_dist, 'miles to',
                          q→next_city→city_name);
        end;
    end;
    end print_all;
```

Fig. 16.1 — A portion of a routing program in PL/I.

```
route(City1, City2, Distance) if
       road(City1, City2, Distance).
route(City1, City2, Distance) if
       road(City1, Somewhere, Dist1) and
       route(Somewhere, City2, Dist2) and
       Distance = Dist1 + Dist2.
```

Fig. 16.2 — A routing program in Prolog.

Prolog 'machine', which searches for all possible solutions; but this is no concern of the programmer.

At a previous point in the program, some 'facts' have been declared about cities:

```
road(bristol london, 120).
road(london, chelmsford, 40).
road(bristol, bath, 12).
```

and so on.

There are several ways of using the two **predicates** listed above. Queries about the database can now be made directly:

```
road(bristol, london, How_far)
```

gives

```
How_far = 120
No (more) solutions
```

and

> road(bristol, Where, How_far)

gives

> Where = london How_far = 112
> Where = bath   How_far = 12

> No (more) solutions

Note that the mechanism which produces these solutions is general, so that there is no problem with 'reverse' queries such as:

> road(Where1, Where2, 12)

which provides the correct response

> Where1 = bristol Where2 = bath
> No (more) solutions

This flexibility is inherent when a knowledge-based approach is taken with the applications language. To the extent that a very large proportion of traditional data processing problems are 'knowledge problems', rather than procedural ones, fifth-generation languages (5GLs) would seem to offer a promising alternative, offering such advantages as transparent syntax, rapid prototyping and easy maintenance.

The impact of 5GLs on systems software will also be considerable, for the following reasons:

(a) Interfaces will become much more easy to design, because development tools will be easier to construct and more powerful.
(b) Complex distributed systems will become easier to manage, as most of the difficulties arise when knowledge about status, privileges etc. has to be established before action can be taken.
(c) The systems software code will be more transparent and readable, hence easier to maintain.

16.3.2.1   *Incorporation with existing system software*
Fortunately, there is no problem in matching existing systems software such as device drivers, system calls etc. to a knowledge-based shell. Rather than considering the system call, for example, as a line of imperative code within a procedure, it can be regarded as a logical predicate which returns 'true' (the operation was a success) or false (some error occurred):

> found(File) if
>   no_error(File) and
>   exists(File).

16.3.3   Object-oriented languages
The concept of attacking the **what** rather than the **how** of a problem can be extended to the way in which its component processes can be visualised. If

the system that is being modelled can be viewed as a community of interacting objects, each with a particular function, and communicating via messages, then the task of developing some kinds of computer-based solutions is eased. The type of language that enables such systems to be developed is called an **Object-oriented language**.

16.3.3.1 Smalltalk-80

This language was developed at the Palo Alto Research Centre (PARC) by the Xerox Corporation to ease the process of developing windowing interfaces to advanced office automation systems.

The basic concepts are quite simple. An **object** (which could be regarded as corresponding to the static part of a process as described in Chapter 13) is considered as being an **instance** (member) of a particular **class**, from which it **inherits** a number of things, most importantly a set of **methods** which enable it to deal with **messages** which are passed to it by other objects.

Instances of a class can share many attributes in common: this saves development time when a group of similar objects is being constructed. For example, two instances of the class 'Graphic_Objects' may share the **class variables** 'Where_X' and 'Where_Y'; but instances 'Line' and 'Circle' may have, respectively, individual **instance variables** 'Length' or 'Radius'. Each of these instances will have its own method for producing a line or a circle.

As mentioned, each object is activated by passing it a message. These are of the form

>   :Circle 100 200 20

At a lower level will be more primitive operations on the graphics screen itself. At a higher level could be a complete windowing interface. An object-oriented system is well suited to the development of such interfaces.

The basic mode of operation of a windowing system is to capture events from the real world and pass them to applications via messages. An event may be a keypress, a pointer entering a rectangle on the screen or the depression of a mouse button.

It is evident that an object oriented language is a very appropriate tool for the development of windowing systems: what is being provided is a very high-level virtual machine whose functionality can be used directly in an application. This virtual machine could, of course, be layered on top of a conventional kernel.

An additional advantage is that user-developed libraries are easy to maintain, and can be made as 'public' as the author wishes, leading to potential savings in development effort.

16.4 OPERATING SYSTEMS

In this section we will discuss how operating systems have evolved, and end with an examination of emerging standards.

We introduced operating systems, conceptually, as a 'shielding' layer between the user or the application and the machine. It would be natural, therefore, to expect the evolution of operating systems to follow developments in technology and in user requirements. This has happened, albeit with a slight lag. Although it is generally easy for technologists to develop hardware products on a 'solution looking for a problem' basis (**technological push**), software products usually need some **user pull** to establish a need and formulate some ideas about the functionality of the product. We thus occasionally have the interesting situation of very powerful processors waiting for software to run on them.

This disparity, however, is likely to become less marked in the future. The reason is that the users of systems, once an oppressed minority subject to the vagaries of unreliable or capricious systems, have become an informed and fairly vociferous majority, to the extent that software houses are showing some evidence of listening to them.

Two areas which reflect the dissatisfaction of users are the ability of the system to multitask and the nature of the user interface.

16.4.1   Multitasking

It is an interesting phenomenon that, after a short period of familiarisation, most users, whether of applications or systems software, begin to customise their system wherever possible. The reasons for this are outside the scope of this book, but have a lot to do with work satisfaction and 'usability'. The customisation takes the form of the acquisition of a set of favourite utilities which enhance the 'vanilla' system, and, particularly with personal computers, of the installation of a number of 'pop-up' personal productivity enhancers. These take the form of 'terminate and stay resident' (TSR) utilities which are activated by a particular hot-key combination, or **chord**. This type of application is very popular because it is very useful — a 'pop-up' diary and notepad can be called up in the middle of any application; or a terminal emulator run; or a section of the display screen can be 'grabbed' and printed.

Significantly, the MS-DOS operating system was not designed initially with such activities in mind; it was merely conceived of as a vehicle for running applications. Consequently, these applications tended to be idiosyncratic in the way they treated the operating system, in the worst case by ignoring system conventions and operating directly on the hardware (an activity which we identified as a 'no-no' in Chapter 11). As a result, an attempt to maintain more than one of these applications in memory often resulted in system crashes or unpredictable behaviour.

Users persevered with these applications because, despite the occasional accident, they enabled people to work with a computer in the same way as they did with their normal office work: in bursts, switching between activities, with the occasional diversion, and with a general need for instant information. What was really needed, of course, was a single-user multitasking system. This would have an advantage over the more primitive 'switching' kind of system in that activities such as file downloading, compilations etc. could run in the **background**, leaving one task (such as a spreadsheet or word processor) to act as a **foreground** task with which the user could interact.

The discussion in this section will be found generally useful as an introduction to windowing interfaces. It is interesting to note that, despite the different lineage of this product and the Hypercard system described earlier, the terminology is similar. Evidently, the object-oriented approach is a general and powerful metaphor.

Firstly, it is important to note that such systems offer much more than a conveniently visual interface with which to run programs. Applications themselves have to be written in a way which makes use of the services offered.

16.4.2 Windowing systems

In terms of our 'virtual machine', we need to add another layer of 'virtualising': not only is the I/O interface hardware-independent (see Chapter 11), but multiple streams of information can be directed to one device. For example, an application can open a number of different windows on one physical display screen, and write text or graphical information to each one independently.Each of these **virtual workstations** is identified by a handle (similar to a file handle) and can be independently moved, sized or closed.

The physical properties of a workstation are of no concern to the application, which handles information in a standardised form known as **normalised device coordinates**. These comprise a display space of 32768 by 32768 points. A **current point** is maintained, and all output is relative to this. In such a system, text and graphics are treated in the same way; a character is a graphic object similar in properties to a circle or polygon. A wide range of primitive graphics shapes and 'fills' is supported.

This concept owes much to the **GKS** (graphics kernel system) which has been running for some years on large computers, and is implemented as a library of routines callable from, say, a FORTRAN program.

16.4.2.1 Messages

These are the 'life-blood' of the system. All information is passed to the running application in the form of messages, which are stored in 'mailboxes', one for each application. All applications have a unique identifier. An application can act on a message or choose to ignore it. Typical messages might be:

> A key has been hit;
> mouse button has been clicked once;
> mouse button has been clicked twice;
> menu item has been selected;
> mouse has entered a virtual workstation;

and so on. Additionally, applications can send messages to one another in just the same way. This would provide, for example, a facility for 'cutting and pasting' between different applications or different invocations of the same application. Pictures scanned from a newspaper could be sent from the scanner application to a desktop publishing package, or comments on a manuscript relayed directly from the reviewer's to the author's screen while an improved version is being edited.

All applications will have a main loop in which the mailbox is inspected at regular intervals and the appropriate action taken. The pre-emptive multitasking of OS/2 will take place transparently underneath the applications.

To conceptualise what is going on in such a system, it is useful to regard the system as an environment which supports (runs) applications, rather than a passive layer. This is especially important when it is realised that, increasingly, environments of this kind will run over local or wide area networks and fully distributed applications will undoubtedly appear before long.

It will probably come as a relief to know that the full set of 'conventional' system calls is supported.

Finally, it is evident that a real 'convergence' is taking place in the way systems and applications are working together. Operating systems such as OS/2 (or, on Apple Macintosh systems, Multifinder, which we have not had the space to discuss) provide a natural virtual machine to very high level object-oriented languages (such as Smalltalk, Actor or FLAVORS). It may be that such languages will constitute an extension to the operating system itself, enabling (for example) knowledge-based applications to run in a supportive and protected environment.

16.5   CONCLUSION

The study of systems software continues to be stimulating and informative, and is likely to be more important in the future as technological possibilities are exploited and as users become more skilled at articulating their requirements.

What we should not forget is that the role of computers is to serve people and organisations, not the converse; and the more attention that is paid to getting the interface right, via good languages and operating systems, the better the users' experience will be.

Increasingly, with the development of very high-level interfaces and functionality within operating systems, the end user will take much more of a hand in designing his/her own systems. Although it is unlikely that the specific 'applications package' as we know it will disappear, the interface between systems and applications program will become easier. The languages and services offered by the operating systems themselves will be of sufficient generality and power to enable users to construct their own solutions, some of which may be idiosyncratic and interesting.

The task of the systems software specialist, therefore, is likely to be an interesting one; information about new devices such as those we have discussed, and probably those which we cannot yet imagine, will have to be assimilated and these devices incorporated into systems which are comprehensible and easy to use. In this connection it is likely that some specialist assistance will be needed from the **HCI** (human–computer interface) community.

There will certainly be no lack of development tools for systems or applications: procedural or declarative languages, conventional or object-oriented methods, windowing or command interfaces, all in a variety of combinations — the main problem may be in making the choice as to what tools should be used!

Although, undoubtedly, problems will occur as a result of the abuse or misunderstanding of this new-found power, it is the authors' opinion that the trend is towards a liberal and skilful community of information users, employing computer systems to add power to their activities, however individual they may be.

FURTHER READING

Kidder, T. *The soul of a new machine* (Penguin Business).
Vallee, J. *The Network Revolution* (And/Or Press).
Papert, S. *Mindstorms* (The Harvester Press).
Gaines, B. and Shaw, M. *Conversations with computers* (Prentice-Hall).

Index

3GLs, 31–33
4GLs, 33, 120, 128–129, 204, 219
5GLs, 33–34, 120, 123–124, 129–130, 219

absolute addresses, 57
absolute program files, 145
absolute symbols, 51
accumulator (AC), 53
Ada, 32, 78
Ada project support environment (APSE), 136, 211
address resolution, 58
admin command in Unix, 210
airline reservation system, 148
ALGOL, 32, 38, 39
APL, 32, 35, 42, 123
application generators, 33
applications packages, 225
applications program interface (API) in OS/2, 186
applications software, 16–17
applicative languages, 33
APSE, 136, 211
arguments, 38
    errors, 102
    in command lines, 139
    in Unix commands, 192
arithmetic expressions, 36
array bounds, checking of, 73
array dimensions, 37, 68, 122–123
array processing operators, 32
array subscripting, 72–73
arrays, 35, 72–73
artificial intelligence, 34, 127, 219
ASCII, 53, 144
assemblers, 46–64
    definition, 56
    tasks, 57–59
assembly language, 31, 46–53, 206
    definition, 47
assignment elimination, 33
assignments, 37, 69–71
asynchronous events, 169

asynchronous system traps (ASTs), 175
automated parsers, 99
automatic library search, 112, 207

background, 167
background task, 224
backup file, 205
Backus–Naur Form (BNF), 39–41, 83, 87
balance set in VMS, 189
bank switching, 178
basic input–output system (BIOS) in MS–DOS, 160, 199, 200
BASIC, 32, 38, 44, 74, 103, 106–107, 122, 130
batch files, 140
batch operation, 137
BBC microcomputer, 150
binary files, 145
binary search of symbol tables, 64
binding delay, 95
biological processing units, 216
BIOS, 160, 199, 200
block I/O, 160
block-structured languages, 32, 39, 69, 83, 105, 123
blocks of statements, 37
BNF, 39–41, 83, 87
Boolean data, 36
bottom-up syntax analysis, 85
breakpoints, 208
bridge model of systems software, 15
buffer, 148, 149, 150, 173, 174
built-in functions, 36, 37–38, 102, 104
byte-oriented machine, 53

C programming language, 16, 32, 33, 81, 193, 206
C-language, 79, 83, 85, 89, 99
cache memory, 181
caching, 149
CALL statement, 37
CASE in software engineering, 208, 211

CASE structure in programming, 125
character codes, 144
character data, 36
character I/O, 140, 162
character set of programming language, 35
character strings, 82
   variable length, 36, 106–107, 108
child process in Unix, 192, 202
Chomsky, N., 41
CICS/VS, 21
class in Smalltalk, 222
clock, time of day, 158, 159, 175
clusters, 150, 152
   in VMS, 188
co-routines in Modula-2, 207
COBOL, 18, 32, 35, 36, 38, 69, 73, 83, 105
code generation, 78, 89–95
code skeletons, 90–91, 103
command file, 135
command line intepreter (CLI), 137, 198
command syntax, 139
command tail, 140
commands, in Unix, 192
   in VMS, 189
   in MS-DOS, 138
   transient, 139
COMMON statement in FORTRAN, 39
communications, 142
compaction, of files, 150
compilers, 18, 30, 66–109
   definition, 66
   efficiency, 77, 95–96, 101
   size, 79
   structure, 78–81, 83
compiler–compilers, 98–99
complex numbers, 36
computer-aided design (CAD), 217
computer-assisted software engineering
   (CASE), 208, 211
concurrency, 149, 164, 174
   in Modula-2, 207
conditional assembly, 53, 58
conditional statements, 71
conferencing, 142
console, 135, 155
constants, 35, 36, 68
context-free grammars, 41
context-sensitive grammars, 41
control statements, 37
controllers, intelligent, 149
convergent technology, 218
coupling of processes, 174
CPU, 18, 29, 164, 165, 166, 170, 174
CPU time, 121
crashes of programs, 101
critical region, 173
cross reference listings, 64, 77
cross-compilers, 67
cursor control in VAX/VMS, 201
cut and paste, 225

data acquisition, 167

data conversion, 58, 74, 82, 103–104
data fusion, 218
Data Interchange Format, 147
data manager in OS/2, 187
data manipulation statements, 37
datastructures, in programming languages,
   32
   logical and physical, 148
data types, 35, 36
   in assembler, 50
   in C, 206
   in Modula-2, 206
   in Pascal, 32
   user-defined, 36
database, *ad hoc* enquiries on, 29
database management system (DBMS), 21
database services in Unix, 194
date manipulation functions, 38, 199
debuggers, 143, 207
debugging, 31, 128
   information, run-time, 77
   messages, 102
DEC, 188
declarative languages, 34, 123–124, 226
declarative statements, 37, 125
definition section in Modula-2, 206
DEFS directive, 49
delta information in SCCS, 210
Department of Trade and Industry (DTI),
   208
descriptor, process, 175
devices, 155
   assignment, 155
diadic operators, 36
Digital Command Language (DCL), 188
direct manipulation, 135
direct memory access (DMA), 149
directives, assembler, 49
directories, 150–154
directory files in Unix, 190
directory structures, 151
   in Unix, 190
disk copy utility, 20
diskette, 152
dispatching, 166
   of processes, 174
distributed operating system, 188, 196
DMA, 149
DO loops, 71–72
DO statement in FORTRAN, 67
driver, 138, 148, 149, 150, 157, 158, 159,
   160, 162, 163, 169, 199
DS directive, 49
dummy arguments, 38
dynalinking, 146
dynamic data exchange (DDE), 187
dynamic linking and loading, 118
dynamic storage allocation, 69, 75, 105

EBCDIC, 144
editing operations, 205

editor/interpreter, 122, 127
editors, 20, 204
efficiency, of 4GLs, 129
 of compiler, 77, 95–96, 101
 of interpreter, 126, 129
 of programming languages, 44
EMACS, 205
embedded systems, 21
emulators, 47
END directive, 49
end user programming, 33
end-of-file value, 152
entry points, 115
environment strings, 146
EQU directive, 49
error handling, by compiler, 101–103
 by interpreter, 127
error messages, from assembler, 59
 from compiler, 76–77
errors, operating system, 141
 detected by operating system, 102
EVAL, 123–124
exception handling facilities, 103
executable statements, 37, 125
export in Modula-2, 206
expressions, 36
 code generation for, 92–95
 definition of, 40
 in assembler, 50
 parsing of, 87
Extended Edition of OS/2, 186
EXTERNAL attribute in PL/I, 39
external procedures, 37, 76, 110–111
external references, 114
external symbol list in object code, 115

FATs, 152, 153
FIFO, 156
fifth generation languages, 33–34, 120,
 123–124, 129–130
file access, 143, 148, 150
file allocation tables (FATs), 152, 153
file attributes, 147
file extension, 111, 144, 147
file handle, 149, 152, 200
file handling in programming languages, 32,
 103
file I/O, 140
file locking, 148
file manager in OS/2, 187
file operations, 147
file permissions in Unix, 190, 193
file pointer, 143, 150, 200
file server, 158
file storage, 143
file structure of Unix, 190
file system operations in Unix, 194
file types, 143, 144
 in Unix, 190
files, 143–154
 application-specific, 147

binary, 145
 data interchange, 147
 general, 147
 hidden, 147
 language processor, 147
 library, 146
 object, 146
 system, 147, 148
 text, 145
first generation languages, 31
fixed format programming language, 35, 48
flag, 169
floating point arithmetic, 104–105
floating point calculations, 142
floating point data, 68
floating point numbers, 36
floating point units, 217
folding editors, 95, 205
FOR loops, 37, 71–72, 90–91
foreground, 167
 task, 224
fork, system service in Unix, 202
formal language definitions, 98
formal parameters, 38
formatted I/O, 199
formatted listings, 77
FORTRAN, 32, 35, 36, 39, 83
forward reference problem, 59, 61
fourth-generation languages, 33, 120,
 128–129
fragmentation, 154
 of disk space, 152
 of memory, 180
 of program storage, 107
free-format programming language, 35
fseek Unix system service, 193
functional programming languages, 33, 44,
 123–124
functions, 37, 74–76

gallium arsenide, 216
garbage collection, 107–108
gathering up of parse trees, 89
generation of machine instructions, 90
generations of programming languages,
 31–34
global data, 39
global optimisation, 97–98
global variables, 69, 106
GOAT computer, 9, 53–56
GOSUB statement, 38
GOTOs, 32, 44, 67
grammars, 39
graphical output, 74
graphics characters, 145
graphics code processors, 217
graphics kernel system (GKS), 224

handler, 138, 148, 157, 158, 159, 160, 163
hardware debuggers, 208

hardware independence, 155
hashing of symbols, 64
header files, 199
heap-based storage allocation, 106–108
Helios, 196
help, command of OS/2, 185
   in VMS, 188
hibernation of processes, 175
hidden files, 147
high-level languages, 31–33
hot key, 185
human-computer interface (HCI), 226
Hypercard, 195, 224
Hypertext, 196, 218
hypervisor, 182
hypothetical machine, 53

IBM, 90, 179, 184, 186, 215
identifiers, 35, 82
IF statements, 37, 71
implementation section in Modula-2, 206
import in Modula-2, 206
incremental compilers, 95
index registers (IX), 54, 106
   use for array subscripts, 72, 73
   use in loops, 91
index variables, 72, 91
indexed addressing, 56
indivisibility of operations, 171
inference engine, 124
information, 226
inheritance in Smalltalk, 222
initialised data, 49
input/output, 170
   character, 140
   control, 22
   errors, 102
   file, 140
   routines, 103–104
   services in VAX/VMS, 200
   statements, 37, 73–74
   stream, 143
instance in Smalltalk, 222
integers, 36
integrated environments, 211
integrated packages, 187
Intel, 80386, 181
Intel 8086 assembler, 47
intelligent controllers, 149
interactive compilers, 95
interactive debugging, 103
interface, user, 135
interleave factor, 148
intermediate code, 78, 99, 128
internal procedures, 37, 111
interpreters, 18, 46–47, 86, 120–130
   definition, 120
interpretive execution, 44
interpretive languages, 121–125
interrupt routine, 167
interrupts, 23, 102, 157, 165, 175

software, 138, 149
IPSEs, 136, 204, 208, 211

kernel, 138, 140, 148, 149, 150, 152, 158, 159, 160
   routine, 198
key words, 82
keyboard, 165
keywords, 36
   misspelled, 76
knowledge base, 124
knowledge-based applications, 225
knowledge-based programming, 219–221

labels, inserted by compiler, 71
language definitions, 39–42, 98–99
language development, 30–34
language features, 42–44
language generations, 31–34
language grammars, 39
language processors, 18, 29–131, 204
   files, 147
language sensitive editors (LSEs), 95, 205
late binding in OS/2, 186
layers of operating system, 19, 155
LET statement in BASIC, 122
lexical analysis, 78, 81–83, 125
librarian, 146, 204, 207
libraries, of object code, 112
   run-time, 136
library files, 146
library routine, 198
library searching, 115
linguistic elements, 35–39
linguistic terminology, 30
linkage editors, 110–119, 204, 207
   efficiency of, 116
linked list, 153
linkers, 110–119, 204, 207
LISP, 33, 120, 123–124, 129, 205
list processing, 36
list structures, 123–124
literal table, 62–63, 82
literals, 36
   in assembler, 51
   in high level languages, 68, 82
LL(1) parsers, 85
load map, 207
load module, 111, 114
loaders, 110, 116–119
   relocating, 117
   simple, 116
local optimisation, 96–97
local variables, 39, 69, 106
location counter, 57, 61–63
locking, files and records, 148
logic programming languages, 34, 124, 220
logical data, 36
logical data structures, 148
logical event flags (LEFs), 175

logical expressions, 36
logical operators, 36
loops, 71–72, 91
low-level languages, 31
LR(1) parsers, 85
Lukasiewiczian notation, 85

machine architecture, 90
machine code, 21, 31
machine, virtual, 164
machine-specific optimisation, 98
macro asemblers, 52–53
macro expansions, 58, 59
macros, 31, 46, 52–53, 198, 205
MAKE, 136, 209
mapping of memory, 179
MASCOT, 211
mathematical functions, 38, 104
mathematical services in Unix, 194
memory, 170
    access, 141
      illegal, 180
    allocation, 176
    chips, 215
    fragmentation, 107, 180
    management, 164, 176
    mapping, 179
    physical, 179
    protection, 141, 180
    requirements of interpreter, 126
    virtual, 149, 179, 185
memory management unit (MMU), 179
messages, 34
    in Smalltalk, 222
    in windowing systems, 224
meta-languages, 39–40
methods in Smalltalk, 222
Microsoft, 184
military languages, 32
MINCE, 205
mixed compiler/interpreters, 128–130
mnemonic operation codes, 48
Modula-2, 33, 110, 173, 174, 198, 206
modular programming, 110–112, 127
monadic operators, 36
mouse button, 224
move of data, 70
MS-DOS, 111, 143, 152, 160, 182, 223
    batch files, 140
    commands, 138
    system services, 199–200
multi-media systems, 218
multi-phase linking, 117
multi-user system, 148, 169
multiple virtual machines, 182
multiplication and division, 94
multitasking, 161, 162, 164, 165, 167, 169,
    174, 181, 185, 223
    operating system, 117
    in OS/2, 187
    in Unix, 190

mutual exclusion, 161, 168, 172
MVS, 179

name, passing parameters, by, 38–39
natural language systems, 29–30
network, 148, 158
NEW( ) directive in Pascal, 105
new technologies, 216
non-commutative operators, 94
non-executable statements, 37
non-procedural languages, 34, 123–124
non-terminal symbols, 40
normalised device co-ordinates, 224

object code, 46, 66
    listing, from assembler, 59
      from compiler, 77
    output from assembler, 59, 63
object files, 146
object in Smalltalk, 222
object-oriented approach, 224
object-oriented languages, 34, 221–222, 226
ON ERROR statements in BASIC, 103
ON-units in PL/I, 103
one-pass assembler, 60
op-codes, 48
    translation, 57
operands, in assembler, 48
    in reverse Polish, 86
operating systems, 18–19, 135–212
    development, 222–225
    differences in methods of link-editing,
      117–118
    layers, 19, 155
operating-system specific code, 74
operation in assembler, 48
operator-precedence grammars, 85
operators, 36, 82
    in reverse Polish, 86
optical processing units, 216
optimising compilers, 95–98
ORG directive, 47, 49, 58
OS/2, 143, 146, 182, 184–188, 225
    Extended Edition, 186
overflow errors, 102
overlays, 118, 178
    of compiler, 79

page fault, 179
page swopping, 119, 149
paged memory, 181
pages of memory, 179
Palo Alto Research Centre (PARC), 222
parallel architectures, 216
parallel processing, 33, 130
parallel processors, 174
parameters, 38, 199
    passing mechanisms, 38, 75
parentheses in expressions, 36

parse tree, 83–84, 85, 87–89, 125
parsers, automated, 99
parsing, 81
   of commands, 141
Pascal, 18, 32, 33, 35, 43, 72, 74, 79, 105,
   149, 198
passes, 59, 78
PC-DOS, 148
PDP-11, 150, 167
PERFORM statement, 37, 38
performance, 24, 46, 101, 121, 126–127, 129
personal productivity enhancers, 233
phases of compiler, 79
physical data structures, 148
physical memory, 179
pick files, 221
Pick operating system, 195
PID, 175
pipes in Unix, 190, 193
piping, 156
PL/I, 32, 36, 39, 78, 103, 108, 130, 219
pointer based structures, 79
pointers, data type, 36
Polish notation, 85
polling, 165, 166
portability, 128, 157
   of languages, 42–43
pre-compilers, 128–130
predicates in Prolog, 220
presentation manager in OS/2, 184, 187
priority levels in OS/2, 186
privileges, 148
procedural languages, 34, 226
procedures, 37, 74–76
   call, 56
   entry code, 75
   linkage, 76
processes, context, 175
   control services, in Unix, 194
      in VAX/VMS, 200
   control, 24, 141
   descriptor, 175
   hibernation and waking, 175–176
   identifier (PID), 175, 202
   in VAX/VMS, 189
   scheduling, 199
   synchronisation, 199
   timing, 199
productions, 41, 85
productivity of programmers, 21–22, 33, 42,
   129
program files, absolute, 145
   relocatable, 145
program proving, 44
program segment prefix (PSP), 145
program selector of OS/2, 185
programmer's workbench, 211
programming languages, 29–44
   definition, 29
project management, 208
Prolog, 34, 123–124, 129, 219–220
proving of programs, 44

protection of memory, 180
protocols, 157
pseudo-instructions, 49
pseudo-operations, 52
PSP, 145

qualifier, in command lines, 139
queries in Prolog, 220
queue, 175
quoted strings, 35, 82

railway track diagrams, 41–42
railways, 168
re-entrancy, 167
real numbers, see floating-point
real-time event handling in VAX/VMS, 200
real-time operating system, 150
record locking, 148
record structures, 36
recursion, 24, 69, 79, 87–89, 123–124, 125
recursive definitions, 40
recursive descent parsing, 85, 86–89
recursive loop, 108
redirection, 156
   in Unix, 190, 192
reduced instruction set computers (RISC),
   98, 217
redundant instruction elimination, 96
reference, parameter passing by, 38, 75
register allocation, 98
relational operators, 36
relational tests, 71
relocatable object code, 76, 111, 113–115
relocatable program files, 145
relocatable symbols, 50–51
relocating loader, 117
relocation, by linkage editor, 115
   by loader, 117
relocation list, 115, 117
report generators, 33, 34
request code, 160
request header, 160
reserved words, 36
resident modules, 119
resolution of external references, 115
restarting of instructions, 179
reverse Polish notation, 85–86, 89
   evaluation of, 92
rich text, 187
ROM, interpreters in, 122
root directory, 152
round-robin multitasking, 175
RT-11, 150, 167
run-time debugging, 103, 128
   facilities, 95
   information, 77
run-time environments, 100–108, 112, 127
run-time errors, 73, 98, 101–103, 128
run-time overheads, 44
run-time routines, 74, 101, 103–105

run-time sevices in VAX/VMS, 201

S-language, 79
  example of, 82–83
scanner, 81, 225
scanning, 79
scheduler, 174, 175
scope rules of variables, 39, 69
  in APL, 123
screen, 165
screen painting, 33
scripts in Unix, 190
second generation languages, 31
sector, 150, 151, 152
segmented memory, 181
self-modifying programs, 123–124
self-relocating programs, 115
semantic analysis, 79
semaphore, 161, 163, 170, 171, 172
serial port, 140
shareable code in OS/2, 186
shared modules, 207
shell, 148
Shell in Unix, 191
  process, 202
  scripts, 193
signal, 171
signal box, 169
signalman, 169
Simula, 32
simulation languages, 32
single user system, 223
single-tasking, 169
skeletons, 90–91, 103
Smalltalk, 34
Smalltalk-80, 222
SNOBOL, 32
software chip, 206
software debuggers, 208
software development, 23, 204
software development tools, 204
software engineering, 17, 111, 130
software interrupt, 138, 149
software maintenance, 42
software packages, 16
sort programs, 20
source code control system (SCCS), 210
source code, 46, 66
source library in Unix, 193
source listing, from assembler, 59
  from compiler, 77
source program, 29
special files in Unix, 190
specialist processors, 217
SSADM, 211
stack-based architecture, 106
stack-based machine, 92
stack-based storage allocation, 69, 75,
  105–106, 108
stages of compilation, 78–79
statement of parentheses, 37

statements, 37, 69
static linking, 118
static storage, 122
storage allocation, 58, 69, 90
storage management, 105–108
storage shortage errors, 102, 105, 108
stream I/O, 143, 160
structured query language (SQL), 219
sub-programs, 37
subroutine call, 56
subroutines, 37
subscripts, 35
  calculations, 73, 97
  errors, 102
Sun 386i workstation, 182
supervisor, 182
switches in Unix commands, 192
symbol table, 59, 64, 69, 74, 78, 82, 85,
  115–116, 122, 125–126, 207
  methods of access, 64, 126
  use of, 61–63
symbolic address resolution, 58
symbolic addressing, 46, 48–49
symbolic back trace, 208
symbolic operation codes, 31, 48
symbolic parameters, 52
symbols, for compilation, 81
  in assembler, 49
  in programming language, 35
synchronisation, 161, 167
syntactic structure of expressions, 40–41
syntax analysis, 78, 83–89, 125
  bottom-up, 85
  top down, 85
syntax, in VMS, 188
  of commands, 137, 139
syntax tree, 83–84, 85, 87–89
system calls, 74, 169
  in OS/2, 186
system files, 147
system services, 19, 135
  in OS/2, 186
  in Unix, 193–195, 202–203
  in VMS, 189
Systems Application Architecture (SAA),
  186
systems software, categories, 17–19
  definition, 15
  languages for development of, 33, 79, 91,
    101, 205–207
  need for, 21–22
  study of, 22–24

task gate, 182, 186
task state segment (TSS), 182
tasks in OS/2, 186
technolgical push, 216, 223
teleprocessing monitors, 20–21, 118
temporary storage, 70, 94
terminal symbols, 40

terminate and stay resident programs
    (TSRs), 177, 223
text files, 145
text formatters, 142
text of object code, 115
text processing languages, 32, 36
third generation languages, 31–33
threads in OS/2, 186
time and date routines, 199
time of day routine, 200
time-slice, 174
timer services in Unix, 194
tokens, in commands, 141
    in programming languages, 35
top-down syntax analysis, 85
track, 41, 148, 150
trade marks, 9
transient commands, 139
translators, 18
transparency, 136, 153
tree for parsing, 83–84
triadic operators, 36
turnkey operation, 137
two-pass assembler, 59, 61–63
type conversions, 104–105
types, see data types

undefined variable errors, 102
uniprocessor, 174
Unix, 33, 143, 157, 184, 189–197
user interface, 17, 136, 223
    in Unix, 190
user of operating system, 155
user pull, 223
user-defined types, 36
utilities, 19–20, 136, 142
    in Unix, 195

VALUE clause in COBOL, 36
value, passing parameters by, 38
value result, passing parameters by, 38
values in assembler, 49–50
variables, 35, 68–69
    declarations, 37
VAX, 179, 188
VAX/VMS, 175, 184, 188–189
    librarian, 207
    systems services, 200–202
version control, 209
video display, 140
virtual machine, 19, 21, 136, 164
    multiple, 182
virtual memory, 119, 149, 179, 185, 195
virtual-memory operating system, 79
virtual workstations, 224
VM/370, 182, 215
VMS, see VAX/VMS
voice input-output systems, 218
von Neumann, J., 33, 164, 216

wait, 171, 172
waking of processes, 176
windowing, 184
    in OS/2, 187
    interfaces, 222, 224
    memory, 178
word-processing program, 20
working set in VMS, 189
workspace, process, 175

xenix, 182
Xerox Corporation, 222

Z80 assembler, 57
Z80 processor, 122
zero division errors, 102